P9-CCX-661

Territories of Philip II

Territories of Philip II's allies

Military supply routes of Philip II

Boundary of the Holy Roman Empire

RMAN

MPIRE

LORRAINE
ALSACE

SILESIA

Prague

BOHEMIA

MORAVIA

Vienna

AUSTRIA

HUNGARY

STYRIA

Graz

LOMBARDY

CARINTHIA

Milan

VENICE

Genoa

OTTOMAN

EMPIRE

PAPAL STATES

NAPLES

Naples

Lepanto

1571

SICILY

Tunis
1574 lost

Malta
1565

Sanderson

Also by Geoffrey Parker

THE ARMY OF FLANDERS AND THE SPANISH ROAD

THE DUTCH REVOLT

SPAIN AND THE NETHERLANDS

The
Library
of World
Biography

THE THREE AGES OF MAN

Philip II as a young man (by Lucas de Heere in about 1550) ; at the height of his power (by Alonso Sánchez Coello in about 1583) ; and in old age (by Pantoja de la Cruz in 1597, the year before the king's death)

Philip II

By Geoffrey Parker

THE LIBRARY OF WORLD BIOGRAPHY

J. H. PLUMB, GENERAL EDITOR

Little, Brown and Company—Boston–Toronto

FIRST EDITION

T11/78

The handwriting specimens on pages 12–13 are reproduced with
the permission of the Haus- Hof- und Staatsarchiv, Vienna.

LIBRARY OF CONGRESS CATALOGING IN PUBLICATION DATA
Parker, Noel Geoffrey.
  Philip II.

  (The Library of world biography)
  Includes bibliographical references and index.
  1. Felipe II, King of Spain, 1527–1598.
  2. Spain — History — Philip II, 1556–1598.
  3. Spain — Kings and rulers — Biography. I. Title.
DP178.P37   946'.04'0924 [B]   78-17122
ISBN 0-316-69080-5

Published simultaneously in Canada
by Little, Brown & Company (Canada) Limited

For John Elliott

Acknowledgments

The research for this book was made possible by generous grants from the British Academy of London and the Travel and Research Fund of the University of St. Andrews. I would like to thank them. I am also very grateful to James Coonan, John Elliott, David Lagomarsino, Angela Parker, Jack Plumb and Lee Smith, all of whom read the whole of my typescript and made many valuable comments. Professor Lagomarsino also advised me on how best to use the rich manuscript collections in the Library of the Royal Palace in Madrid, and most generously lent me his notes; while Dr. Christopher Riley provided me with some useful material on Spanish Milan. I have benefitted from discussing Philip II and his world with many friends and colleagues — notably Fernand Braudel, Helli Koenigsberger, Peter Pierson and Felipe Ruiz Martín — but my greatest debt is to John Elliott, who first aroused my interest in the life and times of Philip II and provided, in his books and articles, a model of how Spanish history ought to be studied.

Contents

Foreword

Although his father, the emperor Charles V, had ruled vaster territories, Philip II of Spain was still the monarch of the greatest empire Europe had known since the Mongols and the first that encircled the globe, stretching as it did from the southern tip of Chile not only to Florida but across the Pacific to the Philippines. Nor was that all. Nearer home there was growing involvement in Africa, along its western coast as well as its northern shores. The Spanish territories in Europe were immense, yet endangered on the one hand by the infidel Turks, on the other by the heretic Dutch and English: situations which the archenemy of Spain — France — enjoyed exploiting.

The problems that faced Philip II were as great as his empire. He was constantly at war — involved not in minor wars but in great wars. The Turks were an unending menace to his kingdoms and principalities in Italy, eating up ships, men, arms, and above all, money; that was eased by the great victory at Lepanto, but the threat remained. The Dutch and the English were officially or unofficially at war with him for decades, for even in times of peace, Philip II could never be sure whether the English pirates might not appear — burning, ravishing and robbing — whilst the Revolt of the Dutch fes-

tered like an ulcer. The difficulties of ruling millions of Amerindians, of keeping some control over the rivalry and jealousies
of his colonial governors, and, at the same time, undertaking
a vigorous campaign of Christianization were as endless as they
were complex. And Spain itself was never docile — regional
jealousies and antagonisms were backed by centuries of tradition. The Spanish aristocracy was the proudest in Europe and
not easily tamed by either monarchy or bureaucracy.

And yet, whatever the problem, ultimately the decision
came to the king. Surely, as Dr. Parker shows in this brilliant
new life of Philip II, the king was aided by his councils and
his councillors, many of whom were of outstanding ability and
efficiency; but in the context of sixteenth-century monarchy,
the final "fiat" was and had to be the king's. And so Philip
worked endless hours at his papers, discharging a heavy burden
of government which few men in the history of the world have
had to sustain for so many years.

Unquestionably, the king and his councillors felt that this
huge, hierarchical, yet diverse empire could be bound together
only so long as its members remained devoted to the Catholic
faith — and that Protestantism and its crusaders could only
bring confusion and chaos — hence Philip's ferocity toward
heretics. The basis of his attitude was not only religious but
also constitutional: Protestantism for Philip II meant disinte-
gration and rebellion; Catholicism meant unity and devotion.
Because of the stridently national element in Spanish Catholicism, a distorted picture of Philip II has been created by
generations of Protestant historians. They have portrayed him
as a dedicated fanatic, sitting like a black spider in his bleak
cell at the Escorial, working endlessly day and night to crush
the Dutch, to reimpose Catholicism on England, to convert or
destroy the Amerindians, and to monopolize all the riches —
gold, silver, spices — of the known world. For these ends he
was prepared to imprison his own children, to assassinate opponents, and to rack and torture all who thwarted him.

In this caricature, as in all caricatures, there are, of course, elements of truth. The repressive powers of the Spanish Inquisition were very efficient and ruthlessly employed. Compared with the rest of Europe, even Italy, Spain was very free from heresy and that was not achieved without ferocity. Cruelty — the rack and the stake — were methods of government in a turbulent world, and it is well to remember that they were used in England as well as Spain. Philip II's ministers, however, were more thorough and more efficient, and they had no fellow travelers to placate. It can be granted that Philip II was completely, wholeheartedly Catholic, deeply religious; it was not by chance that he designed the Escorial as a monastery, and as he worked in his study he was certainly aware of the daily devotions of the monks who surrounded him. That there was an element of austerity in his makeup can be admitted; that he was prepared to toil at the details of government may also be granted. But he was far more complex and much more human than the "ogre" of Protestant historians would allow us to believe.

Dr. Parker has used the letters and accounts of Philip II, which enable a much more rounded portrait to be drawn. Furthermore, Dr. Parker brings to his subject sympathy and understanding, although both the sympathy and understanding are dispassionate — as they should be. And so from this short but remarkable biography a much more interesting and believable portrait of Philip II emerges. The fanatic for work, the remorseless administrator remains, but he is human, often behindhand with his papers because he has been drawn to some of the good things of life. He hunted with pleasure, loved gardens, liked rich food, enjoyed music passionately, and possessed an eye for fine paintings — not only Titian, whom all admired, but the strange contorted genius of Hieronymus Bosch. One painter whom he did not like was the genius on his doorstep — El Greco. But, in general, the king had a quick and discerning eye. He was also imbued with intense intellectual curiosity — the animals of the New World intrigued him and he set up one of the first royal zoos. Nor was he ignorant of science.

So we have a more rounded portrait but not a portrait turned upside down. Philip II remains one of the most hardworking monarchs in all history; year in year out he dealt with mountains of business — on one occasion handling four hundred documents in a day. And the ruthless nature of his actions and total commitment to his religion cannot be denied. He loved an *auto de fé,* the complex ritual of sentencing heretics — and he watched the spectacle with delight. And he was remorseless in his support of the Inquisition. But then to sustain religion and to rule his kingdom were tasks imposed on him by God.

He is by any standards one of the most remarkable men ever to sit on a throne in Europe. He created a pattern of government not only in Spain and his European possessions, but also in Spanish America and the Philippines, a pattern that was to last for three hundred years after his death. He also brought to Spain, and its court, a regal style that lasted far longer.

— J. H. PLUMB

Preface

In an entertaining novel of 1641, *The Light-footed Devil* by Luis Vélez de Guevara, the hero of the story is taken by his engaging companion ("one of your lesser demons") to the top of the watchtower of San Salvador in Madrid in the early hours of a June morning. "Here," the devil announced, "from this perch in the clouds, which is the highest spot in Madrid, I am going to show you everything that is happening in this Spanish Babylon. I shall lift off the roofs of the houses, by diabolical means, so that we can see clearly the meat in this great pie of Madrid as it really is. And we shall start with those of the highest degree." The present observer, writing from the watchtower of Saint Salvator in Saint Andrews, Scotland, has need of more than a light-footed devil to help him to penetrate the life of Golden Age Spain, either at the top or the bottom. The problems of writing a biography of any sixteenth-century person "of the highest degree," like Philip II, are numerous.

Unlike his father, whom he wished to emulate in so many ways, Philip II wrote no memoirs. The reason (according to an ambassador who composed the king's obituary on the day of his death) was Philip's dislike of vanity. For the same reason he would not allow others to write an official "life" of him. The first studies of Philip II were therefore unofficial, more often than not written by his enemies, and they have set the tone for most subsequent biographies, which rely heavily on anecdotal and circumstantial details. Even works based upon archival material have seldom penetrated to the heart of their subject and illuminated the private world of Philip II. This is not surprising: given the king's practice of having all government orders issued in his name and with his signature, it is sometimes difficult to be sure where policy decisions came from, while the well-known addiction of the Prudent King to "secrecy and subterfuge" seriously complicates the task of discovering motives and true intentions.

There would have been little point in writing yet another biography had not a new source of evidence on Philip II come to light: the Altamira papers. There exist in two Madrid archives, the Instituto de Valencia de Don Juan and the Biblioteca de Heredía Spínola, some five thousand holograph letters and working papers of Philip II. There are perhaps as many again in the University Library in Geneva and in the British Library in London. Originally they all belonged to the archive of the counts of Altamira, which was broken up in the mid-nineteenth century, and there can be no doubt that this collection contained a substantial part of what was once Philip II's private archive. Most of his personal papers are there, as are the precious *billetes* or memoranda in which the king expressed his wishes, and often his innermost feelings, to his closest collaborators. Although Philip II kept no diary, he appears to have used these working papers as a sort of outlet for his emotions, his thoughts and his reasonings, as well as for his decisions. The existence of these documents has been known to historians for more than a century, but so far there has been no systematic attempt to use them as the basis of a full biography. However, it is only in these personal papers, with their tortuous ratiocinations about matters great and small, that the private world of Philip II stands revealed.

But is such prying into private lives worthwhile? Can any

reconstruction of the personal habits and tastes of a public figure, however much labor has been expended in the task, produce a work of historical interest and value? This biography includes information concerning the times at which the king ate and slept, his reading and his gardening tastes, and his sexual habits, as well as an analysis of those affairs of state in which he was personally involved. By contrast, important events in which he was not directly involved have been omitted. I have tried to view the world through his eyes. The attention devoted to the apparently trivial details of his everyday life appears to me to be justified by the greater understanding they afford of King Philip as a human being. Time has simplified many a historical problem by destroying the relevant documents, and there are several crucial events and decisions during the reign of Philip II for which there can now be no total certainty concerning what happened and why. It is in situations like these that we need an understanding of the psychology and "normal" behavior of the principal actor, for the more that is known about him and about the way in which he made decisions (large and small), the more likely it is that we shall be able to fill in the lacunae which remain.

Such an approach is not designed to exculpate the king. This biography is not a "whitewash." I have merely tried to treat my subject throughout as a rational being who had good reasons for all of his major actions, public and private. Even in the case of his "crimes" — such as the imprisonment of Don Carlos, the summary execution of Montigny or the murder of Escobedo — I have sought to explain Philip II's role rather than merely to condemn or excuse it. I believe that it is important, as well as interesting, to understand how powerful and intelligent men who profess high moral principles can be persuaded to act drastically against the interests of others.

— GEOFFREY PARKER

Philip II of Spain

Note on Currency, Names and Dates

All sums of money are given in ducats of 375 maravedís. There were, at this time, approximately four ducats to the pound sterling. All proper names are given in the original form unless there is a recognized English version (William of Orange, Don John, Seville, Brussels and so on). All dates up to 4/15 October 1582, when Philip II introduced the Gregorian Calendar, are given according to the Julian Calendar (except that each year is taken as beginning on 1 January, not 25 March); all dates after that are given in New Style (even for those countries, like England, which did not adopt the Gregorian Calendar until later).

ONE

Apprenticeship, 1527–1558

ON 9 MARCH 1526 Charles V, Holy Roman emperor and ruler of Spain, Mexico, the Netherlands and much of Italy, rode into the bustling and fast-growing city of Seville for the first time. Still in his traveling clothes and covered with dust, he dismounted in the courtyard of the royal castle and strode to the room where Princess Isabella of Portugal, his cousin, was waiting. It had been arranged that the two were to marry, and they were betrothed at once. Charles then retired to change and rest until one o'clock the following morning, when he and Isabella were married. After the nuptial mass, they retired together to bed.

The royal couple were in their prime — the empress was twenty-three; her husband was twenty-six and already the father of an illegitimate daughter, Margaret of Parma — and they spent their first summer together in the south of Spain. For most of the time they lived in the Alhambra, the beautiful palace of the Moorish kings in Granada, which Charles ordered to be extended with a new suite of rooms. In fact, the new palace was never finished, and Charles never returned to Granada, but it was there, in the sweltering heat of the Andalusian summer and amid the bustle of building work, that Philip II was conceived. In December his parents moved back to the more familiar surroundings of Old Castile and it was at Valladolid, effectively Charles V's capital, in the building called to this day "the palace of Philip II," that the child was born on 21 May 1527, in the presence of his father and the leading nobles. As is often the case with a first child, the birth was difficult — labor lasted thirteen hours — and his mother asked for a veil to be placed over her face so that her agony would not be seen. "I may die, but I will not cry out" was her firm rebuke to a midwife who urged her to give full vent to her feelings. Two weeks later the child was baptized, and when the ceremony was completed the royal herald cried out in a loud voice three times: "Don Felipe, by the grace of God prince of Spain." But the infant prince was heir to far more than Spain.

Dynastic accident had brought together in the person of Charles V four separate inheritances, each of them a major political entity. From his father's father, Charles received the ancestral estates of the Habsburgs in southeastern Germany and (after 1519) the title of Holy Roman emperor; from his father's mother he inherited the Burgundian lands in the Netherlands. From his mother's mother, Charles received Castile and the Castilian conquests in North Africa, the Caribbean and Central America; from his mother's father he inherited Aragon and the Aragonese overseas dominions of Naples, Sicily and Sardinia. In the course of his reign Charles was to add several more territories to this impressive core of patrimonial states: in the Netherlands he annexed several provinces in the northeast; in Italy he gained the duchy of Lombardy and in North Africa he conquered Tunis (both in 1535); most spectacular of all, in America only a few thousand Spaniards conquered in twenty years (1519–1539) an area eight times the size of Castile, inhabited by one-fifth of the world's population.

At the moment of Philip II's birth, however, most of this lay in the future. In 1527 Charles V was at war with France and with many of the independent princes of Italy (including the pope); the Turks had just overrun Hungary, driving into exile

Charles's sister (Mary, queen of Hungary and Bohemia) and killing her husband, the king. The previous year had seen the formation of the first anti-Habsburg alliance between France and the Turks. The internal situation in Charles's dominions also gave cause for concern. In the Netherlands, the main towns of Brabant, the richest and most influential province, defied government orders and refused to vote money for the war. In Castile the representative assembly (the Cortes) likewise refused to provide the funds requested and it had to be disbanded. Charles V dared not risk a confrontation because only seven years before, in May 1520, a major rebellion had broken out against his authority and above all against his taxes. The revolt, known as the *comunero* revolt, involved most of the large towns of Castile and was only suppressed in 1521 when the nobles, fearing social upheaval, threw their weight behind the crown. Following the rebellion, there were executions, banishments and indemnities; but Charles had learned his lesson. The comuneros had made some reasonable demands, and the victorious emperor was prepared to make some concessions: they had asked him to come to Spain, to learn to speak Castilian, and to make use of Castilian advisers (all of which he did at once) ; they had asked him to marry a Portuguese princess (which he did in 1526) ; and they had asked that any children born of the union should be brought up and educated in Spain (which they were, and all the children also eventually died in Spain). Philip II is often criticized for having been brought up to be "too Spanish." With the memories of the great comunero revolt so fresh in men's minds, Charles V had no choice.

The need to keep Prince Philip in Spain was reinforced by the fact that his father, the emperor, was often absent. From 1529 to 1533 he was in Italy and Germany, trying to organize the defense of Christendom against the Turks. In 1535–1536 he was away again, conquering Tunis. In 1539–1541 he was in the Netherlands. And after he left for northern Europe again in May 1543 he was not able to return to Spain until 1556.

Philip II thus spent many of his formative years apart from his father and, in 1539, when he was only twelve, his mother died. The young prince was obliged by court protocol to lead the funeral cortège from Toledo, where the empress died, to the vault of her ancestors at Granada.* Meanwhile Charles V shut himself up in a monastery to mourn for eight weeks.

Until 1535, Philip was brought up with his sister Maria (only one year younger than he was) in the household of his mother. Life there seems to have been casual and undemanding, for at the age of seven he still could neither read nor write. Shocked by such backwardness, a member of the prince's entourage composed a special book to teach him his letters, and another to teach him Castilian grammar (since young pupils found the standard grammar of the great humanist Antonio de Nebrija too difficult). The same courtier also translated Erasmus's classic *The Education of a Christian Prince* (composed in honor of Charles V in 1516) into Castilian. But this promising beginning was undermined by the choice of Juan Martínez de Siliceo as Philip's tutor, above the heads of such impressive candidates as Juan Luis Vives (the noted Valencian humanist who had been tutor to Mary Tudor in the 1520's). Siliceo, although a scholar of distinction, was not firm enough with his charge for the emperor's liking. "He was not, and certainly is not now, the person who is most suitable for your studies," Charles complained. Nevertheless, Siliceo (who was a cleric) later became Philip's confessor. "I hope he will not want to appease you as much in matters of conscience as he did in matters of study" was Charles's comment. It was to remedy Siliceo's softness that, in 1541, further educational appointments were made: Cristóbal Calvete de Estrella, a classical

---

* The journey was memorable for others besides the prince. The body of the empress decomposed badly in the summer heat so that when the coffin was opened at Granada for a final identification before burial, the marquis of Lombay could not be sure that the corpse was that of his late sovereign. Appalled by this example of "earthly corruption," Lombay renounced the court, took Holy Orders, and rose to become the third general of the Jesuits and, posthumously, Saint Francis Borgia.

scholar, was to teach the prince Latin and Greek; Honorato Juan was to teach him mathematics and architecture; and Juan Ginés de Sepúlveda was to teach him geography and history. Unfortunately, no one was appointed to teach the prince modern languages, and although he learned in time to understand French, Italian and Portuguese, he could never manage to speak them. Toward the end of his life he took special care to make sure that his heir apparent, later Philip III, could speak French. The old king claimed that, although he could understand it perfectly, he could never get the pronunciation right and therefore felt too embarrassed to speak. (This embarrassment explains Philip's oft-cited failure to make a speech in French, which he had prepared, at the abdication ceremony of Charles V in 1555. He only managed to utter two words; the rest had to be read out by someone else.)

The new tutors also taught the other young members of the royal household who were the prince's companions – about fifty pages, almost all of them the sons of Spanish noblemen. All activities in the life of Philip II, from 1 March 1535 onward, took place within the arena of his own personal household. He was seldom alone. Within five years, this household had grown to one hundred and ninety-one persons, including the fifty-one illustrious pages, eight chaplains, a kitchen staff and sundry cleaners. When the household moved, it required twenty-seven mules and six carts to transport all its equipment (one cart for the chapel, one for the tapestry work, three for the privy chamber, one for other things).

Philip's new household was under the stern, strict and Argus-eyed "governor" appointed by Charles V: Don Juan de Zúñiga. Whereas the tutors were in charge of the things of the mind – moral attitudes, letters, virtues, devotions – the governor looked after physical education and behavior. Until 1535 this had been done by the prince's mother, who sometimes had to smack her son when he was naughty. Zúñiga continued the same firm regime, thereby provoking the prince to complain to his father about his governor's severity. But Zúñiga was

supported by the emperor: "If he gave in to your every ca-
price," the prince was told by his father, "you would be like
the rest of mankind and would have no one to tell you the
truth." A special book was composed, at the emperor's command, describing how the last prince of Spain, Don Juan, the
eldest son of the Catholic kings, was brought up and Zúñiga
was told to follow the same regimen "so that my son will live
and die in the same way as the prince his great-uncle" (another
concession to the comuneros?).

Zúñiga did his job well. In 1543, when Philip was made
regent of Spain, his father noted that "up till now, thanks be
to God, there is nothing obvious to criticize in you." Philip
had become, in the words of Martin A. S. Hume, "a Spaniard
among Spaniards": he ate, drank, dressed and acted like a
Spanish grandee. He learned, under Zúñiga's watchful eye, to
do everything with dignity and grace; he acquired an air of
authority which led everyone who met him, even those who
came upon him incognito and alone (for instance, while hunting), to treat him with respect. Zúñiga also taught him self-
control and self-discipline: Philip became adept at concealing
his feelings and restraining his emotions.

Although a great deal of the prince's day was taken up with
reading and study, the account books of his household and the
letters from his tutors to Charles V reveal a good deal about
Philip's developing tastes. From his earliest years, there is
evidence of his love of nature. When his household moved
about, one mule was required to carry a number of caged birds
belonging to the prince; two years later, Zúñiga informed the
emperor that the prince was happiest out of doors, and was
content to do anything "provided he could do it in the countryside." Indoors, he liked to play with toy soldiers, and possessed
a knight in silver armor of which he was very fond. From 1540,
when he was thirteen, he began to buy books of his own, thus
initiating a lifelong habit. His first choices, no doubt influenced by his tutors, were Josephus's *Jewish War,* Ovid's *Metamorphoses* and the Bible (in five volumes). At the same time

"a book of large sheets of plain paper" was purchased "which His Highness asked for so that he could paint in it."

One lifetime addiction which appeared early was music. Orders were issued in 1540 to repair the organs in the prince's chapel and from that time onward Philip refused to travel unless accompanied by his own organs, his own minstrels and his own choristers, so that his ears would hear only music of the highest quality. His sister Joanna learned to play the viol and the vihuela (a sort of lute) with considerable skill, and the prince probably also learned to play. He learned to hunt, too. In 1530, when only three, the prince was asking every day to go to the woods at Aranjuez in order to try out his small crossbow (and when he could not, he quarreled with his sister Maria over which of them owned more clothes). Ten years later he was no less enthusiastic: "He went on horseback into the hills for a good six hours," Zúñiga wrote to the emperor, adding grumpily: "It only seemed like two hours to him, but it seemed like more than twelve to me. . . . His only real pastime is shooting game with the crossbow." The household accounts bristle with orders to supply more crossbows, more arrows, more javelins for the hunt. Wolves and bears, as well as deer and rabbits, were shot down. Before long the emperor found it necessary to protect his game against the ravages of his son, and Philip was only allowed to kill a fixed number of animals every week. To make up for disappointments like this, the prince's valet was given thirty ducats a month as pocket money expressly to buy "things which will please His Highness." Some of these are revealing: in the course of 1540, for example, he bought jewels, perfumes, fencing swords, jousting lances (for "running at the ring"), and "a cup of Venetian glass, which was purchased when His Highness was ill with diarrhea."

The prince's health was not good, and it was a source of constant concern. Throughout his life, Philip looked sickly — his fair hair and pale skin gave him an almost albino coloring — but he avoided major illnesses until the summer of 1535, when he was unable to do any lessons for two months and almost died from what appears to have been salmonella poisoning. Philip's diet was rich, but extremely monotonous. There were only two meals a day (lunch and dinner) and the choice of dishes was exactly the same for each: fried chicken, partridge or pigeon, a piece of game, roast chicken, a slice of venison and a hunk of beef (about four pounds of it), except on Fridays when there was fish. There were soups and white bread with every meal. Fruit was available at lunchtime and salads in the evening but hardly any vegetables were consumed, and the household accounts show that little fruit was actually taken. Later on, Philip obtained express permission from the pope to eat meat even on Fridays and during Lent on account of his weak constitution. "We do not wish to risk changing our diet," he told the pope. He only abandoned his meat on Good Friday. Not surprisingly, the Prudent King seems to have suffered constantly from constipation, and the accounts of his doctors show that doses of turpentine, emetics and clysters had to be administered frequently. A new chamber pot was provided for the royal privy every fortnight, this purchase forming the most regular item in the household account books.

Philip displayed the same fascination with the state of his health as did his great-grandson Louis XIV (who, as is well known, perused the logbook kept by his doctors as he sat upon his commode). In the inventories made of the king's possessions after his death, we find many items that reflect his concern for health and, even more, for personal cleanliness. He had an eyeglass made of gold, a toothbrush made of ebony inlaid with gold, a gold toothpick, and a special box holding all his tooth-cleaning brushes and sponges, bowls to hold toothpowder and toothpaste, special instruments with which to clean out the ears, scrape the tongue, and relieve aching teeth. There was a hairbrush and a brush to clean combs, a bowl for heating water for shaving, special nail scissors and a manicure set, and the inevitable "silver goblet for the purges to be administered to

His Majesty." There were also phials and boxes of special substances for medicinal purposes: rhinoceros horn, coral, amber, balsam, coconut, and "rings made of bone which are said to be good for hemorrhoids." Apart from piles, and the occasional bout of food poisoning, Philip II seems to have suffered from asthma, arthritis (from 1563 onward), gallstones (from time to time in later life) and malaria (producing periodic fevers after the 1560's at least). But in spite of all this, the king was quite handsome. A Scottish observer noted in 1554 that he was medium to small in height, and continued:

> Of visage he is well-favoured with a broad forehead, and grey eyes, streight-nosed and manly countenance. From the forehead to the point of his chin, his face groweth small; his pace is princely, and gait so straight and upright as he loseth no inch of height; with a yellow head and a yellow beard. And, thus to conclude, he is so well-proportioned of body, arm, leg and every other limb to the same, as nature cannot work a more perfect pattern.

It is thus that he appears in the early portraits by Titian and Antonis Mor: diffident, perhaps, but handsome; and every inch a king.

Philip II's intellectual development matched his physical progress. The letters he wrote reveal the development of his distinctive literary style and his even more distinctive script, aptly described as an "all but illegible, loopy handwriting — itself almost a visual image of the circles of command and power — endlessly returning back to the writer" (see the next two pages).

Philip's intellectual interests broadened rapidly under the influence of his new tutors. In May 1541 Calvete de Estrella bought a large number of books in Salamanca for his prince. The majority of these were either classical authors or works of theology — which should not surprise us in view of the fact that almost three-quarters of the works published during the first

PHILIP II'S HANDWRITING

These two extracts show how the king's unique, spidery script changed during his life. The first, from a letter written to his aunt, Queen Mary of Hungary, when he was sixteen, is the earliest example of his writing known to me. It is still fairly regular, although the words are heavily abbreviated and the lines are beginning to run into one another. The second is characteristic of his fully matured calligraphy, achieved during his thirties, and illustrates the decline in legibility. It is from a letter written to Cardinal Granville on 4 August 1579, five days after the fall of Antonio Pérez.

Estamos
con salud, aunq[ue] la p[ri]ncesa no dexa de
tener alguna pesadunbre con su p[re]ñado.
Placera a n[uest]ro señor de continuarle la
salud p[ar]a q[ue] suceda como se desea/ El guar-
de y acreciente la muy real p[er]sona y
estado de v[uest]ra al[tesa]. De V[a]ll[adol]id, a xii de dez[iembr]e
1544.

We are in good health, although the princess [Philip's wife, Maria Manuela of Portugal] is not without some pain because of her pregnancy. May it please Our Lord to preserve her health, so that all may be as we desire; and may He guard and advance the most royal person and position of Your Highness. From Valladolid, 12 December 1544.

/aqui van las cartas en frances del p[rincip]e
my sobrino, q[ue] son una carta suya
y otra de los comisarios de Artues .
q[ue]creo q[ue] e]s duplicada de la q[ue] vino el
otro dia con una postdata de nue-
vo/ y lo uno y lo otro he visto esta
mañana.

Here are the letters in French from the prince my nephew
[Alexander Farnese, prince of Parma, regent of the Netherlands]:
there is a letter from him and another from the commissioners
of [the estates of] Artois, which is, I believe, a duplicate
of the one that arrived the other day, with a new postscript.
I looked at them both this morning.

century of printing concerned religion. But there were other volumes purchased, such as the *Adages,* the *Querella pacis,* and the *Praise of Folly* by Erasmus, all bought in 1542; Aesop's *Fables* (in Greek and Latin) ; and Dürer on geometry and architecture. Later, there were more adventurous items, many of them later forbidden by the Inquisition: in 1543, 144 maravedís were paid in Valencia, where Moorish influence was still strong, "for a book of the Koran which His Highness ordered to be bought." Two years later he purchased books on architecture by Serlio and Vitruvius (both written in Italian) , the collected works of Erasmus (in ten volumes) , the *Immortality of the Soul* by Pico della Mirandola, the *De revolutionibus* of Copernicus (published only two years before) , and works by Marsilio Ficino and Johann Reuchlin. In 1547 there was a bulk purchase of one hundred and thirty-five books from the Aldine press: one hundred and fifteen in Greek, seven in Latin (including Pliny's *Natural History*) and thirteen in Italian (including Dante and Petrarch). The same consignment of books included works on music, mathematics, astronomy, history, geography, magic, theology and philosophy, ranging from Agricola's *De rebus metallica* to Reuchlin's *De arte cabbalistica.* By the time of his death, Philip II possessed at least two hundred books on "magic" — hermetic, astrological and cabalistic — and it was partly this interest in the occult (to which we shall return) that made it necessary for him to appoint a special censor to "expurgate" the library at the Escorial in order to keep out the Inquisition in 1585. Thanks to the erudition of Calvete de Estrella, Philip II received a wide and enlightened education, and the books he bought as a boy always remained on his shelves. They provided him with that encyclopedic knowledge which appears in so many of the marginal notes he scribbled on the reports of his secretaries. A reference to historical precedent, a fact of geography that had been overlooked, a deeper understanding of the ways of men, often saved Philip, and his ministers, from error.

Philip II remained a great reader all his life, but in his early years he also kept up a practical interest in tapestry weaving and in needlework. He danced, too, he played card games, he learned to play quoits (a new game in Spain, it would seem, since special sieves had to be purchased "to shake sand on the table where His Highness played quoits in the German manner"), and he had a number of buffoons and dwarfs to entertain him. The young prince also spent a lot of time, as he was to do throughout his life, in prayer. At Pentecost 1541 he received his first communion, and from then onward he paid close attention to his chapel. Some years later, seventy-seven ducats were given to his chaplain and his court painter, who had, respectively, written and lavishly illustrated a book of vespers and other offices for the prince to use in his chapel. For Holy Week, he always went on retreat to some monastery founded by the royal family — again, a lifelong habit — although in these early years he took plenty of hunting equipment along with him so that the journey to and from the retreat would be more enjoyable. He was also much given, at this stage, to tournaments and jousting. Some of these were very grand occasions, modeled upon the heroic combats narrated in chivalric novels such as *Amadis of Gaul,* one of Philip II's favorite books. Fact, however, seldom lived up to fiction. On one occasion in 1544 a great tournament was arranged on an island in the river Pisuerga near Valladolid. It ended badly. The prince and his team, splendid in their armor, set out in a small boat for the island, but it sank under their weight. After a time it was refloated and the bedraggled warriors set off again. Again the boat sank, and the tournament had to be called off. In July 1546, there was to be another spectacular combat, this time on an island in a lake at Guadalajara. Again it ended badly, for the prince injured both his legs and had to walk with a stick for some weeks afterward. But Spanish celebrations were famous for failure: visitors from abroad during Charles V's reign were always critical of them. It was only when the prince went to the Netherlands, and especially to the remarkable "festivals of Binche," that he discovered what spectacles really were.

The great voyage to the Netherlands, which was chronicled in a large tome written by Calvete de Estrella, marked a milestone in the development of Philip II. Already he was maturing fast. In 1543, at the age of sixteen, he had become effective regent of Spain for the first time and he had married his first wife, Maria Manuela, princess of Portugal. Before long he also faced his first rebellion: in May 1545 news arrived at the Spanish court of a revolt in Peru by the European colonists. The rebellion was serious, in view of the risk of Peru's breaking entirely free of Spanish control, and so Prince Philip convoked his leading advisers to consider the correct policy to follow. The duke of Alva put forward the solution he was to suggest later on other, similar occasions: to send an army and crush the rebels by force. The other councillors pointed out that this was impossible. Peru was over three thousand miles from Spain, and the rebels controlled the sea. Alva was overruled, although his policy, which was founded on his deep distaste for the insult to royal authority posed by a revolt, may well have appealed to the young prince. Twenty years later, in a different context, Philip was to adopt it. But in 1545, at the age of eighteen, the final decision was not taken by him but by his itinerant father, the emperor.

Charles V was absent from Spain but he was not idle: in 1543 he occupied the lands of the duke of Gelderland, his only rival in the Netherlands; in 1544 he defeated and made peace with the king of France; in 1545 he made peace with the Turks; and in 1546–1547 he defeated the German Lutherans, who had opposed him with impunity for twenty years. With so many successes behind him, the emperor had the leisure to consider the possibility of transferring his enormous empire to his son, and in 1548 he gave orders for Prince Philip to leave Spain and join him in the Low Countries, there to meet his future Netherlands subjects and to receive practical instruction in the art of government from his father.

In fact, the political education of the prince had already begun by letter. Charles V was painfully aware, as were all his less exalted contemporaries, of the fragility of life. His own father had died in 1506 (when Charles was only six) and his mother had almost immediately passed irrevocably into insanity. Charles's first will and testament, in French, was composed in 1522 "in the knowledge that nothing is more certain than death and nothing more uncertain than the time of it." In 1554, his last will and testament (significantly, composed in Spanish) contained the same phrase. It was in this spirit that the emperor wrote four sets of "instructions" to guide his son and heir should death suddenly claim him. The first was written at Madrid in November 1539, just before the emperor set out for the Netherlands; the second was written at Pálamos, north of Barcelona, in May 1543, as Charles left Spain to direct the war against France; the third and longest was written at Augsburg in January 1548, after the defeat of the German Protestants; the fourth and shortest was written in Brussels in 1556 as the emperor prepared to return to Spain to die. These papers of advice reveal, better than almost any other source, the political skill and competence of Charles V. The instructions, especially those of 1543, are a synthesis of the art of government and a blueprint for the actions of a good prince. They constitute, in the words of the great Belgian scholar L. P. Gachard, "a monument of prudence, of foresight, of consummate experience in government, of profound knowledge of men and of the world. They would, by themselves, suffice to give Charles V the reputation of being the leading politician of his time."

The instructions of 1543 were the most important, and they were designed to do two things: to lay down precise rules for Prince Philip's conduct of government, and to offer advice on the problems that were likely to arise. Written in the emperor's own hand, the documents sparkled with incisive and subtle insights into the art of government and the intricacies of sixteenth-century politics. Immediate problems, such as the strengths and weaknesses of individual councillors, were discussed in detail — for on these matters the young prince had no one else whose judgment he could trust. The duke of Alva, for example, who was twenty years older than Philip and who was to play a prominent role in government until his death in 1582, was admitted to be the best military commander in Spain, but the emperor advised his son to keep him out of the administration because of his dynastic ambition: "He has always laid claim to great things and tried to make more of everything that he has, although he always does it with great humility and self-abasement. Beware, my son, of what he does with you who are much younger." Charles V warned his son about the factions that had grown up among his servants, one of them led by the duke of Alva, and urged him to avoid becoming identified with any single faction or faction leader: "Transact business with many, and do not bind yourself to or become dependent upon any individual, because although it may save time, it does no good." There were many similar pieces of general advice, which the young prince was to take to heart: never trust anyone, never show your emotions, always have fixed hours in which to appear regularly in public, be devout and God-fearing at all times, be just in all things.

The emperor did not stop here. He also gave advice about more intimate matters. He reminded Philip that his sisters were now growing into women and should be treated with appropriate decorum and respect for their sex; he asked that the prince get rid of the buffoons and simpletons who filled the court (a piece of advice Philip did not follow) ; and he advised his son to avoid excessive sexual indulgence (an imminent problem, since Philip was about to marry his cousin of the same age, Maria Manuela of Portugal) . "When you are with your wife . . . be careful and do not overstrain yourself at the beginning, in order to avoid physical damage, because besides the fact that it [intercourse] may be damaging both to the growth of the body and to its strength, it often induces such weakness that it prevents the siring of children and may even kill you." Philip must remember, the emperor continued, that he was not marrying to enjoy sex, but to produce heirs. And "for this reason you must be very careful when you are with your wife. And because this is somewhat difficult, the remedy is to keep away from her as much as you can. And so I beg and advise you strongly that, as soon as you have consummated the marriage, you should leave her on some pretext, and do not go back to see her too quickly or too often; and when you do go back, let it be only for a short time." Naturally the emperor did not leave matters there. He told Philip's governor, Don Juan de Zúñiga, to make sure that this advice was followed (and he told Philip of Zúñiga's orders). He also placed his daughter-in-law in the care of relatives, who had strict orders "to keep her away from the prince except for the times which his life and health can stand."

This remarkable piece of paternal advice concluded with an injunction that Philip was not to use his separation from his wife as an excuse to consort with other women: "Since you have not, I am sure, had relations with any other woman than your wife, do not commit any further wickedness after your marriage because . . . apart from the discomfort and ills that may ensue from it between you and her, it will destroy the effect of keeping you away from her."

The young prince appears to have followed this advice to the letter. The reports of Zúñiga to the emperor, which normally listed Philip's shortcomings in meticulous detail, recorded no sexual excesses until the birth of Don Carlos, the young couple's only child, put an end to the princess's life in July 1545. In almost all other things, too, the emperor's advice was religiously followed, which is not surprising, given the credentials of the adviser: no other person had as good a title to be believed and respected. Charles V knew the problems facing a prince of Spain as no one else did or could, and the fruit of his experience had a uniquely forceful influence on his son, who kept the 1543 instructions all his life.

The longer instruction of 1548 was also full of valuable advice on governmental methods, personal behavior and dynastic affairs. This time the emperor envisaged a marriage between his son and a daughter of the king of France (actually effected in 1560), between his daughter Maria and his nephew Maximilian (effected in 1548) and between his other daughter Joanna and another nephew, Prince John of Portugal (effected in 1552).* There was also a bird's-eye view of the European political scene, underlining the policies and developments most advantageous to the Habsburg empire.

But, the emperor began to wonder, could any of this make sense to his son, who had never set foot outside Spain? Philip knew nothing about the geography of Europe, nor of the extent of his future inheritance. And the people of Charles's empire beyond Spain had never seen their future sovereign. The emperor therefore resolved that his son should make a "Grand Tour" through Italy and Germany to the Netherlands where, on the one hand, he could be recognized as heir apparent by the provinces of the Low Countries and, on the other, he could be introduced directly to the problems of government and diplomacy by his father. Accordingly, Prince Philip left Valladolid, the town where he was born, in October 1548, and traveled via Barcelona and Genoa to Milan, capital of the state of Lombardy. The prince spent Christmas and the New Year there, before moving on through Trent, Innsbruck, Munich and Heidelberg to Brussels, the capital of the Habsburg Netherlands, where the prince was reunited with his father on 1 April 1549.

Something of a cloud lay over the meeting, however. Some observers believed that the prince had behaved badly on his journey, standing on ceremony and appearing cold and arrogant. An English observer of the prince's entry into Mantua

* These alliances are graphically displayed in the genealogical charts on pages 80–81.

noted that when the duke of Ferrara and the Venetian ambassador came in person to pay their respects, "the prince made small countenance to anie of them, wherupon he obtayned throughe all Italye a name of insolencye." There had also been reports from Zúñiga in Spain that the prince was acquiring bad habits. In a remarkable letter the emperor singled out for criticism "the disorder and the time wasted in getting up and going to bed, in dressing and undressing . . . because although at present it may not be of great inconvenience, it bodes ill for the future if all this becomes a habit and custom." Charles then launched into a long list of crimes his son had committed: he had become cool toward his wife, he came home very late from hunting, he was becoming negligent in his devotions and in confessions; and then there was "what happened in Cigales at the house of Perejón and going out by night," and "other little things that have begun during my absence." The emperor intended to take a strong line on these matters (although perhaps his severity was mitigated by his own shortcomings: before his son could reach the Netherlands, Charles had an affair with an eighteen-year-old girl from Regensburg, the fruit of which was Don John of Austria, born in February 1547).

For several reasons, therefore, Charles V was glad to have his son once more under his direct scrutiny, and he labored to improve his manners, his understanding of politics and his knowledge of the Low Countries. In 1549 the prince, accompanied by his father and the leading courtiers, made a leisurely tour of the Netherlands to meet his future subjects. This time, it would seem that everyone was favorably impressed. Philip now appeared affable, he danced well, he flirted with the ladies, and did his best to drink as much beer as the Netherlands nobles. And he was certainly favorably impressed with the Low Countries. He was delighted by the formal and ornamental gardens and the distinctive red-brick and black-slate building style, both of which he successfully introduced into Spain on his return; and he fell in love with Flemish art and music, sending pictures like van der Weyden's *Descent from the Cross* back to Spain and collecting Netherlands musicians and instruments for his household. But what made the most lasting impact was the obvious wealth of the cities of Flanders and Brabant, especially Antwerp, and the sumptuous magnificence of the old Burgundian court, especially as displayed in spectacles like the festivals held at the palace of Binche in Hainaut. In August 1549, in honor of the prince, an elaborate presentation of "the Castle of Darkness," a passage from *Amadis of Gaul,* was staged in the magnificent grounds of the palace, the property of Queen Mary, sister of Charles V and his regent in the Netherlands. Even twenty years later, men still talked about court festivities as being better or worse than "the festivals of Binche." Philip II never forgot them.

The prince remained in the Netherlands until the spring of 1551, when he returned to Spain. Now twenty-four years old, he began to take a direct share in government. There were no more long papers of paternal advice; instead, there were regular and intimate letters from Charles asking the prince's opinion on almost every major issue. Decisions were made by the king and his son together, without reference to any other "watchdog" in Spain. The prince had come of age, and was ready to take his father's place whenever need should arise. It is even possible that Charles intended to abdicate almost at once. As early as 1542 he had sent some of his advisers to find a suitable place for him to retire to if, like Marcus Aurelius, he could lay down the cares of office. The Hieronymite monastery of Yuste, in Estremadura, had seemed particularly appropriate. However, any plans Charles might have made were destroyed by the European war that began at the end of 1551.

A major rebellion broke out in Germany, where the Protestant princes managed to drive out the emperor's troops. At the same time the French invaded Italy and the Turkish fleet attacked Spain's bases in North Africa. Although he mobilized more than 150,000 troops in 1552, Charles V was unable to defeat his enemies. In 1554 he therefore ordered work to begin at Yuste to build a small palace to which he could retire and spend his last years on earth in spiritual meditation. In the same year he bestowed the kingdoms of Naples and Sicily on his son, and organized Philip's marriage to his second cousin, Mary Tudor, queen of England. Philip became "king consort." In October 1555 Charles made him ruler of the Netherlands, and in January 1556, king of Spain. The emperor had abdicated.

Yet Philip's apprenticeship was still not quite over: for some time he continued to stand in the shadow of his father. The psychological burden of being the son of such a great man must always have been oppressive; but for his first year as king, Philip's position was intolerable because Charles V continued to reside in Brussels until the end of 1556, openly directing his son's policies. Even after that, from his retreat at Yuste, he bombarded the young king with orders, opinions and peremptory letters of advice on what to do. When Philip desired to make peace with his enemies in order to save money, the emperor overruled him. (And, in this, events proved the emperor right, for in the war that followed, the Habsburgs' armies gained complete control of Italy and inflicted two crushing defeats on the French: at Saint-Quentin in August 1557 and at Gravelines in July 1558.) Philip II only ceased to be an "apprentice" and escaped from his father's tutelage in September 1558 when, clutching his wife's crucifix and his own scourge, his eyes fixed on Titian's great *Gloria* painting, the emperor Charles V died. His son was at last free to govern his great inheritance in whatever way he chose.

TWO

The King at Work

PHILIP II has sometimes been compared to a spider sitting at the center of a web. Certainly his style of government stood in marked contrast to that of his globe-trotting warrior father; but Philip firmly believed that too much mobility in a monarch was a bad thing. His last paper of advice for his son and heir, written in 1598, was explicit on this point: "Traveling about one's kingdoms is neither useful nor decent," he wrote. The right place for the king of Spain was to be always in Spain. Philip was particularly opposed to sovereign rulers' moving around at the head of an army (as Charles V had so often done). In 1586, when his son-in-law, the headstrong duke of Savoy, proposed to lead an attack on Geneva, the king issued a stern rebuke:

> The duke must not be present in person, nor even nearby [he thundered], above all for reasons of prestige. If the venture succeeds, his prestige will be enhanced whether he is present or not — and perhaps he will be respected even more if he is absent — but if it fails to achieve its objective (as it may do, for these things are in the hands of God, not men), he will lose more prestige by far if he is there in person.

Philip II deliberately chose to govern his far-flung empire, and his armies, from Castile. Despite criticisms, and although he delegated considerable power to his servants in America, Italy and the Netherlands, he insisted throughout his reign that all important decisions (and many unimportant ones) should be referred back to Spain for his personal scrutiny and sanction.

This desire for a high degree of centralization (by sixteenth-century standards) created serious administrative problems. First, the volume of business always threatened to clog the wheels of government; second, the enormous distances separating the outlying provinces of Philip II's empire from Madrid created the constant risk that a decision, once made, would be overtaken by events before it could be put into effect. It took a minimum of two weeks for a letter from Madrid to reach Brussels or Milan; it took a minimum of two months for a letter from Madrid to reach Mexico; and it took a minimum of a year for a letter from Madrid to reach Manila in the Philippines. "Distance," it has been said, "explains a good half of the actions of Philip II." Even if this is a slight over-statement, the battle to overcome the problems posed by distance, and by the excessive volume of business, certainly goes a long way toward explaining Philip's unique style of government.

The sixteenth century was the golden age of conciliar government all over Europe, and Spain was no exception. At the center of Philip II's administrative system was a complex structure of fourteen councils, five of them created by his great-grandparents, Ferdinand and Isabella, four of them created by his father, Charles V, and five of them created by himself (see the accompanying chart). From 1561, when Philip decreed that Madrid should become the permanent location of all central government offices, each of his councils met at fixed times on fixed days in a separate room of the new royal palace, especially extended by the king.

His most important councils were those of Castile (a sort of "Home Office" responsible for justice, public order, economic

The Councils of Philip II
(with the dates of their creation)

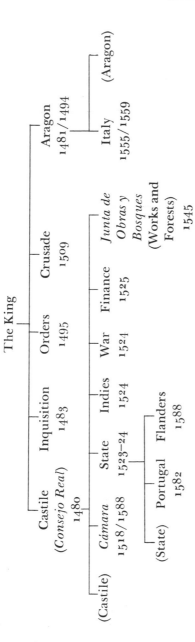

By the time of his death in 1598, Philip II was advised by fourteen central councils (the equivalent of modern government departments), each with its own sphere of competence: the Council of State dealt with foreign affairs; *Cámara*, with patronage in Castile; Orders, with the affairs of the three military orders in Castile; Crusade, with administering the clerical tax of that name; and so on. All of the councils continued into the seventeenth century.

The repetition of a council in parentheses means that it continued in operation even though some of its responsibilities were assigned to new bodies, which then functioned independently. Two dates of creation separated by a slash indicate that the council's competence was changed at the later date, so much so that the council could be said to have had two "birthdays" rather than one.

matters and ecclesiastical affairs within the kingdom of Castile), the Indies (which had similar responsibilities for the
New World) and the Inquisition (which controlled the
twenty-one tribunals of the Holy Office established throughout
the Spanish empire, from Peru to Sardinia and from Navarre
to Sicily). The councils were primarily administrative departments, and they were staffed (except for the Council of State,
which dealt with foreign affairs) mostly by lawyers trained in
the universities of Castile. Of eight presidents of the Council
of the Indies appointed by Philip II, seven were lawyers; of
thirty-nine councillors appointed by him, every one was a
lawyer. The universities of Spain, with their *colegios mayores*
or "graduate schools," were used by the Spanish Habsburgs as
a sort of seminary wherein future administrators could be
trained.

A complex conciliar structure and an embryonic bureaucracy were essential for the effective government of an empire
as vast and as diffuse as Philip II's. But the councils were only
advisory bodies, and the bureaucrats were no more than administrators. Philip II did not adopt the "cabinet" style of
government favored by most later rulers, with the heads of the
various government departments meeting together to discuss
policy and make collective recommendations to the sovereign.
Such a system would have deprived him of a considerable
amount of authority. Instead, the king insisted that all orders
should be issued bearing his personal signature, and the final
decision on most issues was taken by him alone and in person.
The basic document of the Spanish central government was
therefore the *consulta,* the paper which every council sent to
the king after each meeting with a formal note of its recommendations on all items referred to it. Early in the reign
these consultas and any other relevant papers were brought to
the king and read to him either by the secretary or by the
president of the council. The officers of the more important
councils had a daily audience, after which the papers were left
for the king to scrutinize at leisure. In time they were returned

with holograph responses, notes or memoranda attached. To some extent this part of the government's activity was automatic. With their spheres of competence, their fixed procedures and their trained ancillary staffs, the councils could cope admirably with the mass of routine, ordinary business which the central government had to transact every week of the year. But not all of Philip II's business was ordinary, predictable and routine. Periodically there were emergencies, demanding constant attention while they lasted; there were also matters requiring the attention of more than one council; and there were other items that, for various reasons, the king did not wish any council to see. Even before he returned to Spain in 1559, he invited his ministers to write to him directly. "When you wish to write something for my eyes alone," he informed one official, "whether it is a matter of state or anything else, if you put on the envelope that the letter should be delivered to me in person, it will be done."

The king's insistence on seeing personally and in secret a considerable number of incoming papers in this way at first created many problems for his ministers. In April 1560 the secretary of the Council of State, Gonzalo Pérez, a man with thirty-five years of experience in government, complained that his council had only met twice in full session since its return to Spain the previous September. "I have been ill these past few days," he wrote, "but that has not prevented me from attending to business punctually, since decisions are taken so slowly that even a cripple could keep up with them." The fault, Pérez contended, lay in the system: "Truly with sixteen councillors who are so different in background and in other things, I do not see how they can agree. I believe His Majesty will see the light and will realize what should be done. I hope to God he does so soon." But five years later Pérez was still complaining: "His Majesty makes mistakes and will continue to make mistakes in many matters because he discusses them with different people, sometimes with one, at other times with another, concealing something from one minister and reveal-

ing it to another. It is therefore small wonder that different
and even contradictory decisions are issued."

This situation could not last, and with the coming of open
war to the Mediterranean, the Netherlands and even the south
of Spain after 1566, changes in the system of government had
to be made. One innovation was the creation of informal com-
mittees, known as *juntas,* to discuss and advise the king on
particular policies and situations. For example, a committee
of three senior ministers met throughout 1571 to handle the
campaign in the Mediterranean that ended in the great victory
of Lepanto. By the end of 1572 death had reduced this particular body to "the two" and before the end of the next year
both of them were also dead. But there were many ad hoc com-
mittees of this sort, some existing for only a few weeks, others
continuing for far longer, like the great committee created in
November 1573 to prepare for the state bankruptcy decree of
September 1575. This "junta system" meant that some advisers
became very familiar indeed with large areas of the king's
business and acquired, in effect, the position of cabinet ministers. Some of them were officials of the royal household, with
an existing right to communicate directly with the king, but
most of them were bureaucrats. Courtiers like Ruy Gómez da
Silva or the duke of Alva were concerned more with patronage
and foreign policy than with administrative routine. Supervision of everyday government was entrusted to men of humbler station, such as Francisco de Erasso, a minor nobleman
of Navarrese extraction who had been a government official
since 1523, and had by 1559 become secretary to no less than
six of Philip II's central councils and a member of two more.
In 1565 he fell from grace, however, and the following year he
was found guilty of fraud and fined 13,000 ducats. After a
time, his mantle seems to have fallen on a man of even
humbler origins, Diego de Espinosa (1502–1572), a priest
trained in law at the University of Salamanca who became
president of the Council of the Inquisition in 1564 (and later
inquisitor general) and also president of the Council of Cas-

tile in 1565. From then until his death in 1572 Espinosa was, in the words of an influential (and perhaps slightly jealous) courtier, "the man in all Spain in whom the king places most confidence and with whom he discusses most business, both concerning Spain and foreign affairs." When he died, everyone speculated on who would succeed to "the superintendence of matters of war, state and finance, the handling of consultas and all the rest of the burden which the cardinal carried." The king, however, was not willing to trust anyone else with as much power as Espinosa had held. "I believed that it was wise to entrust many matters which concerned my royal office to the cardinal," he informed Espinosa's successor as president of the Council of Castile. "And perhaps there were good reasons for it then. But experience has shown that it was not a good thing; and although it meant more leisure and less work for me, I do not think it should be allowed to continue." Philip II had come to appreciate the wisdom of his father's advice, tendered almost thirty years before: "Do not bind yourself to or become dependent upon any individual, because although it may save time it does no good."

Yet the fall of Espinosa did not bring about a return to the chaotic governmental style of the 1560's. The clock could not be turned back because the volume of official business with which the government had to deal had increased enormously. The central councils were meeting more often — from 1571 onward the Council of the Indies had to meet three afternoons a week as well as every morning in order to get through its agenda — and the quantity of paperwork they produced grew prodigiously. The Council of War, for example, which produced only two or three bundles of working papers a year in the 1560's, turned out over thirty a year in the 1590's. The business of all the fourteen councils seems to have increased in proportion, as did the copious volume of business that never passed through the councils at all. The number of memorials and petitions asking for favors and rewards was staggering. In

May 1571, when Espinosa persuaded the king to take on a special private secretary to handle them, 1,252 separate memorials were presented to the crown — over forty a day. The king had to make a decision on each one.

It was small wonder that at times Philip II seemed to feel that he would never finish his work. "Although I have 100,000 papers in front of me, I thought I ought to remind you that . . ." he began a desperate note to one of his secretaries. On another occasion he stoically read and signed in a single day the four hundred separate documents that had been allowed to accumulate on his desk. Philip II was indefatigable: he could work at all times and in all places. When the weather was fine, he took his papers with him (although he would have preferred not to) : "So far I have been unable to finish with these devils, my papers," he announced. "But I am taking some with me to read in the country, which is where I am off to right now." The king often read dispatches as he traveled, even on board ship. When the royal family went sailing on the Tagus at Aranjuez, Philip "took a small desk with him and dealt with and signed some dispatches which his valet brought him." Meanwhile, on the banks of the river, the court ladies danced and a Negro band strummed guitars.

Naturally business could seldom be so delightfully combined with pleasure. Sometimes the king found the pressure of work too great and simply gave up. On one occasion, for example, he complained to his secretary: "Because I have been dealing with Low Countries business until late this morning, and afterward signing a lot of papers that came in, I cannot cope with any more. I am therefore going off into the country. If I can manage anything afterward I will call you." The refrain was much the same on other occasions: "I have just been given this other packet of papers from you. I have neither the time nor the strength to look at it, and so I will not open it until to-morrow. It is already past ten o'clock and I have not yet dined. My table is full of papers for tomorrow because I cannot cope with any more now." Or again: "It is already ten o'clock and I am going to pieces and dying of hunger because it is a fast day. These papers will have to wait until tomorrow." Very often the king complained about eyestrain — he was writing "with awful pain in my eyes" or "with my eyes half-closed" and so on — no doubt caused by long hours and poor candlelight. He never seems to have worn glasses, although he possessed two pairs of "traveling spectacles," probably to protect his eyes against dust (until the art of lens grinding was refined in the seventeenth century, spectacles were of little use to most people). The king's shaky and irregular handwriting (see pages 12–13) no doubt owed as much to eyestrain as to the arthritis which, from the 1560's onward, affected his writing arm and slowed his script down.*

The pressure of official business was taking its toll on the king's health and temper, and it was becoming essential to reduce his personal involvement in less important affairs. In April 1573, Espinosa's former secretary, Mateo Vázquez, proposed to the king one simple method of reducing his burdens. He wrote to Philip directly: "It does not seem that Your Majesty has a personal secretary, with the result that there is a great deal of unavoidable reading and writing; and from this employment and effort we must fear the damage to health which we know occurs in most people who deal with papers." Vázquez proposed that he should deal with all incoming mail intended for the king's eyes alone, not for a council, so that "much reading and writing by Your Majesty in person can be avoided." It was a good idea, and for the next eighteen years Vázquez was to fill the role he had described, serving as the king's personal private secretary. He was allowed to prepare and even to write out the king's replies to incoming papers. According to a colleague:

* Concrete evidence of the king's writing speed is, of course, almost nonexistent. However, we know that on 11 April 1578 he began writing a note to Mateo Vázquez "just after 9 P.M." and that he was still writing when the clock struck ten. He had only written 450 words (on 2½ sides of paper!).

They were dealt with in this way. His Majesty used to sit down at his table and the secretary came up to it with his papers. Sitting on a stool, Vázquez would make a report to His Majesty on what the secret letters and memorials on serious matters contained. When His Majesty had listened, he decided what he wished to be done in each case. . . . The secretary at once took a note of His Majesty's resolutions, and subsequently turned these into memoranda for the ministers concerned, in His Majesty's name. . . . If the matter was serious, the memoranda were written by Vázquez but initialed by the king. . . . When His Majesty dealt with consultas, Secretary Vázquez would read out the substance of them with the council's recommendation and His Majesty, having heard their contents, took the decision which seemed best in each case, in the presence of the secretary. The latter noted down the decision on a sheet of paper and afterward, using the most clear and concise reasons, he put the decision in the margin of the consulta in his handwriting, which the king subsequently initialed.

Vázquez also served as coordinator of the various informal juntas that Philip created with increasing frequency after the 1560's. The king and his secretary determined who should be included (and when they should be dropped), the times of the meetings, and the agenda. Vázquez attended to take minutes, to relay the findings of the committee to the king, and the latter's instructions to the committee. Without Vázquez, it has been observed, "the junta system would not have worked": his role was essential if the king was to maintain his principle of "confuse and rule" by concealing most areas of his policies from most of his ministers, so that no one would know more than he did.

A perceptive Venetian ambassador noted in 1574 that Philip II never entirely trusted anyone — "They say that the king suffers from the same malady as his father: that is, suspicion." Even Philip's adulatory biographer Lorenzo van der Hammen admitted that "suspicion, disbelief and doubt were the basis of his prudence." Nowhere did these negative qualities emerge more clearly than in the king's remuneration of his servants. Few of them received an adequate salary. Many ministers complained of their impoverishment through service to the crown, especially powerful aristocrats like the duke of Alva, who (probably correctly) claimed that he had spent 500,000 ducats of his personal fortune in carrying out the tasks assigned him by the king. It seems that this was precisely Philip's intention. In 1575 the duke of Medina Celi, another nobleman who had served the king faithfully for years, lay dying. He expressed his chagrin at all the debts he had incurred in the royal service. The king was informed of this by his secretary but replied: "You are well aware that I prefer to do more for the dead than for the living; and when he is dead I shall not fail to settle my debt to him."

The king trusted no one, and this was the real reason for his insistence on seeing every state paper for himself. Of course he could not spot every mistake, fraud or ambiguity, and every minister knew this; but they never knew in advance what the king's eye might light upon. One small example of iniquity discovered by Philip's personal involvement in government concerned the son of an official of the Council of the Indies, who used his inside contacts to steal some four hundred ducats of silver off a ship newly arrived from America in 1580. He was found out, and sentenced by the Council of the Indies in 1582 to four years' exile and a fine of 20,000 maravedís (fifty-three ducats). This was, in itself, lenient, but on appeal the sentence was reduced to two years' exile and 10,000 maravedís. In July 1583 the condemned man appealed to the council again and, no doubt out of respect for his father, they favored further clemency. The king was sent the relevant paper to sign, but by chance he read it first. He was furious. "The offense was serious," he reminded the council, "and deserved severe punishment. Seeing that the sentence has already been moderated on appeal — which should not have happened — there is no reason why we should now reduce it by a single

day more, nor why we should pardon him. Let him serve his
sentence to the full."

Through incidents like these, which became the talk of the
court, Philip II became famous far and wide as the "king of
paper," the monarch who was happiest when scribbling notes
to a secretary who was sitting next door. Certainly Philip far
preferred reading and writing to speaking and listening. "If
you are near at hand," he wrote to one courtier, "it might be
advisable to hear the details [on Portuguese developments]
from you by word of mouth. . . . But since you can send them
to me by letter in complete security, I think it would be best if
you did so." Even with his intimates the king could be tongue-
tied. When his daughter Catalina left him in 1585 to become
duchess of Savoy: "I was unable to say goodbye as I had wished
either to you or the duke, nor could I say some of the things I
was thinking about." So, after he had climbed a nearby church
tower in order to catch a last glimpse of his daughter's galley
sailing away, he sat down to write her a letter in which he
was able to express his inner thoughts.

This habit of transacting business by writing has excited
much criticism both from contemporaries and from historians.
To the people of the sixteenth century, most of whom could
read only with difficulty (and, when they did so, they generally
read aloud) , Philip's preference for the written word was all
but incomprehensible. "God did not give kings authority over
men so that they could withdraw to their study to read and
write, nor even to meditate and tell their rosaries," the king's
almoner told his master one day, alleging that Philip preferred
written communication, "mainly so that Your Majesty can
have a better excuse for getting away from people." There was
a grain of truth in this — the king sometimes confessed that he
disliked having people around him all the time — but it was
not the only explanation. He also hated to make a decision on
the spur of the moment: if a matter came to him on paper he
could take his time. Furthermore, although his secretaries,

architects and ministers came to see him at fixed times on most days, and although he gave regular audiences to foreign diplomats, he sometimes found it difficult to remember what was said to him. Once, when a prominent minister asked the king's secretary to arrange an audience for him, the king was reluctant to agree: "I would be glad to see him but, really, I do not have the time, and little of what is said to me at audiences stays in my head — but don't tell anyone that. I mean in most audiences, not all." Finally, and most important, there was simply not time for the king to deal with all the business he chose to supervise unless he could have every matter summarized and prepared beforehand with a covering note from the appropriate secretary. Anyone who has had anything to do with administration knows how much time is wasted in meetings. Given the complexity and the size of the Spanish empire, and given Philip's II's insistence that he should vet every order issued in his name, the elaborate paperwork of his secretaries and himself was indispensable. The proof of the system's success lies in the large number of papers sent to the king which were returned with a decision within one or two days. Some even came back the same day: "At 6 P.M. a courier arrived with a letter for the king from Antonio Pérez and he returned at eight o'clock with his reply" is a fairly typical entry in the logbook of the king's private secretary.

The cost of such administrative efficiency to Philip II can only be guessed at. In 1590 a well-informed courtier estimated that the king had written enough letters and papers in his life to fill more than four mule loads — and at that time the king still had eight more years of life ahead of him! At about the same time, a Florentine ambassador asserted that Philip spent eight or nine hours of each and every day toiling at his desk, following the same strict routine that he had always followed. He woke up spontaneously, normally at about eight in the morning, and then spent an hour or so reading papers in bed. He only rose at around nine-thirty and was shaved by his barbers and dressed by his gentlemen of the bedchamber. Im-

mediately after dressing the king went to chapel and heard
Mass, then gave audience to anyone who wished to see him
until the hour of noon, when he ate lunch. After that he had
a nap and then began the main work of the day, which kept
him at his desk until dinnertime. The meal was normally
served at around 9 P.M., but it could be delayed if the king
was not ready to eat. Bedtime was also a flexible hour, again
dependent on the volume of business on hand. The king's
whole day was geared to the rhythm of his administration,
which began to function at eight o'clock in the morning in
order to generate a sufficient quantity of papers by the time
the king started work after lunch. Pleasure had to be fitted
into this rhythm of work. Even Philip's daily visits to his wife
were sandwiched between his business commitments: before
going to Mass, after dinner, and just before going to bed (the
royal couple normally slept — as royal couples normally did
at that time — in separate rooms). In Philip II's life, recreation and leisure activities tended to take place only when one
was too exhausted to do any more work.

THREE

The King at Play

Find out how the pheasants are doing at the Casa de Campo and if anything more is needed for them, and if it would be better to let them all free at once, or only some of them, or whether we should keep them cooped up. Let me know about this, and tell me whether they have started building any of the walls at the Pardo, and how work there is getting on. And write to Aranjuez and ask them about the buildings there and about the hedges, and whether they can hear the pheasants there . . .

This characteristic holograph note, at the end of a routine letter from one of his secretaries about public works, betrays some of Philip's deepest and most passionate interests: birds, gardens, building, the sounds of nature. But it reveals even more about the king's almost boyish excitement and enthusiasm for the new secluded world he was creating for himself in the heart of Spain.

As soon as he returned from his long voyage to the Netherlands and Germany he knew what he wanted. Almost from the moment of his arrival in Spain in 1551, although technically still only prince regent, Philip began to issue orders that were intended to make the royal palaces of Castile and their gardens "like those of the Low Countries." He sent his architects and head gardeners to tour France and other countries for ideas on how to overhaul his Spanish patrimony and make the king's private world more secluded and luxuriant. The traditional aim of growing trees and shrubs in the royal gardens for their fruit was abandoned. In 1553 the custodian of the royal palace at Aranjuez was ordered to pull up all the olive trees, to level the land where they grew, and to sow grass. Almond and mulberry trees too were to be uprooted, leaving only a few big ones "and these are only to remain because they improve the view; they are not to be cultivated nor is their fruit to be picked. There is to be no sowing of crops or cultivation of vegetables." All mud walls were to be replaced by hedges, and an entirely new network of streams and rivers was to be created, including some artificial lakes which, the king hoped, "would encourage birds to come and improve our hawking." Before long there were orders to create similar "Flemish" gardens at other royal palaces: at the Casa de Campo (four thousand acres of gardens laid out by Philip near Madrid); at the Pardo, also near Madrid; and at El Bosque near Segovia. Alas, these early efforts were unsuccessful. During the king's second absence in northern Europe (1554–1559) the new trees were all allowed to die (because the Spanish gardeners did not appreciate the need for irrigation) and the old habits of gathering fruit returned. Philip was horrified at what had happened when at last he returned to Spain, and he decided that the only way to have Flemish gardens in the Iberian peninsula was to import Flemish gardeners to make them. Experts in making dikes and artificial lakes, skilled seedsmen and growers were therefore brought to Spain, forming a colony of some thirty Netherlanders, many of whom chose to settle in their new country. Their labor was directed by the king in person, and throughout the 1560's he was forever visiting the various gardens, giving oral directions on the spot about where to plant trees and how to lay out individual flower beds. Letters to the custodians of his palaces often ended with the command: "Do not do anything more until I can come and see for myself."

The operations on the royal gardens were undertaken on a large scale. Trees were brought from far and wide, from France, Flanders and America, as well as from all over Spain, and they were brought en masse: 65 bundles of trees and saplings from the nurseries of Holland in 1561 and a further 36 "chests" in 1565; 1,500 jasmines and 3,000 myrtles from Valencia and 1,775 trees from Arcos in January 1562; 50 orange trees from Plasencia the next month; and so on. By the time of the king's death there were no less than 223,000 trees in the royal gardens at Aranjuez alone, almost all of them planted under Philip's personal supervision. It was the same elsewhere. In 1565 he drew up his own plan according to which the gardens of El Bosque were to be planted and began importing shrubs and trees. At the Escorial, he ordered the gardens to be begun at the same time as the building of the monastery, and he so contrived matters that in every one of the twelve beds there were some flowers in bloom at all times of the year. And when in 1581 the king went to his newly conquered realm of Portugal, one of his first orders was for gardeners to be sent to the royal palaces at Almeirim and elsewhere to put the gardens there "in the same order and perfection as those at the Casa de Campo and Aranjuez." The king was justifiably proud: both were unique in Spain, the Casa with its fountains, topiary work and great artificial lakes (large enough to stage a mock galley battle in 1570 in honor of the king's marriage to Anne of Austria) ; Aranjuez with its island-gardens, its shaded walks and its lush lawns. He would sometimes eat picnics there, surrounded by the fragrance of the flowers he had planted, and as in all his palaces, he made sure that the desk at which he toiled over his papers was placed in a window overlooking his gardens.

The gardens were not only equipped to satisfy the king's love of flowers. At Aranjuez there was also a small zoo. It started with four camels, which were brought to the palace in the 1570's from Africa. They were encouraged to breed since they proved useful with building work as beasts of burden, and by 1600 there were about forty of them. There were also ostriches. In 1584 the king was excited about the arrival of a number of specimens from Africa, and he considered what sort of cage to put them in. Perhaps the wrong decision was taken, because four years later one of the birds got out and attacked a gardener, injuring him so severely that he was off work for several weeks (characteristically, the incident has been preserved for posterity only because the king ordered the man to be given twenty ducats in compensation for lost wages, and the payment was noted in the accounts). At the Casa de Campo there was a larger zoo with elephants, rhinoceros (a rarity in Europe) and lions (again, security was less than perfect because in 1563 a lioness escaped and almost mauled a courtier to death while the royal family looked on helplessly from their coach). There was also a special flock of swans, imported from the Netherlands, which floated majestically on the artificial lakes constructed by Dutch experts (and carefully stocked with both perch and carp, also imported in special containers from the Low Countries).

Philip was a keen fisherman, always ready to throw his line into the Tagus at Aranjuez or into the Eresma at El Bosque (the Eresma was rich in trout), as well as into his private lakes. The fish were protected by draconian legislation: anyone caught fishing in the royal ponds would receive one hundred lashes for the first offense and would be sent to the galleys for the second; anyone caught swimming in the pools would be fined 3,000 maravedís (eight ducats). The king did not intend to spend the whole day fishing and catch nothing: life was too short. So before he went to the Pardo in February 1566 he gave orders that "the water level in the small lake should be allowed to fall overnight so that it will already be lower tomorrow and I can fish there if I want." The fish could expect no mercy.

He had much the same outlook when he went hunting. There was the same effort to breed game, and to observe a "close season," and the same savage penalties against poachers: a fine of 10,000 maravedís, six months' banishment from the village of residence, and loss of gear (plus one hundred lashes if the poacher resisted arrest by the forest guards) were the standard penalties. For poaching a royal pheasant, the fine was increased by 5,000 maravedís; for poaching a royal swan it went up by 10,000. Sometimes matters became more serious, as in 1569 when a guard at the Pardo caught two poachers red-handed with seven rabbits. The poachers drew their swords, half-killed the guard, and escaped. The king himself gave judgment in this case: the two poachers were sentenced to death (for resisting arrest, not for poaching — "There is no doubt that poaching is not a capital offense," the king admitted) and were fined 2,000 ducats; their wives were fined 4,000 maravedís (about eleven ducats) and exiled from their village for two years. The king was a little reluctant to condemn the women. "With wives one has to be moderate, on account of the obligation they have to their husbands in such matters," he noted. And, furthermore, "a wife should not lose what should be her own because of a crime committed by her husband." But these wives had actually been out poaching themselves, and the king's game had to be protected. As with his fish, Philip's satisfaction lay in the quantity, not the quality of the "bag." His favorite hunting technique was to go with his family into the forest, to a blind camouflaged with nets, toward which a herd of deer was driven. When the deer became entangled in the nets, the royal hunting dogs were set loose on the herd and so most of them were torn to death just where the royal family was watching, to their great enjoyment. "In less than no time," noted a delighted foreign visitor, "thirty of the deer, or even more, were killed." With such an active owner there was no place for poachers. In the 1590's, when arthritis scarcely allowed him to move, the king and his family would go to a clearing in the woods in their coach;

there they waited until their numerous huntsmen (there were over sixty attached to the royal household) drove the game in to them to be dispatched either with crossbow or arquebus. The king's love of nature did not lead him to neglect the inside of his royal residences. The registers of his "Ministry of Works" (the Junta de Obras y Bosques) contain over five thousand closely written folios of orders concerning the royal patrimony, most of them about constructing or reconstructing his palaces. Philip II lived a large part of his life in the middle of a building site. He employed a team of resident architects, whom he saw twice a week, to keep an eye on the work in progress. However, the ideas, and often the original plans, came from the king himself, not from his architects. The teaching of Honorato Juan and a careful study of the books of Vitruvius and Serlio had given him a sound grasp of the principles of architecture, and his voyage to the Netherlands had shown him the sort of buildings he wanted: Flemish country houses. From 1559 onward his builders at El Bosque, at the Pardo and at the Madrid palace were given detailed instructions on how to build with red bricks and slates, and a special team of Flemish slaters were brought over to carry out roofing operations. The "Philip II style" was born.

The king's insistence on supervising every stage of the design and construction of his works could produce problems, however. He was capable of intervening after building had begun in order to introduce expensive changes of plan. His ministers tried to bridle their master's enthusiasm but to no avail: "I am sorry to fatigue Your Majesty with such trifling matters," the secretary of works wrote hopefully, as he sent a list of minor building matters to the king for approval, but Philip did not take the hint: "They do not fatigue me, they delight me!" he replied, and checked every item. The king intended to make sure that he got his own way. He was also resolved to exact his pound of flesh from all building workers. In 1564 he expressed concern that workers at El Bosque were turning up for work half an hour late "because the local clock is half an hour slow, and their work for that time is lost. Put up a new clock and set it by the sundial in the garden." The king expected his workmen to be at their posts by seven o'clock sharp at all times — except when he himself was present, for he did not wake up until around eight. "Since I am sleeping in the room with the blue bed in it," he instructed his secretary of works, "see to it that until eight o'clock there is no hammering or great noise."

At other times the king was prepared to put up with a lot, provided his buildings could be completed more rapidly. He was angry and disappointed when the work took longer than he expected, as in 1565, when he reached El Bosque only to find that not enough had been built to accommodate him: "I arrived here this afternoon, where I found far less done than I either expected or desired. . . . I could not help losing my temper a little, and I swore that if the work was not finished in fifteen days, I would go back to Madrid." Next it was the glaziers who enraged him: "I tell you that nothing is getting done . . . and so, if they do not finish this week, we shall just have to get rid of them." But the king's special wrath was reserved for his architects. His principal one in the early years, Juan Bautista de Toledo (1500–1567), who had worked with Michelangelo and seems to have resented somewhat the king's architectural pretensions, often crossed swords with his sovereign. In 1565 he was suspected of having altered the plans approved by the king and Philip exploded with anger: "This is no good at all . . . and it is no less than an insult that instead of finishing the work, as I had expected and ordered . . . he has not even done the half of it." The architect was unruffled, both by accusations of altering the plans and by his failure to finish the building work. "Buildings are like plants," he crooned. "They only grow if they are watered, and the water they need is money." The king was somewhat appeased. "Here is fine philosophy," he commented, but gave orders for all available funds to be sent to the master of works. Philip was able to dominate his later architects, Juan de

Herrera and Francisco de Mora (uncle of the king's biographer Balthasar Porreño), rather more effectively; but during the 1560's he felt it necessary to move tirelessly from one building site to another to make sure that everything was under control. So regular and predictable were his movements that a little book was composed by a courtier (some said by the king's wayward son Don Carlos) entitled *The Great and Notable Voyages of King Philip*, which ran: "From Madrid to the Escorial, from the Escorial to the Pardo, from the Pardo to Aranjuez, from Aranjuez to Madrid, from Madrid to the Escorial, from . . ."

Even the briefest glance at Philip's itinerary over these years is enough to show that the jibe contained much truth. But there were good reasons. Apart from the different attractions of the gardens of each palace at different times of the year — the superb hunting at the Pardo in the autumn; the fragrance of Aranjuez in the spring — Philip II was a born collector and each palace held a part of his "treasures." El Bosque boasted a "hall of mirrors" and a selection of valuable paintings, their precise arrangement determined by the king himself. At the top of the "new tower" of the Madrid palace, built to Philip II's personal design in the Flemish style, there was an art gallery which contained many of the pictures he was most fond of — the Bosches, the Brueghels, the Titians and the rest, most of which now hang in the Prado Museum. In all, there were 181 paintings, and in the Escorial there were a further 250 religious pictures and 220 "Flemish paintings" and portraits of great men. Finally, the Pardo palace contained a series of forty-five portraits of the king and his relatives, all by Titian, Antonis Mor and Sánchez Coello.

As a child, Philip had always been fond of painting and in later life he is reported to have done some sketches himself and, it is thought, at least one full-scale canvas (the *Saint Joseph*, which until the Spanish Civil War hung in the parish church of the town of El Escorial). Not surprisingly, he had a very clear idea of what he did and did not like in art. He was fond of most Flemish Renaissance artists, whether their subjects were religious or secular. By 1574 he possessed thirty-three paintings by Hieronymus Bosch. On the other hand he seems to have cared little for the Italian contemporaries of Scorel, Patinir and van der Weyden: his "art gallery" contained no quattrocento work. He liked Titian, among his contemporaries, and he commissioned many works from him, including a series of eight large canvases known as "The Poesy," based on scenes from Ovid's *Metamorphoses;* but he did not like at all the allusive, mystical paintings of El Greco. Philip kept a number of artists fully employed throughout his reign, and he provided them with a special studio in a building near the Madrid palace and connected to it by a secret passage through which he could come at any time to supervise their work.

Beneath his art gallery at the top of the "new tower" in the Madrid palace was the king's library. Already in 1553 he possessed 812 volumes of his own, several of them manuscript, and they filled twenty-three bookcases. In 1576 the number had swollen to 4,545 volumes, 2,000 of them manuscript, and there were yet more in the royal library in Brussels. By the time of Philip's death his collection contained 14,000 volumes, including 1,150 Greek, 94 Hebrew and about 500 Arabic codices. It was the largest private library in the Western world. But the king did not want it to remain that way. He wished to make his books available to scholars by turning the Escorial library into a research center. Accordingly, in the hope of encouraging serious study, he created a "college" at the Escorial in 1575, with teaching in arts and theology. Alas, this intention was thwarted: the monks showed little interest in their library after the king's death, and they would not allow others to work there either. Regret at the "interring" of valuable books and manuscripts in the monastery mounted, but to no avail, and inevitably many began to criticize the monarch whose action had brought about this state of affairs. But this was somewhat unjust. Philip had, in fact, granted access to some scholars; and in any case, the books were *his* books. Until the end of his days he "often liked to read to pass the time that was left after all his many and important occupations in the tasks of kingship." He was certainly at home in his library. He annotated some of his books, he quoted from them in his letters, and he was so familiar with the volumes he owned that in 1566, when one item went missing from a consignment of 473 sent to the Escorial, the king was at once able to identify and describe it. In May 1575, when over four thousand of his books were in the Escorial library, the king was able to lead his family on a conducted tour of all the "paintings, tapestries, and silverware, which with the books were of great value. . . . The king our lord was the one who did all the talking about things in the library, instructing his children and talking to the queen, so that they should see everything properly and slowly." The king is also said to have written a book himself — *The Order of Creatures,* about the diversity of nature — in 1560, and two sonnets, both of some elegance, are attributed to him. He never wrote history, even though he much enjoyed reading it. (By contrast his father dictated his memoirs, and his grandson, Philip IV, translated part of Guicciardini's *History of Italy.*)

It was not only books and pictures that King Philip collected. He was also fascinated by geography. In August 1570 he instructed his Flemish painter "Antonio de las Viñas" (Antoon van den Wyngaerde) to make sketches of the leading towns of Castile. Although Wyngaerde was forced to stop work in 1572 because both his hands became crippled (for which the king awarded him a generous disability pension), a considerable collection of "views" was assembled, and they were displayed in frames in the Pardo palace. In 1566 orders were issued to the mathematician Pedro de Esquivel "to note down by personal observation the actual location of all places, rivers, streams and mountains, however small they may be," in order that "the description of Spain may be as exact and complete, as detailed and excellent, as His Majesty desires and Master Esquivel can achieve." Esquivel designed special portable instruments to carry out triangulation, and he made many of the observations himself so that the maps, which are today preserved in the Escorial, were extremely accurate. Although never published, they were certainly used by the government, for instance, in organizing the *Relaciones topográficas*. These were the fruit of two extensive surveys carried out by the government in New Castile in 1575 and 1578. Printed questionnaires, of fifty-seven and forty-five articles respectively, were issued to every community and the returns were carefully copied into eight large registers (again, preserved today in the Escorial), providing priceless information on the location, population, economy and history of around six hundred settlements. They were intended both to enlighten the king about his subjects and to form the basis of a historical geography of Spain (alas, never completed).

Philip II's mania for collecting things knew no bounds. He owned a horde of over five thousand coins and medals, all in special cabinets; he owned jewels and works of art in silver and gold; he had 137 astrolabes and watches; he owned musical instruments, trinkets, precious stones, and 113 statues of famous people in bronze and marble; finally, he owned a large collection of arms and armor, much of it assembled originally by Charles V, which he had moved from Valladolid to a special building, the armory of the royal palace in Madrid, where it has remained to this day. In all, the private collections of Philip II were worth well over seven million ducats in 1598, and the cost of the buildings he had undertaken was well over double that sum (the Escorial alone had cost five and a half million).

The collector-king was no mere dilettante, however. He had a genuine and almost inexhaustible curiosity. When in the winter of 1587 a man arrived from the Netherlands with a pair of skates, the king arranged for a skating display and took his children out in a warm coach to watch. Afterward he summoned the new arrival, Jehan Lhermite, who was later to be his valet and unofficial chronicler, and spent some time examining the skates and how they worked.

The king was no less fascinated by science, alchemy and magic. When in 1562 the construction of the Pardo palace was held up for lack of water, he welcomed the suggestion that a water diviner should be used and he went in person to watch the diviner, a Moorish boy, at work. The boy did not need rods; he just "saw" water underground, and he found a source twenty-four feet under the surface, to Philip's delight. Later on, the king expressed interest in reports that it was possible to communicate with absent people by means of their image. At other times (especially at times of financial need) the king eagerly followed attempts to make silver and gold from other elements. In 1567 he confessed that he dared not put too much hope in the trials: "Truly, although I am skeptical about all these things, I am less so about this one. But it is no bad thing to be skeptical, because if it does not succeed one feels less regret." The skepticism was justified on this occasion — no gold was produced from lead and copper — but there was more success with the production of "essences." Philip created a sort of laboratory at the Escorial, where a series of stills, retorts and alembics produced concentrated rosewater and other perfumes, and also medicines and drugs for the court apothecary. In December 1594 the royal apothecary's department was reorganized with an official "distiller" to look after the "distribution and preservation of essences and, at the time when the roses and herbs are ready, to distill the necessary liquids." There were special medicinal herb gardens at Aranjuez, the Casa de Campo and the Escorial, all laid out under the king's personal supervision. By 1582 the royal gardens at Aranjuez were producing 180 arrobas (5,400 pounds) of rose petals, all of it used for medicinal purposes.

The only area of the occult in which Philip reputedly had no real interest was astrology. According to his biographer Porreño, he liked to act in ways that ran against superstition:

in 1580 he took a particular delight in having a "Horoscope for 1579" published because not one of its predictions had come true; on another occasion, again according to Porreño (a priest), he had a book of horoscopes torn up in his presence, page by page, to prove that he did not believe in astrology. And yet this cannot have been the whole truth because the king is known to have had five horoscopes cast for him, and until his dying day he kept by his bedside the *prognosticon* or prediction made for him in 1550 by the German magus Matthew Haco. Perhaps he was impressed by the accuracy of some of the predictions: that he would marry three or four times, that he would have seven children (his wives bore him eight live children) and that only two of them would reach maturity (only two survived him). Philip's interest in these matters is reflected in one of the frescoes painted in the library of the Escorial (in the ceiling bay devoted to "astrology"), which shows the stars in the sky as they were at the moment of the king's birth. This was deliberate, for the preliminary sketches of the frescoes have survived and they bear the holograph annotations of Philip's chief architect and confidant, Juan de Herrera.

Herrera was a mathematician and he possessed an extensive collection of books on astrology and magic; he may even have been a magus or wizard like that other eminent mathematician of the later sixteenth century, Dr. John Dee, who advised both the Holy Roman emperor Rudolf II and Queen Elizabeth of England on the occult. Certainly Philip sometimes followed the advice of someone who was familiar with astrology, for the foundation stones of both the main building and the church of the Escorial were laid at precise, predetermined times when the planetary aspects were favorable. It has been pointed out that the entire plan of the Escorial resembles Herrera's reconstruction of the pre-Christian and "magical" Temple of Solomon. Perhaps Philip was influenced by astrology in other ways. He may, for example, have preferred to wear black because that was the color associated with the planet Saturn, with which the king felt special sympathy; certainly the treatise on magic known as the *Picatrix*, of which he possessed a copy, claimed that dressing in black clothes was an effective means of drawing down on the wearer the beneficent influences of Saturn. This supposition may be a little fanciful (it certainly cannot be verified) but there is nothing ridiculous about the idea. As René Taylor has observed in his fascinating study of the Escorial as a "magical" temple: "That the king should have been interested in astrology and the occult is surely in keeping with his introspective character. Indeed, at this period it would hardly have been possible for a monarch to be otherwise."

Philip II, like his great-grandson Louis XIV, was also a great patron of scholars. His tastes, however, were far more narrow. To begin with, he did not really approve of popular theater. According to Cervantes, he forbade the portrayal of any monarch on the stage and, in 1598, he forbade the performance of plays in Madrid altogether. During his reign there were no subsidies for dramatists, no court theaters (except for religious plays), no patronage of players. Poets did a little better — Juan Rufo received a subsidy of 500 ducats toward the cost of publishing his *Austriada*, an epic poem about the Habsburgs — but most of the king's largesse for literary endeavor went to those working on the classics or on history (like Justus Lipsius or Jerónimo Zurita, both of whom received a pension); on the Bible (like Benito Arias Montano, who was maintained by the king for most of his life, or Christopher Plantin, who received 10,500 ducats toward the five-language, eight-volume "Polyglot Bible," which he printed at Antwerp in 1572); or on "scientific subjects." Alonso de Santa Cruz (who first described magnetic variation), Juan López de Velasco (who described the lunar eclipses of 1577–1578), and the Antwerp cartographer Abraham Ortelius all received regular salaries from the king. In 1567 Juan Plaza of the University of Valencia was appointed professor of botany and was ordered to keep a botanical garden and to forage for specimens

for thirty days each year. Shortly afterward Francisco Hernández, another botanist, was sent out to the Indies to survey its
flora and fauna. He collected more than eight hundred plants
never seen before in Europe, at the king's expense. They were
carefully pressed and sent back to be bound into eighteen
volumes, together with drawings and commentary. In 1582
they were moved from the office of the Council of the Indies to
the Escorial, and the possibility of printing the drawings was
discussed. A proof was made, but the cost of printing was estimated at fifteen hundred ducats. Nothing more was done
and the priceless collection was destroyed in a fire in 1671.
There were other times when the king felt that enough was
enough. Thus, when in 1582 his "chronicler of the Indies,"
Juan López de Velasco, asked for a second grant toward the
cost of printing one of his books, the king refused: "You can
tell him to be satisfied with what has been done for him already."

On the other hand, the king's largesse was frequently extended to humble scholars, to enable them to continue their
work, especially when the work was connected with religion or
mathematics. Perhaps because he himself was not very good at
sums, Philip II was particularly keen to encourage others to
study mathematics. In 1582 he founded the "Academy of
Mathematics," later having the Madrid palace especially extended in order to accommodate it, and he provided the money
to found four chairs. All teaching in the academy was in Castilian (not Latin, as in other universities), and the subjects
taught included architecture, artillery, hydraulics, fortifications, geography and navigation as well as mathematics. Its
first professors included Juan de Herrera, the architect of the
Escorial, and Juan Bautista de Labaña, a Portuguese cartographer, and their salaries ranged between two hundred and
four hundred ducats a year (a village laborer earned eighty
or less). In 1588 Herrera sent a proposal to the Cortes of Castile, with royal backing, that academies of mathematics should

be erected in every main town. Sad to say, most towns in the Cortes voted the proposal down on the grounds of cost. The king was disappointed, but the matter was allowed to rest.

Only one thing brought more consolation to Philip II than all these leisure and pleasure activities, and that was his religion. The king took his religion very seriously, and his modern biographer must follow suit, but with one important reservation: political figures of the sixteenth century, like their modern counterparts, were wont to use religion as a cloak or an excuse for political actions. Thus, when Philip II boasted to the pope on 12 August 1566 that "rather than suffer the least damage to religion and the service of God, I would lose all my states and a hundred lives if I had them; for I do not propose nor desire to be the ruler of heretics," he was exaggerating for the benefit of his audience in Rome. In fact, on 31 July he had conceded a limited measure of toleration to the Calvinists in the Netherlands, and he did so again in 1577. As a head of state, he even found it necessary, from time to time, to make alliances with non-Catholic princes: for many years he protected Elizabeth of England against the threat of papal deposition, and in 1566–1567 he relied on Lutheran troops (with their own Lutheran chaplains) to suppress the Calvinist rebels in the Netherlands. Most notorious of all, in 1583 and again early in 1584 he approached Henry of Navarre, leader of the French Huguenots, and offered him a subsidy if he agreed to declare war on the Catholic Henry III of France.

These were exceptions, however. On the whole Philip the Prudent was a faithful and devout son of the Catholic Church. In his private life there is no doubt of his sincere and deep religious faith. The visible monuments to his piety — the monasteries, the pious donations, the beautification of holy places — do not stand alone. He kept a large library of religious books, and the jottings of his librarian reveal that these items were in demand. One evening, for example, he called for a concordance to the Bible that he wanted to read before going to bed. Of the forty-two books the king kept in a bookcase by his bed, all but one were religious. He attended Mass daily, heard sermons once a week at least, and confessed and received Communion four times a year. He went to a retreat regularly in Lent and also at other times of severe mental strain (for instance, just before ordering the arrest of Antonio Pérez and just after the death of his third wife, Elizabeth de Valois). Attendance at divine service was for him a pleasure, although he always insisted on meticulous observance of his particular taste in matters of ceremonial: at the Escorial, the monks found to their cost that if they did not place the altar ornaments correctly, or if they put out the wrong frontal, or if they opened the church late, the king sent a disapproving message. He knew more about sacristy affairs than the sacristans, one monk claimed, perhaps with a touch of irritated disdain.

Naturally such things did not mean·that the king was only concerned with appearances and externals. He was deeply aware of his duty toward God and of the need to secure and retain God's favor. The monks of the Escorial noticed that on occasion tears would roll down the king's cheeks when he was at prayer or in contemplation. On Christmas night, 1566, the king sang the watch-night offices with the monks in the half-finished choir of the Escorial, bareheaded in the freezing cold. On Corpus Christi Day, 1570, the king again walked bareheaded in the blazing heat of Córdoba and when someone warned him of the danger of sunstroke, he replied: "Today the sun will do no harm."

Deeply religious people were particularly quick to recognize the faith of Philip II. As early as 1549, Saint Ignatius Loyola, founder of the Jesuit order, wrote of the "breath of goodness and sanctity" that emanated from the young prince. Almost thirty years later another Spanish saint, Teresa of Avila, met the king and also commented on his deep spirituality. No doubt the king detected a kindred soul in Saint Teresa: her "angelic spirits," like Philip's own, "found their consolation in solitude." The king protected her against all accusations of heterodoxy, and when she died he made sure that her books and papers were secured for his library at the Escorial. He kept some of her works by his bedside until his death.*

Inspired by the example of his pious parents (and especially his revered father, who retired to a monastery and died there, as Philip himself was to do), Philip never appears to have wavered in his deep faith. He believed, indeed, that all his work as king was God's own work. Just after Christmas 1577, his faithful secretary Mateo Vázquez made a pilgrimage on foot to Barajas, ten miles from Madrid, where he had been enchanted by the peace of village life. He even thought of retiring there, if the king could spare him. The royal reaction was understanding but firm:

All this was very good, although so much exercise all at once for someone who normally does so little may not be a good thing. In order to keep up the good you have done, it would not be a bad thing for you to set aside a short period on fine days to take some exercise: do not leave it and then do it all at once as you have just done. Certainly village life is good for bodily health, and far more relaxing; but for the soul I believe that one can do more for God's service here [at court] than there.

For Philip II, as for most of his European contemporaries, God intervened daily and visibly in the affairs of the world. Although when he heard of the Armada disaster he maintained philosophically that "in the actions of the Lord, there is no loss or gain of reputation: one should simply not talk about it," with great victories the king always saw evidence of divine

---

* According to tradition, the redoubtable Teresa was far from overawed by the king. At her first audience she is said to have begun: "Sire, you will be thinking to yourself: 'I see before me this turbulent, gadabout woman.'" Later she dared to remind Philip of the fate of King Saul when he disobeyed God's commands.

favor. In 1583, following the defeat on Saint Anne's Day of an Anglo-French attack on the island of Terceira in the Azores, Secretary Vázquez wrote jubilantly to the king:

> The care, zeal and resources with which Your Majesty attends to the service of Our Lord ensures, as we see, that He attends likewise to the affairs of Your Majesty: much has been gained and conserved with this victory at Terceira. To have the sea under our control is, as Your Majesty knows, most important for the affairs of the Low Countries; but more important still is the promise of more fortunate successes which we may expect from God's hand in return for the care with which Your Majesty has sought the honor of God and of his religion.

Then he added in a postscript:

> It has just crossed my mind that it must have been the late Queen Anne, our sovereign lady, praying God for victory [the queen had died in October 1580].

Philip shared these sentiments. He agreed that Saint Anne must have been on the side of Spain, "but I always thought that the queen could not be without a share in our good fortune. And what gives me greatest pleasure is that it seems that this victory is an indication that there is something in what you say." It would be almost impossible for a man to feign faith like this, and to his private secretary there would be little point. Philip clearly did believe sincerely that his cause was God's cause, and for this reason he feared from time to time that unless Spain's people were living godly lives, they would offend and alienate his divine supporter.

In 1578 and again in 1596 Philip ordered a public investigation into sin and called upon the clergy of his realms to admonish their flocks to improve their ways and to pray to the Lord for forgiveness of their sins (and for some Spanish victories in war). The king paid more immediate attention to the morals of his ministers: the king's confessor was instructed to reprove the duke of Feria for gambling; the king himself rebuked the president of one of the royal councils for writing love letters to a nobleman's wife; and he insisted on punishing the count of Medellín for living in sin in his country house (even though he did it discreetly). The king's advisers must be above reproach before both men and God.

Perhaps such overt righteousness sometimes encouraged Philip II to convince himself that God would always be on his side. Certainly godly zeal on occasion induced him to abandon his habitual prudence, especially with regard to England. Not only in 1588 but also in 1571 he claimed to have divine revelation that Spain was charged to regain England for the faith: he overrode all the practical objections to invasion posed, in turn, by the duke of Alva and the duke of Parma — the men who were to command the invasion forces — with confident assurances that God would provide. "I am so keen to achieve the consummation of this enterprise," he wrote to Alva in September 1571, "I am so attached to it in my heart, and I am so convinced that God our Savior must embrace it as his own cause, that I cannot be dissuaded from putting it into operation." Parma was later subjected to the same sort of battery: disobedience — even skepticism — was made to seem like treason against God as well as treason against the king.

If there was any bitterness in Philip II's religious cup, it was caused by his relations with the papacy. The king was almost always disappointed in his popes. His reign commenced with Paul IV's declaration of war against him and it ended with Clement VIII's support for his enemies, the French. Gregory XIII tried to prevent the annexation of Portugal in 1580; Sixtus V refused to contribute to the invasion of England in 1588. Above all, Philip resented the scant aid the papacy provided in his struggle to regain and recatholicize the Netherlands. In 1581 he let off steam to his trusty minister Cardinal Granvelle:

I assure you that [the pope] is wearing me out and has me on the point of losing my patience, great though it is. . . . It is clear to me that if the Netherlands were ruled by someone else, the pope would have performed miracles to prevent them being lost to the Church, but because they are *my* states, I believe he is prepared to see them lost, because they will thus be lost to me.

It was a very shrewd point. The papacy had to consider the political implications of its actions, and Philip II was already powerful enough to attempt to dictate to the College of Cardinals who should be the next pope (he did it successfully, twice, in 1590). Philip's dominions hemmed in the Papal States to both north and south; in 1527 his father's army had sacked Rome and taken the pope a prisoner; in 1556 Philip's own forces had invaded papal territory again. The popes had to temper their respect for the king's piety, great though it was, with fear of his power.

At least, however, Philip II was powerful *and* pious. He wished to be just in all things. A good proportion of the anecdotes in the biographies of Porreño and van der Hammen concern the king's anxiety not to wrong anyone. After his death, his devotion to fairness and justice became legendary. For example, the playwright Pedro Calderón de la Barca made the entry of Philip II as a supreme lawgiver into the climax of his most popular play, *The Mayor of Zalamea,* written in the 1630's.

There can be no doubt about the quality of justice in Philip II's Spain. Many visitors commented on the lawfulness of the people, and noted that it was possible "to go from one end of Spain to the other with one's purse in one's hand, and no one will molest you." Although civil lawsuits could drag on for years, criminal cases were often dispatched with exemplary speed. In many towns a new prison was built during Philip's reign to hold the swelling number of apprehended criminals. In Seville the "royal prison," constructed between 1563 and 1569, permanently held between five hundred and a thousand prisoners, all allowed to roam loose in one of the three large halls while they awaited trial, "a picture of hell on earth," wrote one chronicler, although he added that many ordinary citizens liked to drop in to view the spectacle.

Philip II's personal role in the routine administration of justice was minimal. He saw to it that there were enough judges and that they were constantly kept in check by the supreme court, the Council of Castile. From time to time he sent the council reminders that justice must be seen to be done: "Although doing the just thing is important," he told his ministers in December 1575, "as you know, the way of doing it also counts for a great deal." Philip regarded the law with very great respect, and was almost always content to let it take its course. The only cases in which he overrode the normal course of justice concerned the exercise of clemency — thus he once obliged a woman who had traveled far to plead with him for the release of her son; on Good Friday, 1579, he pardoned many men condemned to death, "in order that Our Lord might pardon my sins." Even more remarkable, when he traveled to Lisbon to claim his new kingdom in 1580, he freed all the prisoners in the jails of the towns through which he passed. This was an unashamedly arbitrary use of the royal prerogative, but it was most unusual.

There were only two types of lawsuit in which the king in person intervened regularly: those involving his ministers and those involving his private estates. The first variety included such celebrated cases as the execution of Baron Montigny in 1570 and of Secretary Juan de Escobedo in 1578, dealt with below; the second variety were far more numerous and ranged from poaching cases to complicated lawsuits about watermills near royal gardens. The count of Cifuentes built a watermill on the Tagus, near Aranjuez, in 1558. The king claimed that the mill reduced the water available for the royal gardens and asked the count to remove it. He refused, so the king in 1569 took the case to the local court at Toledo. In 1571 he won, but the count of Cifuentes appealed to the high court at Valladolid. This move clearly irritated the king (whose beloved gardens were suffering) and he therefore wrote a peremptory note ordering the high court "to deal with his matter with diligence and care so that it may be settled as quickly as possible because it is our personal suit and affects our royal patrimony and treasury." If this was an attempt to tamper with the normal course of justice, it failed, for in 1579 the case was still pending and the king sent another letter urging speed. Concern for his patrimony led the king to intervene with the high court once again in 1577. He had received notice from his gamekeepers that the judges had let off a number of poachers, with the result that they had started to poach again. The judges were ordered to be more stern. This was Philip's constant refrain as a landlord: more prosecutions, stiffer penalties, more vigilance and more gamekeepers. Against all who resisted arrest or opposed one of his officers in the execution of his duty, he was merciless and always pressed for the harshest punishments the law allowed.

This severity was the product of more than a simple love of justice. It also stemmed from the king's desire to preserve the heritage he had received from his father, to ensure that his successors would enjoy the same benefits he had known. This desire extended far beyond the private sphere. On a simple level, the king enjoined the planting of young trees and saplings wherever possible "so that our successors do not blame us for the lack of trees which we now see." More seriously, this determination to conserve and defend the rights, powers and preeminences he had inherited made him inflexible and implacable when faced by political opponents and demands for political concessions. He had succeeded to a vast inheritance and he had no intention of allowing anyone, whether neighboring prince or discontented subject, to challenge or flout his authority in any part of his lands.

FOUR

The Delicate Years, 1559–1567

CHARLES V's tearful abdication in 1555, and the ceremonies which followed, made Philip II the ruler of the most powerful empire the world had seen since that of the Mongols: all of Spain, half of Italy, England, the Netherlands, Mexico and Peru. Although England was to be lost forever with Mary Tudor's death (November 1558), Philip's inheritance remained impressive. His subjects numbered perhaps fifty million, in America and Europe, and their wealth was enormous: from the rich merchant-bankers of Medina del Campo and Seville to the commercial capitalists of Antwerp and Amsterdam; from the silver mineowners and great sheep ranchers of America to the grain-producing barons of Sicily and the sheep owners of Castile. The different parts of the empire were linked by strong political, economic and cultural bonds. In the first place, there was the common dynastic loyalty to the monarch shared by all the states, whether acquired by inheritance or by force. Then there were the commercial interests, which connected Seville and Andalusia with America; Bilbao and Old Castile with Flanders; and Valencia and Murcia with Naples. Finally, certain cultural exchanges created intellectual affinities between Spain, in particular, and the rest of the empire. Throughout the sixteenth century America lay in total cultural dependence on Spain: although by 1600 there were six universities in the New World, the professors came out from Spain; and although there were about twenty printing presses in America, the books they produced were almost all written in Spain. In Italy, too, Spanish language and literature achieved great diffusion — "God has turned into a Spaniard" was a common saying in sixteenth-century Italy — while even in the Netherlands the great nobles and some literary figures wrote and read Spanish. But the cohesion and harmony of Philip II's empire was by no means total. In the 1580's a wise veteran minister, Don Bernardino de Mendoza, compared the Spanish monarchy to one of the great religious orders such as the Franciscan or the Dominican: on account of their size and geographical extent, both monarchy and orders resembled loose federations with "nations" and "provinces" which, in practice, had to be accorded a great measure of independence.

Philip's inheritance also suffered from certain other problems not normally shared by the great religious orders: financial exhaustion and political unrest. Charles V's wars against his enemies had been extremely expensive, especially during the 1550's, when he had been compelled to fight on several fronts at once, and by 1555 all the states of his empire had accumulated huge debts. Philip's financial advisers tried hard to balance the books but, unfortunately, their efforts coincided with a period of economic disaster. The war disrupted trade and industry to an unprecedented degree, while a run of bad summers (with, alternately, floods and droughts) destroyed agriculture. Food became scarce; the cost of bread rose to famine prices; and a lethal epidemic, almost certainly influenza, spread across Europe. This combination of high taxation and a rapidly deteriorating standard of living created a tense situation. There was rioting in Aragon in 1558 and also unrest in the Low Countries, where the States-General of the provinces refused to provide any money. And yet, almost miraculously, Philip managed to surmount all these obstacles and collect an army with which he was able to defeat the French (at Saint-Quentin in 1557 and at Gravelines in 1558) and force them to sign a peace with him at Cateau-Cambrésis on the Franco-Netherlands border.

The Peace of Cateau-Cambrésis was a very great victory for Spain. "Truly," wrote one of the Spanish negotiators, "these peace talks have been directed by God himself because, although we have settled things so much to our own advantage, the French are delighted with it." The treaties, which were signed in April 1559, proved to be the bedrock of Spanish preponderance in western Europe for almost a century and allowed Philip II to act as "the gendarme of Europe" for most of his reign.

However, this position of superiority occupied by Spain and her king owed a good deal to accident. Cateau-Cambrésis remained in force for so long not only because Spain, with her vast resources of territory, men and money, was so strong, but also because France, her principal rival, was so weak. The chance death of the energetic French king, Henry II, in a joust held in Paris to celebrate the peace, left his inheritance to four young, sickly sons, none of them capable of holding together the divisive religious and political forces which already threatened to undermine royal authority. In the course of 1559, the great family of Guise gained control of the government, while their rivals, the house of Bourbon, made an alliance with the militant Calvinist minority in Paris and the provinces. In January 1562, after a hard struggle, the Calvinists persuaded the government to grant them a measure of toleration, but only at the cost of alienating the Guise family who, outraged, abandoned the court. Within a matter of weeks the wars of religion began, with Guise and the Catholics competing with Bourbon and the Protestants for control of the government at both local and central levels. The troubles were only terminated in 1598, the year of Philip II's death: throughout his reign, the paralysis of France afforded him a unique freedom of action. One cannot understand the political history of the age of Philip II without constant reference to the changing internal condition of France.

Philip II's Spain possessed other assets in international affairs. One was the "Madrid–Vienna axis," that set of close family bonds linking the descendants of Charles V with those of his brother Ferdinand I (who succeeded Charles as Holy Roman emperor and reigned from 1558 to 1564). Philip's sister Maria was married to Ferdinand's son, later the emperor Maximilian II (1564–1576), and Philip II himself later married one of their daughters, Anne. Most of Anne's brothers spent considerable periods of time residing at Philip's court and, if the king had died without surviving issue, he made it clear in his will that one of his Austrian nephews was to inherit his empire (and both of his surviving children, Philip III and Isabella, married Austrian Habsburgs in 1599).* Although neither Maximilian nor his son and successor Rudolf II (1576–1612) were particularly ardent in their support of Philip II's policies, especially his policies toward the Netherlands, at least they never actively opposed or challenged them. Spain could count on the benevolent neutrality, if not on the positive assistance, of the emperor and his relatives. In return, Philip and his successors were almost always ready to supply men and money for the defense of the exposed Habsburg provinces of Styria, Carinthia and Hungary.

Other princes were more reliable in their support of Spain. In Italy, the republic of Genoa and the duke of Savoy were constant allies, providing the vital link that allowed the transfer of men and money between Spain and Lombardy and from Lombardy along the "Spanish Road," which led from Milan across the Alps to Franche-Comté, another of Philip's possessions, and thence to the Low Countries. Further north, the Road was kept open through the favor of the duke of

* See the family tree, p. 81.

Lorraine, the Catholic Swiss cantons, and the Catholic house of Guise, whose power was paramount in the areas of France adjoining the Spanish Road.* The French Protestants, on the other hand, were Philip's implacable foes and they lost no opportunity of assisting Spain's enemies elsewhere: the bandits of Catalonia, the Moriscos of Valencia† and the Protestants of the Netherlands could all count on the support of the Huguenots (as the French Calvinists were known). The Huguenots also tried to influence the Valois court, weak though it was, to cooperate with these dissident subjects of Philip II and also to ally themselves with his enemies abroad. Thus between 1570 and 1574, the French king provided substantial subsidies to the Dutch while the French ambassador at the Ottoman court did his best to arrange a formal treaty between France, the Dutch, and the Turkish sultan.

The Turks were indeed Philip's principal enemy, and his main headache, throughout the first two decades of his reign. The war that began in 1551 dragged on until, in 1560, persuaded largely by the Knights of Malta, Philip undertook a campaign to recover the city of Tripoli, lost by the Knights nine years before. The expedition proved a disaster: twenty-seven galleys and ten thousand men were captured by the Turks. Just as these losses were being made good, in 1562, twenty-five more galleys were destroyed at sea in a freak tempest. These reverses were serious. Without galleys and veteran troops, Philip could not guarantee the safety of his Mediterranean empire. In 1563 the Turks attacked the Spanish outpost of Oran and in 1565 they besieged Malta: on both occasions the king experienced great difficulty in beating them off. The problem of defending Italy and Mediterranean Spain was therefore uppermost in Philip's mind throughout the

---

* See the endpaper map.
† Moriscos were people of Moorish descent who had, at least outwardly, adopted the Christian religion when the Moorish states were reconquered in the later Middle Ages.

1560's. It was unfortunate for him that, while the Turkish menace was at its height, a major crisis developed at the other end of his empire, in the prosperous and strategically valuable Netherlands.

The unrest in the Low Countries, which culminated in the Dutch Revolt, stemmed from two separate sources. The first was the penetration of Protestant ideas — Lutheran and Anabaptist but above all Calvinist — into most areas during the reign of Charles V. For a while the government seemed able to hold its own, and constant persecution kept numbers down. But in the 1550's the religious aims of the central government began to diverge from those of its local officers. Persecution began to falter and in some provinces it ceased altogether: no heretics were condemned to death in Holland after 1553, and very few were executed in Friesland or Gelderland. From about 1560, the defiant stand by the local authorities began to receive some support from the aristocratic members of the central government.

It is important to realize that the reasons for this opposition to the crown's policies, both at the center and in the provinces, were largely political, not religious. The Netherlands territories ruled by Philip did not form a monolithic organism with a long history of unity. On the contrary, many areas had only been brought under Habsburg rule, either by purchase or conquest, by Charles V, and the different provinces had only been formally united in 1548. There was therefore little consensus on the role and powers of the central authority in this new state. However, almost everyone in the Netherlands agreed on two political principles: the provinces should retain control of their local affairs, and matters of general importance should be determined, or at least discussed, by the traditional ruling class of the Low Countries. The government's religious policies broke both these principles. They interfered with provincial autonomy because the Inquisition wished to extradite heretics for trial outside their particular provinces; and they were evolved in secret in Spain and then forced onto the political elite in Brussels.

As it happened, the political leaders of the Netherlands, mostly noblemen like Lamoral, count of Egmont, and William, prince of Orange, were already alienated by other aspects of Philip II's style of government — the treatment of religious heterodoxy was only one of several issues of importance on which they were not being consulted — but the religious question was the one they chose to take up because they realized that it was the matter which would cause Philip the greatest embarrassment. Noncooperation over the heresy laws would worry the king and therefore, they surmised, would produce concessions on the other points at issue. At this time, none of the leading Netherlands nobles were Protestants; they merely wished to use the Protestant problem as a lever to force the king to grant them political benefits. In particular they wished Philip to delegate to them far more control over the formation of policy, and they wanted him to appoint some of their aristocratic supporters to the Netherlands council of state, on which they sat. At the end of 1564 the count of Egmont was chosen by his colleagues to go to Spain and persuade the king to sanction a more moderate policy toward heretics, to accord more authority to the council of state, and to appoint more nobles to it. Egmont arrived at court to bargain with his sovereign in February 1565.

It is of some importance to understand the failure of the Egmont mission, and the king's part in it: first, because the need to deal with the count presented Philip with his first real test of political skill; second, because his failure to retain control of the Netherlands represents the biggest blot on his reputation as a statesman — and that failure began with Egmont.

Egmont's mission placed the king on the horns of an extremely difficult dilemma. Until the count's arrival, Philip had been able on the whole to ignore the Low Countries. He could pretend that the erosion of his authority there was not serious and could easily be reversed. But with Egmont at court, things were different. He could not disguise the fact that a group of his subjects were attempting to negotiate with their sovereign. Moreover, the main matter at issue was the religious policy to be followed in the Netherlands, about which the king held uncompromising views: as far as he was concerned, religious policies were not negotiable. The problem was that Egmont, having come all the way to Spain, could not be told the truth in such plain terms. "If we refused outright," Philip noted at one stage, "we should never get rid of him."

The king struggled to keep Egmont happy at court for as long as possible. Only after six weeks did he have the courage for a confrontation. Until then, his mood oscillated between confusion — "I have so much on my mind that I scarcely know what I am saying or doing" — and rage — "I think we have reason to look into the motives of those, both here and in the Netherlands, who have put Egmont up to this." But time was running out. The situation in the Mediterranean was fast becoming serious: in mid-March news arrived at court that a large Turkish fleet was about to set out to attack some Christian objective (in the event, this turned out to be Malta). It was therefore essential to find some way of getting rid of Egmont. At the end of March the king decided to try to bluff his way out: he would appear to comply with the count's wishes, but without making any concrete concession. He informed his secretary: "I have drafted my answer in this way so that Egmont will not be able to force me into a decision. . . . My intention is, as you will have gathered, neither to resolve these demands of the count, nor to disillusion him about them, for then he would worry us to death and we would never be finished with him." The king proposed to tell Egmont that no decision could be taken on the political issues — the powers and membership of the Netherlands council of state — until he had sought the advice of Margaret of Parma, his regent. On the religious question the king was prepared to set up a committee of experts to discuss the best way to punish heretics. This was an important concession, and the king was at pains to define precisely the functions and composition of this new body. It was to be a small committee, he told his secretary, even though Egmont had wished for a large one, because the king was anxious that there should be no chance of its developing into a forum where the Protestants might present their case themselves, as had happened at the Colloquy of Poissy in France four years before. On the contrary, the king wanted there to be no discussion of toleration or of changing the heresy laws: "Under no circumstances do I wish the punishment to stop: I only wish the method [of punishment] to be examined. And although it seems to me that Egmont wants the punishment to be mitigated, I do not wish this to be considered or interpreted in that way. Only the method is to be discussed." And with that, the king concluded, "All the rest appears fine to me: please God that Egmont will be satisfied with it and go." But it was getting late, and the king began to worry that he had made a mistake, so he ended his draft with characteristic diffidence: "If anything seems unwise here, you can amend it. It is one o'clock in the morning and I keep falling asleep."

The next stage was to deceive Egmont into believing that his proposals had been accepted in principle. It was decided that it would be easiest to pull the wool over his eyes at a personal audience with the king. The audience was duly arranged for 4 April. First, Philip announced that he had some personal favors to confer on his faithful vassal: he confirmed Egmont's title to the lordship of two towns of Brabant, Ninove and Enghien, and agreed to let him accept an honorarium offered by the province of Flanders. Together, these were worth about 50,000 ducats. When the count had been softened up by these windfalls, the king moved on to business. His words — which had been carefully scripted by his secretary Gonzalo Pérez — impressed upon Egmont the need to maintain the exclusive exercise of the Catholic religion, but promised great things from the committee of experts. On 6 April the count rode off for Brussels "the happiest man in the world," his wildest dreams of personal wealth and political success fulfilled. By contrast, the king was left drained by his performance. It was the sort of personal confrontation and public role he loathed. "I am so busy," he told his secretary, "and so starved of sleep because I need to spend most nights looking at papers which other business prevents me from seeing during the day. So I am just starting to look at these papers of yours now, which is after midnight." Four days after Egmont's departure the king gave up: he had had enough. Leaving orders for all his councillors and all ambassadors to remain in Madrid, Philip rode off to spend some time with his queen at their country house near Segovia, El Bosque. The king had — he thought — won a valuable breathing space, and he meant to make the most of it. It was not his fault if no good came of it.

Egmont returned to Brussels at the end of April and at once reported to the council of state on his visit. Despite the fact that he had brought no firm resolution in writing, he assured his colleagues that the king had expressed his verbal consent to a relaxation of the heresy laws and to the supremacy of the council of state. In any case, Egmont continued, "being pre-occupied with the war against the Turks, who are expected to attack Malta, His Majesty finds it impossible to come to the Low Countries this year." (Malta was in fact besieged from 18 May to 7 September.) The council, encouraged by this news, felt free to proceed as it wished without fear of interruption from Madrid: the "committee of experts" was convened and given a brief to find ways of "moderating" the heresy laws (which was precisely what Philip had wished it not to do). The Netherlands leaders knew that the king could not stop them until Malta was preserved: "The Turks press us hard this year," one of them noted in April, "which will mean, we believe, that the king will not come to the Netherlands." Nevertheless, it was not long before they discovered that their actions did not have the king's consent. In the middle of June a packet of letters from the king, dated 13 May, arrived in Brussels. Their contents revealed that Egmont had completely misrepresented the king's wishes, especially concerning the punishment of heretics. One of the letters quashed the appeals of six repentant Anabaptists condemned to death: the king insisted that they should be burned, proving that he intended to make no change in the heresy laws. Egmont was totally discredited. He was made to look a fool. The nobles on the council of state once again ceased to cooperate with the regent and an important group of lesser nobles held a series of informal meetings at Spa, near Liège, in July and August to discuss what action should be taken if the king refused pointblank to moderate the heresy laws.

The king had not foreseen or desired the chaos that resulted from the apparent contradiction between the impression he had given Egmont on 4 April and the tenor of his letters of 13 May. He had not anticipated that the count would so grossly misrepresent his views and he had certainly not intended to precipitate a crisis of authority in the Netherlands at a time when all his energies were engaged in arranging the relief of Malta. His notes to Gonzalo Pérez revealed his mystification at what had happened and his perplexity at what to do about it. The explanation, however, was simple: the letters of 13 May had not been prepared by Gonzalo Pérez but by Philip's French-language secretary, Charles de Tisnacq. Tisnacq was a ruthless scourge of heretics. He had tried and sentenced to death an important lieutenant of John Calvin's in 1544 and he had organized the largely successful campaign of repression that followed. His dogged loyalty to the Church endeared him to the king (although not to the extent of making him privy to important royal policy decisions: "Of the dispatches which arrived yesterday from the Netherlands, I sent the ones that did not matter to Tisnacq" was a comment which typified the king's attitude). The poor secretary was therefore unaware of the duping of Egmont. When Tisnacq drafted replies to the outstanding letters from the Netherlands on 13 May he did so in the normal way: according to the law. Anabaptists were burned, so a short, routine letter to this effect was presented to the king for approval. Philip appears to have been unaware of the significance of his signature. The fat, however, was now in the fire, and in July Margaret of Parma wrote to the king insisting on a clarification of his position: "On several matters which Count Egmont had heard from the royal lips, Your Majesty's letters [of 13 May] appear, at certain points, to contradict the report he has made." She also sent the recommendations of the committee of experts, which had come out strongly in favor of relaxing some of the heresy laws, and she asked the king for a decision. This package from Margaret arrived at court early in August but the royal reply was not signed until over two months later. The long delay was not due to uncertainty about the correct policy. On the contrary, the king had been consistent throughout 1565: he wished there to be no change in matters of religion, and a stern answer to the letters of Margaret and a blank rejection of the proposals of the theologians was drafted for him by Gonzalo Pérez as early as 3 September. But the king was not yet ready formally to endorse such an uncompromising statement, and he sought to delay the final resolution. First, he ordered the matter to be discussed by two lawyers from the Council of Castile who specialized in ecclesiastical affairs. Then he claimed that he was too ill to transact business with Pérez — he had, he said, "awful headaches" — and he did not discuss the Netherlands problem with Pérez, or with anyone else, until 30 September.

These serious delays were only partially the consequence of the king's ill health. "Headaches" were just a convenient excuse: as at certain other moments of crisis when the king took to his bed, one feels that the malady was feigned in order to delay the evil hour of decision. According to one shrewd contemporary at court: "Whenever the king receives unpleasant and bad news, he suddenly feels ill and suffers from diarrhea, just like a sheep or a rabbit." In the autumn of 1565, illness was prudent: the king dared not lay down the law to the Netherlands until he was sure that Malta was safe, and the long-awaited news did not arrive at court until 24 September. Philip was now free to state his position loud and clear. There was to be no change in the heresy laws; heretics were still to be burned; the Inquisition was to continue its work. The letters — there were six of them — incorporating these decisions were drafted on 4 October and, after more severe headaches, the king supervised the preparation of the final versions, which he signed on 17 and 20 October.

Although there were some personal favors to the leading nobles, the king's letters of October — normally known as "the letters from the Segovia Woods" because they were signed at Philip's country house of El Bosque ("The Wood") near Segovia — were a slap in the face for Egmont in particular and for the other Netherlands ministers who had unanimously favored changing the political and religious organization created in 1559. It was realized at court that the decisions would not be popular — "some people will be surprised," one minister at court wrote laconically to his colleague in Brussels — but no one in Spain could have expected the dramatic reaction that rapidly followed.

Early in December the group of nobles who had met at Spa in the summer decided to prepare a petition calling for the abolition of the Inquisition and the moderation of the heresy laws. Six copies of the document, known as the Compromise of the Nobility, were circulated, and about four hundred signatures were eventually obtained — about one-tenth of the entire aristocracy of the Netherlands. The great nobles would not sign, but they lent tacit support by refusing to carry out the king's orders: William of Orange resigned all his offices in January 1566, and the rest threatened to follow suit. They only came back to court when the organizers of the Compromise determined to present their petition to Margaret of Parma, in person, in Brussels on 5 April. On the appointed day, three hundred confederates, fully armed, rode into Margaret's palace and laid their demands before her. No one lifted a finger to hinder the confederates, and Margaret, abandoned by everyone, her authority flouted, was compelled to do as she was bidden. She instructed the inquisitors to stop their work and commanded the magistrates to cease enforcing the heresy laws until further notice.

The "heretics" lost no time. Everywhere they "began to prick their ears up," as one Catholic put it, at the new sounds emanating from Brussels. Protestant exiles streamed back from France, England, Germany and Geneva, ready and willing to spread their "true faith" to the ignorant multitude. Thanks to Margaret's orders, the magistrates did not molest them and open-air Calvinist services were soon attracting enormous crowds, six or seven thousand at a time, every Sunday and holiday. The warm summer evenings, the absence of persecution, and the widespread unemployment provided the opportunity; the network of Calvinist churches in exile provided the leaders to exploit it.

Lenin wrote of the nineteenth century: "Politics begin where the masses are; not where there are thousands, but where there are millions. That is where serious politics begin." In the sixteenth century, however, the masses were numbered in thousands, not millions, and concentrations of people on the scale of the Calvinist "preach-ins" of the summer of 1566 were beyond the capacity of any early modern government to control. For a few months the masses, led to some extent by their preachers, held the initiative, until on 10 August a small group of Protestants, about half of them exiles newly returned from England, began to smash all the images in the churches of West Flanders. Within two weeks the "Iconoclastic Fury" had spread over most of the South Netherlands and within a month, in almost all the provinces, numerous churches had been devastated. Wild reports circulated to the effect that half the population had gone Protestant and that there were two hundred thousand people up in arms against the king's authority. Now the Calvinist leaders, supported by a considerable number of the nobles, demanded complete religious toleration. With the world collapsing about her ears, Margaret felt that

she could not refuse, and on 23 August she granted full toleration to all the Protestant communities then in existence.

Every stage in the collapse of royal authority in the Netherlands was reported back to the king in the increasingly strident,
despairing and alarmist letters of his sister but, as in 1565, it
seemed essential for the king to buy time until he was able to
send an army. Accordingly, on 31 July, Philip signed a letter
which permitted the suspension of the heresy laws (although
he promptly placed on record before his personal notary that
this concession had been extracted by force and was therefore,
in his opinion, not binding) and at the same time he signed an
order authorizing Margaret of Parma to raise thirteen thousand soldiers in Germany (and he sent her a letter of credit
worth 300,000 ducats to pay for them).

Philip had decided that the time had come to impose his
will on the Netherlands by force. His overall position had improved since 1565. To begin with, he had more money: a fleet
from America arrived at Seville in September with silver bullion for the king worth 1,500,000 ducats. Also, the Mediterranean situation had become less tense. In 1566 the Ottoman
fleet entered the Adriatic, rather than attacking Tunis or
Corsica; then in September the victorious Sultan Suleiman I
died, precipitating rebellion and military mutiny in several
parts of his empire. The Turkish menace had thus abated, and
this in itself made the Netherlands problem somewhat easier
to solve. Finally, the very fact that the opposition in the Low
Countries was now in the open and was linked to Calvinism
also simplified the choice of the policies which Philip could
adopt. No sixteenth-century monarch could tolerate the sort of
challenge to his authority posed by the Compromise or the
Iconoclastic Fury, and at the meetings of the Spanish Council
of State in October 1566 every one of the king's advisers agreed
that force would have to be used to restore government control. The only discussion concerned the amount of force required and the timetable of repression. Although some councillors wished the king to go to the Netherlands in person at the

head of an army, it was decided that the risk of assassination or mishap was too great. Instead, orders were issued to mobilize 60,000 infantry and 12,000 cavalry, and supreme command of the new army was entrusted to the duke of Alva.

Unfortunately for Philip and the duke, it was already too late to move all the troops to the Low Countries before the snow closed the Alpine passes. The expedition therefore had to be postponed until the spring of 1567, and the king began to make preparations for a voyage of his own to the Netherlands, by sea, in the following autumn. Meanwhile, in the Netherlands, although the rebels tried to recruit reinforcements in France and Germany, they failed, and in March 1567 government troops were able to crush the main rebel army at Oosterweel. This forced all the towns in revolt to submit. By May it was clear that there would be no need to mobilize all the 72,000 men intended and it was therefore resolved that Alva would take with him only 10,000 Spanish veterans from Italy. The duke took his leave of the king in April and he arrived at Brussels with his troops in August. Almost at once he began to deal with the dissidents: on 9 September he had Egmont and a number of other political opponents arrested and imprisoned, and he created a new judicial tribunal, the "Council of Troubles," to try all cases of suspected rebellion or heresy. At the beginning of Lent, 1568, a large number of people accused of complicity in the rebellion were arrested on the same day all over the Netherlands. It was a formidable achievement, but it was not enough: many of the opposition leaders, and most notably the prince of Orange, had taken refuge in Germany, where even Alva's long arms could not reach them. Alva feared (quite rightly as it turned out) that these exiles were plotting a new uprising with foreign aid. He wrote to the king warning him not to leave Spain until all his enemies were either dead or defeated.

The king had not been idle since Alva's departure. A large fleet had been collected at Santander; special banners had been woven for it; provisions had been embarked aboard it; and the royal guard was standing by. The archives of Simancas had been combed for all state papers that it might be useful to take to Flanders, and patents had been drawn up naming the queen (Elizabeth de Valois) as regent during the royal absence. Almost 200,000 ducats had been spent on preparations for the voyage. However, late in September 1567, when Alva's letters discouraging the king's journey arrived, the whole expedition was called off. In the event the king never went.

Although it is possible to argue that all the preparations were a sham and that Philip never intended to go, there is much evidence (apart from the extensive and detailed preparations themselves) to suggest that he fully intended to visit the Netherlands in 1567. In the first place, it was the obvious solution to the Netherlands problem, one upon which everyone agreed. In the second place, it was his *duty* to go, and the king was nothing if not dutiful. In the third place, there is the evidence of his other voyages when occasion demanded: to Andalusia in 1570, to Portugal in 1580, to the kingdoms of Aragon in 1585, to Old Castile and Aragon again in 1592, when the king was scarcely able to walk. The evidence for supposing that Philip never intended to go to the Netherlands is far less substantial. Admittedly he asserted that this was the case to the French ambassador, laughingly claiming that everyone should have suspected that so many ostentatious preparations must have been meant to deceive. But the king loved to appear wise after the event, and he loved to deceive ambassadors, the French ambassador in particular: what he said to him can never be automatically relied on. The real weight of the argument that he never intended to go derives from the personal tragedies of 1568, which made it impossible for the king to leave Spain however much he had wished to do so. But none of the catastrophes were visible in September 1567, let alone in May. They could not have influenced the king's decision to stay in Spain. Philip's failure to visit the Netherlands at this stage was a critical mistake, for whch he was to pay heavily; but it was not a mistake for which he can fairly be blamed. The real culprits were his only son, Don Carlos, and his third wife, Elizabeth de Valois.

FIVE

Family Life—and Death

THERE WAS SOMETHING curiously cold about all the children of Charles V. None of them exhibited the hearty yet tender love which clearly united the emperor with his sisters, especially with Mary of Hungary, undoubtedly the ablest member of the family. Philip II certainly felt strong emotions from time to time, but they seldom lasted long. Thus when his sister Maria, his childhood companion, came back from Germany in 1582 after an absence of thirty years, Philip became very excited. According to his own account of their meeting, when his coach came within sight of hers, both of them hurried out, ran toward each other, and shared a long embrace in front of all their courtiers. It was a touching reunion, but before long Maria found court life empty and oppressive, and went into a nunnery. Philip, for his part, rarely went to see her. Their younger sister, Joanna, also opted for the solitude of a convent, having abandoned her only son, Don Sebastian of Portugal, at the age of three months, never to see him again. She died there in 1573. It is true that in 1559 a rumor went around the court that she had become the mistress of her spiritual adviser, Francis Borgia (later canonized), but this was almost certainly untrue: Joanna, like her brother, was renowned for

The House of Habsburg in the Sixteenth Century

The Habsburgs tended to produce either huge families or none at all. Of the fifteen children of Maria and Maximilian II (only seven are included here for reasons of space), only Anne had children. And of Charles V's other grandchildren, only two, besides Anne, produced heirs: Catalina and Philip III. The rest either married too late to have children or did not marry at all.

In the charts below, a short line under a name indicates childlessness; a downward-pointing arrow indicates otherwise. A broken line denotes illegitimacy.

I. The Family of Charles V

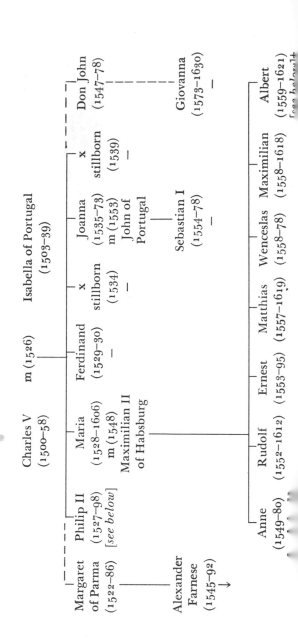

II. The Family of Philip II

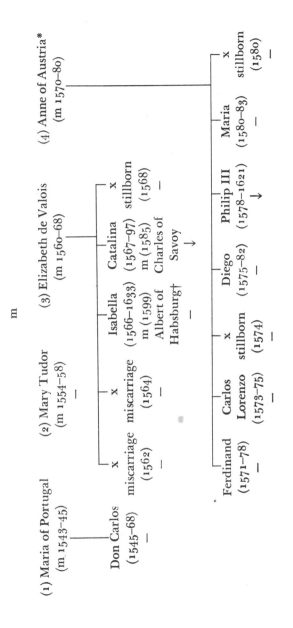

Philip II
(1527–98)

m

(1) Maria of Portugal
(m 1543–45)

Don Carlos
(1545–68)
—

(2) Mary Tudor
(m 1554–58)
—

x
miscarriage
(1562)
—

x
miscarriage
(1564)
—

(3) Elizabeth de Valois
(m 1560–68)

Isabella
(1566–1633)
m (1599)
Albert of
Habsburg†
—

Catalina
(1567–97)
m (1585)
Charles of
Savoy
→

x
stillborn
(1568)
—

Ferdinand
(1571–78)
—

Carlos
Lorenzo
(1573–75)
—

x
stillborn
(1574)
—

Diego
(1575–82)
—

Philip III
(1578–1621)
→

(4) Anne of Austria*
(m 1570–80)

Maria
(1580–83)
—

x
stillborn
(1580)
—

her coldness toward other people. She, like the king, preferred to be alone. Even when they were living under the same roof Philip, his wife and his sister usually ate alone, walked in the gardens alone, and went hunting alone. "Being by himself," a Venetian ambassador acutely observed of Philip II, "is his greatest pleasure."

Everything suggests that, despite the insinuations of certain scandal-hungry foreign ambassadors, Philip II was simply not interested in women, either for their companionship or for their sexual charms. If he felt lust at all strongly, he seems to have kept it, like the rest of his emotions, under strict control. Although he was married four times, he never seems to have been at ease with any member of the opposite sex. His first wife, Maria of Portugal, survived marriage by less than two years (1543–1545); and within only a few months of marrying her, Philip was reproached by both his father and his parents-in-law for treating his young wife coldly. There were no children from this union except Don Carlos, whose birth in July 1545 caused his mother's death. Philip's second wife, Mary Tudor, failed to conceive at all and felt abandoned by her husband – and not without reason, for Philip spent only fifteen months of the four-year marriage (1554–1558) with his wife. Relations with his third and fourth wives, Elizabeth de Valois (1560–1568) and Anne of Austria (1570–1580), were considerably better, and with Anne at least there was a real family life; yet even then an odd coldness could sometimes be seen. It was reported that, in the early years of her marriage, Elizabeth de Valois would lie awake at night hoping in vain for a visit from the king. At other times he was said to come to her room very late, after she had fallen asleep, and then creep away again feeling virtuous at having "done his duty" so easily. Matters appear to have been the same with Anne of Austria. When the couple had been living together for four months, a well-informed household officer wrote: "God keep them in the palm of his hand and grant that we may soon see the fruit that we desire [namely, a son and heir]. They sleep together every night and there is now no trace of the things which kept them apart, thanks to God and to the queen. . . . I do not know if they make love often or not, since neither of them talk much." The writer concluded with a tantalizing reference to "some things I have heard [about the royal couple] which I would tell you if only they could be put on paper." Whatever these things were, they did not last long. After a year or so the relationship became more formal, with the king visiting his wife in her room at fixed times. It was almost as if Philip had taken too seriously the advice given to him, as a young adolescent, by his father — that when a marriage had been consummated "do not go back to see your wife too quickly or too often; and when you do go back, let it only be for a short time." Royal marriages, it would seem, were for procreation not pleasure.

This very un-Freudian interpretation is supported by the history of Philip's conjugal relations with Elizabeth de Valois, about which we happen to know a great deal. The young queen, born almost twenty years after her husband, had come to Spain in 1560, when she was still a child. She reached puberty only in August 1561, at the age of fifteen, and she began to sleep regularly with her husband early in the following year. In June 1562 it appeared that Elizabeth was pregnant and the royal couple celebrated by going hunting together every day at El Bosque near Segovia. It was a false hope, however, and there was no further evidence of pregnancy before Philip left his wife for a six-month visit to his kingdoms of Aragon in August 1563. Catherine de' Medici, queen regent of France and Elizabeth's mother, was becoming impatient to have her first grandchild and she officiously instructed her ambassador to seek an audience to remind Philip of "the desire we have to see some children" and to express the hope that he would endeavor to "justify the opinion we have that he is a good husband." At this the king could control himself no longer. He burst out laughing and begged the ambassador to assure his mother-in-law, who was acting out the traditional role so well, that "he would be at pains to keep up the reputation he had acquired in France." Philip was as good as his word. When he returned to Castile in May 1564 he took his wife to Aranjuez and there he and Elizabeth spent a second honeymoon, eating picnics out together alone in the secluded gardens. The queen had no time to write to her family, she told the French ambassador, because her time was almost entirely spent with the king. His love, she said, filled her with happiness. By July, Elizabeth was clearly pregnant and the king ordered public celebrations in Madrid: the whole city was lit up and crowds gathered outside the palace in her honor. Alas, there were complications. The queen took to her bed on 5 August; on the ninth she had a serious nasal hemorrhage, and at once the court physicians closed in. A succession of purges, clysters and blood-letting quickly weakened the young queen and produced a miscarriage. She was savéd by the intervention of an Italian doctor, but only after his Spanish colleagues had given her up, speechless and comatose, for dead. By the end of September she had recovered, although her health was delicate and her body still showed the scars of the incisions and the tourniquets to which it had been subjected.

Throughout the illness, Philip remained at his wife's side. Not once does he appear to have left the palace and he spent several hours a day, morning and evening, by her bed. When she recovered he went off with her permission to spend a few autumn days at the rising pile of the Escorial, but in November he was on his way back, writing to ask the doctors if he might sleep with her again. The same month, after assuring the French ambassador of his great sorrow at Elizabeth's illness and his enormous pleasure at her recovery, he asked whether her mother, Catherine, had been ill during her first pregnancy. The ambassador told him that Catherine had never had any trouble with childbearing and the king, relieved, said that in the future his wife should do everything his mother-in-law ordered in that respect. But Catherine still had some time to wait for her first grandchild, doubtless because of the period of infertility which in women normally follows a serious illness. But then Catherine's dreams came true: the queen conceived again, and by February 1566 was clearly pregnant. Once more there was public rejoicing, and the king showed even greater affection for his wife. The royal couple moved to Segovia and Elizabeth's pregnancy passed without mishap until a false alarm on 1 August, when she thought her labor had started and the king leaped up from his bed to be with her. After that, she was sometimes feverish, which brought the king to her room to see her as many as five times a day. When labor began some days later, the king at once came to his wife's side, and stayed throughout the birth, holding her hand in his and giving her a special potion sent by her mother to ease the pain at the moment of birth. Afterward, although he had hoped for a son, the king could not disguise his pride and pleasure at having sired the delightful baby Isabella, the person who was in later life to mean more to him than anyone else in the world. Some days after the birth the queen almost died of puerperal fever, and recovery was slow, but before long she was pregnant again and on 6 October 1567 another daughter was born: Catalina Michaela. Amidst the preparations surrounding his proposed visit to the Netherlands, Philip was away during this pregnancy, but he did return for the birth in order to be with his wife.

Perhaps the king was disappointed that once again he had sired a daughter. It was noted that he went by himself to Aranjuez a few days after the birth, failing to return to attend his daughter's baptism on 19 October, although if the child had been a boy, there would have been major festivities. But Elizabeth was young (just twenty-one) and fertile, and by May 1568 she was pregnant once more, spending her days playing at cards, quoits and dice, listening to the jokes of her buffoons, or watching little plays in her privy chamber. She went out to lunch with her ladies-in-waiting almost every day in the Casa de Campo or in the woods near Madrid, and so the summer passed. But then the queen became seriously ill: she fainted repeatedly; she was miserable, often crying for no apparent reason; she had trembling fits; she ate and slept poorly and irregularly. The Spanish doctors, as in 1564, began to apply clysters and tourniquets, which precipitated a miscarriage on the morning of 3 October. It was another girl. The queen died later the same day.

The king spent his time in melancholy vigil by the bed of his dying wife, holding her hand, soothing and comforting her during her last hours. He heard Mass with her for the last time and was present when she was prepared for burial, dressed in the habit of a Franciscan (she died on Saint Francis's day). At her death he moved into the monastery of Saint Jerome in Madrid, a royal foundation, where for over two weeks he remained in retreat, refusing to see papers, ministers and ambassadors, joining the monks as they said Masses continuously for the soul of the late queen. Philip did not emerge until 21 October and even then only to go to the Escorial for a further period of seclusion. For several months he was so upset that he could not bear to hear talk of marriage. In December the French ambassador, who had orders from Catherine de' Medici to offer the king Elizabeth's sister, Margot de Valois, as a new bride, was warned that the king was in no mood to listen to such proposals, and when, on Christmas Eve, the ambassador read out Catherine's letter of condolence to him, tears came to the king's eyes. He wore mourning for his dead bride for a whole year and still in June 1569 referred to Elizabeth's two daughters, aged two and three, as "the only consolation that remains for me, since Our Lord deprived me of the company of the queen their mother." He described her as irreplaceable and on his deathbed he gave Isabella the wedding ring of Elizabeth de Valois, his beloved spouse, and enjoined her never to part with it.

Although in 1570 Philip married his niece, Anne of Austria, and although he found companionship with her for longer than with any of his other wives, it seems clear that he was driven to a fourth marriage solely by the need to produce an heir. In May 1569 he wrote for the benefit of his late wife's mother, but probably sincerely:

> I would very much like to avoid talking about remarriage because, having lost the company I have lost and with my sadness and grief still keen, I very much desire to remain as I am; however, the succession problem being as it is, and . . . with the obligation we princes have to our kingdoms in this respect, I cannot avoid complying with . . . the suggestions that have begun to be made to me on this point.

There were, of course, good reasons for Philip to take this stand with his former mother-in-law, especially since she was trying to persuade him to marry her tempestuous daughter Margot. But the succession problem was real enough. The two infant daughters of Elizabeth de Valois were the only children left to Philip. His only other child, Don Carlos, had also died in 1568.

Great controversy has always surrounded the personality of Don Carlos. His mother only survived his birth by four days in 1545. In addition, Philip was out of the country from 1548 to 1551 and from 1554 to 1559, so that neither parent played much part in bringing up the boy. It is unlikely, however, that parental care could have achieved very much; for it seems clear that Don Carlos shared the mental abnormalities displayed by several of his relatives. His great-grandmother Joanna the Mad had been a whimpering lunatic locked up in Tordesillas castle from 1506 until her death in 1555, whipped and beaten into submission by her keepers (with the express approval of her son, Charles V). Joanna's own grandmother Isabella of Portugal had also been locked up because of insanity, ending her days in 1496 a demented prisoner in Arévalo castle. Don Carlos, like his cousin, the unbalanced Sebastian of Portugal (also tragically abandoned by his parents), had a double dose of Joanna the Mad's inheritance, thanks to the inbreeding of the royal families of early modern Europe.

There appear to have been three stages in the deterioration of Don Carlos's personality. The first was in 1554, when Philip left for England. We have a touching account of father and son fishing, hunting and dining together as Philip moved toward the coast and his marriage with Mary Tudor. Up to that point, Don Carlos seems to have been a fairly normal small boy, but there was a distinct regression during Philip's five-year absence. The child was very late in learning to read and write (even at twenty-one his script was irregular and malformed) and in October 1558 his tutor, Honorato Juan (who had also taught Philip II), admitted to the king that there was nothing he could do to make the young prince learn. Ministers like Gonzalo Pérez could be tactful and argue that "Habsburg children are always late developers," but as the years went by and the prince still showed little interest in anything except wine, women and food, such explanations became patently threadbare. From 1560 on, he was subject to prolonged feverish attacks, perhaps from malaria, which also affected his father and grandfather, and which undermined his health. Then in 1562, while in Alcalá de Henares attending lectures at the university, he fell down a flight of stairs and suffered serious head injuries: he lost his sight for a time and only a trepanning operation carried out by the great Vesalius saved his life. After six months he was able to walk, but he was never the same again. The imperial ambassador, Baron Dietrichstein, who was well disposed, observed that whereas Don Carlos was sensible in some things he was like a child of seven in others. This was probably as favorable a judgment as it was possible to make. The prince's tantrums and rages became notorious. Ambassadors advised their masters not to contemplate a marriage between any member of their family and the prince: "He is usually so mad and furious," wrote the French ambassador, "that everyone here pities the lot of the woman who will have to live with him." He threw out of a window a page who crossed him; he attacked with a knife his father's ministers, even the duke of Alva; he almost killed his horses by the brutal ill treatment he gave them; and he made a shoemaker who presented him with a pair of boots that were too tight eat them as a punishment.

Despite these unpleasant developments, the king had by no means written Don Carlos off as insane; nor did he yet dislike the boy. On the contrary, during Don Carlos's long illness at Alcalá the king was regularly in attendance at his son's bedside and seems to have wished and prayed sincerely for his recovery. Later on, he encouraged the prince to take an active interest in affairs of state, to attend council meetings, and to correspond with ministers abroad, and these suggestions were certainly taken up: the prince's attendance at the Council of State was often recorded and he wrote regularly to his aunt, Margaret of Parma, about Netherlands affairs. But none of this could conceal the underlying defects. In 1564 Philip informed the duke of Alva, then away from court, that "in intelligence and personality as well as in judgment" the prince "lags far behind what is normal at his age." Gradually the king's attitude hardened. A revealing incident occurred in 1564, when Don Carlos asked his father's minister of works to repair the roof of the house where he stored some of his possessions. The minister was favorable: "From what I hear, new tiles are very necessary. If Your Majesty pleases, it would be as well to do something so that nothing should be damaged." The king was reluctant and grudged the effort: "You can do it," he conceded, "so long as it can be done cheaply and that you only buy ordinary tiles. . . . Where tiles have to be replaced, put on the old ones which were taken off the Pardo during rebuilding." It was well known that, in building materials, Philip II made use of nothing but the best, and therefore this obvious meanness was significant.

Incidents like these no doubt poisoned relations between father and son to a considerable degree, and the king seems to have become more ashamed of, and hostile toward, the prince. But matters did not get out of hand until 1567. By August of that year, according to the French ambassador, who got some

of his information from the queen (Elizabeth de Valois):
"But for what the world would say, the king would lock up
Don Carlos in a tower to make him more obedient." Everyone
was aware that a crisis was brewing. Throughout the autumn
of 1567 Don Carlos was amassing money and, apparently, making secret preparations to leave the court. In addition, the
prince told his confessor that he intended to kill "a man";
everything suggested that the "man" was Philip II. Finally,
Don John of Austria informed the king that Don Carlos was
planning to flee to the Netherlands (and Don John had himself demonstrated that it could be done: in 1565 he had escaped from the court to join in the relief of Malta). The king
now had to act. There was still rebellion in the Netherlands,
and there were men at court who could remember the danger-
ous comunero rising of 1520–1521, when the leaders of the
rebellious towns of Castile had used Joanna the Mad as a figure-
head and played off her authority against that of her son,
Charles V. Philip could not run the risk of anything similar
happening again.

On 13 January 1568 Philip ordered public prayers to be
said in all monasteries and churches to ask for God's grace to
be shown to him — although it was not specified why or for
what. On 17 January the king arrived in Madrid from the
Escorial, where he had spent Christmas, and almost at once
convened a meeting of his senior policy advisers and certain
theologians to counsel him on the correct course of action.
Their advice must have been clear because the following night
the king in person, with helmet and sword, led a party of
councillors and guards to place his son and heir under arrest.
Don Carlos was held in confinement, as Joanna the Mad had
been; he was to be transferred to the same place as Isabella of
Portugal, Joanna's mad grandmother, the tower of Arévalo
castle, which had been repaired about a year before; and he
was given as his keeper the son of Joanna the Mad's brutal
jailer. These coincidences were all noted by observers at court.

Few cherished any doubts concerning the reason for the

prince's confinement. Don Juan de Zúñiga, the Spanish ambassador in Rome, put it concisely: "The king did not give
any special reason to His Holiness for his action, but I do not
think there was anything more than what we all know of the
prince's condition." The queen also hinted at insanity as the
reason in a cryptic letter to the French ambassador: "God has
willed his nature to be made public." Philip's inner feelings
are far harder to ascertain. His only full statement was a letter
written to the pope in May. It was not, the king averred,

> the passion or the fault of the prince, nor any intention on my
> part to chastise or correct him, for if this had been my motive
> I would have taken other measures, without going to this ex-
> treme. . . . But since, for my sins, it has been God's will that
> the prince should have such great and numerous defects, partly
> mental, partly due to his physical condition, utterly lacking as
> he is in the qualifications necessary for ruling, I saw the grave
> risks that would arise were he to be given the succession and
> the obvious dangers that would accrue; and therefore, after long
> and careful consideration, and having tried every alternative in
> vain, it was clear that there was little or no prospect of his con-
> dition's improving in time to prevent the evils which could
> reasonably be foreseen. In short, my decision was necessary.

It is fair to guess that, in the face of this personal tragedy,
Philip's sense of embarrassment and shame at the incapacity
of his only son outweighed any feelings of sorrow and sympathy. He forbade the queen to weep and he ordered Don
John to take off the mourning he had donned at the prince's
arrest. In March he wrote to the grandees of Spain forbidding
them to mention Don Carlos in their conversations and even
in their prayers. In April he ordered the prince's household to
be disbanded "because the poor young man is becoming more
deranged every day." The prince, observed the French ambassador, was "rapidly passing into oblivion, and is spoken of
scarcely more often than if he had never been born." Don
Carlos was fast becoming depersonalized, a purely administra-

tive problem. Orders were issued for the archivists of the crown to search out a precedent for King Philip's predicament, and they found one: Prince Charles of Viana was disinherited by his father, John II of Aragon, in 1461, but died in confinement within a matter of months. This discovery was kept secret, especially from Don Carlos, who was forbidden to leave his rooms and even to show his face at the window, until the tower at Arévalo was ready.

Confinement did nothing to improve the prince's condition. He went on hunger strikes and he became appallingly thin, with great bulging eyes. Occasionally he was force-fed with soup. Then he started swallowing things — even a diamond ring — and his general behavior became yet more disordered. By July 1568 it was clear that there was little hope of his survival. Philip now began to betray some emotion. He shut himself away and sat, melancholy and taciturn, in an armchair for days on end. When the prince died on 24 July, having starved himself to death, Philip decreed a general mourning for nine days and ordered his court to wear mourning for a year. There was not, however, general regret at Don Carlos's passing. The duke of Alva's agent at court observed that "there were few signs" of sorrow among the population at large, while the prince's keeper actually rejoiced: "His removal to heaven was a great boon to all of Christendom because certainly, had he lived, he would have destroyed Christendom. His mental state and his habits were entirely disordered. He is very well up there; all of us who knew him thank God for his death."

No one at the time appears to have doubted either that Don Carlos was kept in confinement for good reason or that he died of natural causes. But the story gradually gained ground that there was more to the prince's untimely end than that. One version (favored by playwrights such as Otway and Schiller) centered on a treasonable liaison between Don Carlos and the rebels of the Netherlands, especially Baron Montigny, who was at court in 1566–1567. A more fanciful variety, which had the prince killed because he was having an affair with Philip's wife

Elizabeth de Valois, originated in the *Apology* of William of Orange (published in 1581) and passed from there into most Protestant biographies of the king. The first suggestion is not implausible. There was certainly contact if not conspiracy between the prince and Montigny in 1566, and the baron was arrested in September 1567; perhaps some information came to light that justified the arrest of Don Carlos three months later. Even so, involvement in the Netherlands problem can only have strengthened the case against the prince; his behavior alone gave sufficient cause for alarm. It is possible to be more definite about the supposed "affair" of Don Carlos and the queen. It is true that the prince and his stepmother were very fond of each other and spent much time together. The prince was in the queen's chamber on the night before his arrest: he went to play cards with her, taking one hundred crowns in his purse, "and when he came back again his purse was empty." Don Carlos gave the queen many gifts and he normally wore an agate medallion engraved with her likeness. But a closer relationship with the queen of Spain was scarcely possible: she lived in the midst of her "ladies of the bedchamber," headed by the formidably austere duchess of Alva, hardly the person to turn a blind eye to a liaison which (if discovered) would have cost both women their heads. Even for royalty, privacy was a concept virtually unknown in the sixteenth century. If the queen wept for two days when the prince was imprisoned and again when he died, it was no doubt because she had lost one of the few friends of her own age at Philip's court. Apart from her daily hour or two with the king, Elizabeth de Valois had scarcely anyone of her own rank with whom to relax. Her life must have been unbelievably tedious and, whatever else he was, Don Carlos was not boring!

The main support for the dark suspicions concerning the death of Don Carlos comes from circumstantial evidence: certain other persons whose continued existence was "inconvenient" to Philip II mysteriously disappeared. The murder of Juan de Escobedo in March 1578 (discussed in Chapter 8 below) was almost certainly ordered by Philip; the murder of William of Orange in July 1584, by an assassin, was encouraged by the king and later (if posthumously) handsomely rewarded by him; and the judicial murder of Montigny in October 1570 was unquestionably carried out at the king's command. But in each of these three cases, pressing reasons encouraged the king to exercise that absolute power of life and death which the law gave him over all his vassals. In the case of Don Carlos there was no hurry at all. If Joanna the Mad could be kept in Tordesillas for half a century, Don Carlos could be confined in Arévalo for just as long. The prince's death was convenient to Philip, but it was not necessary. There is no reason to suppose that the king had any part in it.

Nevertheless the tragic end of Don Carlos, following the troubles in the Netherlands and followed by the death of Elizabeth de Valois, seems to have shaken the king's serenity. Early in 1569 he wrote a remarkable letter to his chief adviser, Cardinal Diego de Espinosa, which betrayed the deep depression into which he had sunk. Things had reached such a state, he felt, that he wanted to abdicate. So many things were going wrong that

> they cannot fail to cause pain and exhaustion, and, believe me, I am so exhausted and pained by them, and by what happens in this world, that if it were not for the business of Granada and other things which cannot be abandoned, I do not know what I would do. And perhaps I do not really regret the delays in our negotiations in Germany [for the marriage with Anne], because certainly I am no good for the world of today; I know very well that I should be in some other station in life, one not as exalted as the one God has given me, which for me alone is terrible. And many criticize me for this. Please God that in heaven we shall be treated better.

This letter, betraying the king's anguish when God appeared to have forsaken him, would have shocked any reader of the time with its frankness. But the king reassured his correspondent: "Do not be sad at what I have written, for as I cannot unburden myself with anyone but you, I cannot refrain from doing so." The recipient's secretary, who diligently filed the letter away, noted on the dorse: "This letter must be seen by no one except His Majesty." The Prudent King had good reason to let himself go: 1568 had been the worst year of his reign. Apart from the tragedy of Don Carlos and the death of his wife, there was more trouble in the Netherlands and, worst of all, a major revolt within Spain by the Moriscos of the kingdom of Granada — "the business of Granada" to which the desperate letter above referred.

SIX

Years of Crusade, 1568–1572

ONE OF PHILIP II's most cherished dreams was to Christianize — or rather to Catholicize — all his dominions. He had played an important part in convening the third session of the Council of Trent and his Spanish priests and theologians — over one hundred of them — had been prominent in all the deliberations of the council from September 1562 until December 1563. He also took a keen personal interest in the evangelization of the New World, in the reform of ecclesiastical discipline in Spain and in the diffusion of the Word of God to the "dark corners of the land" in Spain, America, Italy and the Netherlands.

The early efforts of the king to crush heresy in the Low Countries, culminating in the dispatch of the duke of Alva in 1567 with ten thousand Spanish troops, have already been noted. With the support of his troops, Alva was able to enforce a number of new measures designed to preserve the Netherlands for the Roman Church. Fourteen new bishoprics for the Low Countries, created by papal decree in 1561 but bitterly opposed by the Netherlands nobles in the time of Margaret of Parma, were now given definitive form. Following the decrees of the Council of Trent, each diocese began to establish a seminary in which to train priests, and the bishops began the enormous task of eliminating abuses among their diocesan clergy and purging heretics from among their diocesan schoolmasters. In Antwerp alone — with 150 schools — at least twenty-two schoolmasters lost their jobs because of heresy in 1568–1569. In addition, Alva managed to increase substantially the taxes paid by the Netherlands for their own defense. From a total of 750,000 ducats received in the biennium 1566–1567, the tax revenue rose to 4.4 million in 1570–1571. The cost of the Netherlands to Spain fell in precise proportions: 2 million ducats arrived from the Castilian treasury in 1566–1567, but only 550,000 in 1570–1571. The "Netherlands problem" appeared to be well on the way toward its final solution.

Admittedly, the duke of Alva's "new order" provoked some opposition. In 1568 four armies of exiles, reinforced by French, English and German mercenaries under the direction of William of Orange, invaded the Low Countries. But before the year was out, all had been defeated and expelled. Those who escaped to fight another day, like Orange, were thoroughly discredited; those who fell into Alva's hands were severely punished. Perhaps fifteen hundred persons (including prominent nobles like the count of Egmont) were executed; many were outlawed; and about nine thousand had some or all of their property confiscated.

Although many of the transgressors were pardoned and much property was restored by the crown in 1570 and 1574, there has been considerable criticism of the severity with which Philip II suppressed the troubles in the Netherlands. However, the criticisms have generally been based on distortion and exaggeration of the facts. J. L. Motley, for example, wrote of the "torrents of blood" that flowed from the duke of Alva's purges; but in fact, by sixteenth-century standards, the number of executions was relatively small considering the scale of the troubles. No government at that time voluntarily chose to leave traitors and rebels alive once they were captured. Queen Elizabeth's treatment of the northern rebels after 1569 was no different from Alva's behavior (except that Elizabeth's victims were Catholics and Alva's Protestants). Under the circumstances, with their former colleagues invading the Low Countries at the head of an army of thirty thousand men, it is hard to see how Philip II could have spared Egmont and the rest in the summer of 1568. The only really controversial execution seems to have been that of Floris de Montmorency, Baron Montigny. The baron was sent as an envoy to the court of Spain in June 1566 by Margaret of Parma; he was thus absent from the Low Countries when the real rebellion began. However, it was subsequently discovered that Montigny, on his way to Spain, had stayed with his uncle, the constable of France, Anne de Montmorency, and that the two men had reached and signed an agreement to provide troops and money to each other should need arise. This treasonable liaison, long suspected by the Spanish ambassador in France, was subsequently confirmed by the count of Egmont during his interrogation. Montigny was placed under house arrest in Spain in September 1567, and after a long trial he was sentenced to death in March 1570. The sentence was carried out in secret, by garroting, at two o'clock on the morning of 16 October 1570 in the castle of Simancas, where Montigny was a prisoner. The baron was then dressed in the habit of a Franciscan monk, to hide the scars around his neck, and it was claimed that he died of natural causes. He was bundled into his coffin and buried in great haste.

Almost at once, Philip II's enemies spread the story that Montigny had not died of natural causes but had been basely murdered. William of Orange even published the story in his *Apology* (1581). But neither Orange, nor anyone else outside the king's inner circle of advisers, really knew what had happened. The truth, indeed, only came to light in 1848, when the documents concerning Montigny were discovered in a locked chest in Simancas and published. Philip II always denied that the baron had been executed.

This secrecy and deception are curious, since on the face of it the dead man had been tried for treason and found guilty, and the sixteenth-century penalty for treason was death. However there were other urgent reasons for concealing the truth. Reports arrived from the Netherlands that the baron's wife and some of his friends had been lobbying Philip's betrothed, Anne of Austria, as she passed through the Low Countries on her way to Spain, and it was alleged that the princess had promised to do her best to secure the baron's release. She arrived on Spanish soil, at Santander, on 3 October. An "accidental death" before Anne reached him saved the king from an unpleasant choice: either to release a convicted traitor or to offend and alienate his wife-to-be.

The drive against heresy and rebellion in the Netherlands was but one part of a consistent policy followed by Philip in the years around 1570. In all areas he and his ministers moved against non-Catholic or disaffected groups. In the New World, where many communities still practiced their pre-Columbian religious ways, orders were issued to extirpate all "idolators." In Spain there were two large suspect minorities: the *conversos* (Jews who had abandoned their former faith for Christianity) and Moriscos (Moslems who had done the same). The Inquisition had been created at the end of the fifteenth century to control the behavior of these new converts, and gradually its activities grew. By the seventeenth century there were twenty-one tribunals of the Holy Office, fifteen of them on the peninsula and six elsewhere in the Spanish empire. All of them were controlled by the Council of the Inquisition (known as the Suprema), which met in the king's palace in Madrid.

Philip II gave the Holy Office his full support throughout his reign and he made his support public. He presided in person at five *autos de fé* (pageants of the faith — the ritual sentencing of a group of notorious heretics, often followed by some executions): at Valladolid in October 1559 and at Toledo in February 1560 after his return to Spain; at Barcelona in February 1564, at Lisbon in 1582 and at Toledo in February

1591. There is even evidence that he enjoyed the occasions: in 1586, when he was thinking of going to Toledo for a few days, Philip informed his secretary: "We might be able to go to a pontifical Mass, which is really something worth seeing. I also remember that about this time they used sometimes to have an *auto* of the Inquisition, and although I have heard nothing about it, it is possible that there will be one this year. It is something really worth seeing for those who have not seen one. If there is to be an *auto* during the time I am there, it would be good to see it." The king did not merely attend as an observer. At the great *auto* in Valladolid in October 1559, the royal family all swore in public to protect the faith and to support the authority of the Inquisition in all things. It is said that when one of the aristocratic victims at this *auto* was led past the king to his death he mouthed the rebuke: "How can you let me burn?" To which the king retorted: "If my son were as wicked as you I would carry the wood to burn him myself." The condemned man was Don Carlos de Seso who, as *corregidor* (chief magistrate) of Toro, had given the official protection which the Protestants required in order to spread their faith. This story may be apocryphal, but the spirit which underlay it was real enough. The king's apostils on the reports of the Council of the Inquisition are entirely consistent: "The Inquisition's will be done." By way of illustration we may take the case of Don Alonso Enríquez, scion of one of the foremost Castilian families, who in 1578 had insulted the inquisitor general in a letter. "Proceed against him as the council proposes," wrote the king, "and let the same justice be done which is usual and which is carried out in the rest of the affairs of the Holy Office." In another note written a few years earlier, the king assured his inquisitor general that "I shall always favor and assist the affairs of the Holy Office, knowing (as I do) the reasons and the obligation which exist for so doing, and for me more than anyone."

Between 1550 and 1700 the twenty-one tribunals of the Holy Office heard about 150,000 cases, some of them involving several people. The total for the reign of Philip II was probably in the region of 40,000, or a thousand a year. Although most of these cases concerned religious deviation (whether of the Protestant, Moslem or Jewish varieties) a considerable number — perhaps fifteen percent — arose from 'social crimes," such as bigamy, homosexuality and fornication. The Inquisition was, like the presbyteries and kirk sessions of the Calvinist church in Scotland and elsewhere, an important instrument of social control and it played a crucial role in the preservation of order, discipline and subordination in Spanish society. However, the bulk of its work was directed against religious offenders and in this it was extremely effective. Its efforts against Protestantism were particularly impressive. In 1558 two Lutheran cells were discovered in Castile, one in Valladolid and one in Seville, both with around one hundred members (many of them wealthy and influential). Although both were systematically destroyed by the authorities, the government was afraid that other groups might continue to lurk undetected. Suspects were therefore rounded up and interrogated, especially in the areas near to Protestant France: the tribunals of Barcelona, Logroño and Zaragoza alone heard fourteen hundred cases involving Protestants (most of them French) between 1540 and 1700 (and this in spite of a shortage of funds so acute that on one occasion, at least, the Barcelona tribunal was compelled to advance the date of an *auto de fé* in order to economize on food for the prisoners). There was also a drive against heretical books. In June 1559 an Index of prohibited books was prepared by the Spanish Inquisition. It was a hasty compilation: there were errors of title, and even books without a title ("A certain work by . . .") because the inquisitors had only managed to get hold of an imperfect copy. About five hundred works were proscribed. The next Spanish Index, published in 1583, contained almost twenty-five hundred titles and was far more systematic. But by then Protestantism in Spain was a thing of the past: the persecution of 1558–1559 may have been an overreaction, but it had been effective.

The Inquisition was rather less successful against the Moorish minority, partly because they were so much more numerous. At the accession of Philip II there were perhaps 400,000 Moriscos in Spain, equivalent to about six percent of the total population. But this ethnic minority was not evenly spread across the country. About 200,000 of them lived in the kingdoms of Aragon, where they made up around twenty percent of the population, while perhaps 150,000 more were concentrated in the kingdom of Granada, where they comprised over half of the total inhabitants.

The government was worried about the Morisco problem. Ever since the expulsion of all the Moors who would not accept Christianity (in 1492), the authorities had striven to integrate those who remained. By the accession of Philip II, it was clear that the policy of integration was not working. At the same time, there was increasing evidence of collusion between the Moriscos and their cousins, the pirates from Algiers, whose raids upon the Christian villages of Spain's Mediterranean coast became ever more daring. Some also feared cooperation between the Moriscos of Aragon and the Protestants of neighboring France, based on their common hatred of Catholicism. Certainly most observers feared that the Moriscos might act as a "fifth column" if ever the Ottoman fleet landed a Turkish army on Spanish shores.

Not everyone feared the Moriscos, however. The landlords of the east and south of Spain prospered through the skill of their Moslem tenants in irrigation, silk cultivation and silk weaving. There was a proverb, "A man with a Moor is never poor" (*Quien tiene moro tiene oro*), and the noblemen of Granada in particular were anxious to protect their source of wealth against the vexations of the Inquisition and the law courts. In May 1528 they had helped to secure an agreement by which the Moriscos were given permission to enjoy their traditional customs, dress and language. However, after about 1550 this privileged position came under attack. Of all Inquisition cases heard in Granada city in 1550, only fifty percent involved Moriscos, but of all Inquisition cases heard in 1566, ninety-two percent involved Moriscos. The rising intensity of persecution is better illustrated in the accompanying table.

ACTIVITY OF THE INQUISITION IN GRANADA, 1520–1570

Years	Number of Autos de fé	Total Number Condemned	Number of Moriscos Condemned	Moriscos as Percent of Total
1520–1529	1	89	3	3
1550–1559	4	377	271	72
1563–1569	4	420	368	88

Although most of those condemned by the Inquisition were not burned, the majority suffered a long period of imprisonment (at their own expense) and many were subjected to torture. Most were eventually sentenced to lose all or most of their property (which was appropriated by the Inquisition).

The substantial increase in the persecution of the Moriscos was no accident: it was deliberate royal policy. In his last paper of advice to his son, the emperor Charles V had urged the expulsion of all the Moors from Spain, and in 1559–1560 three important anti-Morisco steps were taken. First, the crown refused to accept the offer made by an assembly of Granadine Morisco elders to pay 100,000 ducats in return for a renewal of protection against the Inquisition. Encouraged by this decision, the inquisitors began to make visits of inquiry to areas they had previously neglected and they began to condemn Moorish customs they had previously tolerated: attendance at the traditional festivals, or special ways of killing meat, were now taken as evidence of heterodoxy. At the same time, the central law court for Granada (the Audiencia) initiated a series of inquiries into landowning, challenging the title of many Moriscos to their land. There were many other petty vexations. In 1560, the Cortes of Castile issued a law forbidding all Moriscos to own slaves (on the grounds that the slaves would be brought up Moslems) ; in 1561 an increase in the duty upon silk produce, the mainstay of the Morisco economy, reduced its profitability; and in 1563 a royal proclamation ordered the disarming of all Moriscos.

The anti-Morisco campaign gathered further momentum with the rise to power of Cardinal Diego de Espinosa. He became inquisitor general in 1564 and, in addition, president of the Council of Castile in 1565. He was thus in supreme control both of the Inquisition and of the Audiencia in Granada, and he encouraged their harassment of the unfortunate Moors. On 1 January 1567, by a royal proclamation drawn up at Espinosa's behest and published by town criers in both Arabic and Castilian, all Moriscos were commanded to abandon their dress, language, customs and religious practices within one year, on pain of fines and imprisonment. The Inquisition and Audiencia were jointly charged with enforcement.

The leaders of the Morisco community spent the year 1567 trying to obtain a new agreement with the authorities which would preserve their way of life. They warned that ruthless enforcement of the new laws might produce armed resistance, especially since the harvest of 1567 failed completely in the south and threatened many Moorish smallholders with starvation, debt and flight. The representations of the Moriscos, who petitioned the king, were seconded by the captain-general of the kingdom of Granada, the marquis of Mondéjar, whose family (to which the king's favorite, Ruy Gómez, was allied) had always protected the Moors against persecution. It was to no avail. In 1567 the more tolerant policies of Ruy Gómez and his friends were out of favor in Granada, as they were in the Netherlands. In March, the captain-general was ordered to take his forces to the coast and to leave all power in the hinterland to the Audiencia and some specially raised militia units. In November 1567 Espinosa, basking in the king's full favor, wrote to the ecclesiastical authorities in Granada requiring them to prepare for the vigorous enforcement of the new orders on Morisco dress, language and customs in the new year. As had been predicted, from April 1568 onward, realizing that no further concessions could be expected from the crown, a group of Moriscos began to plan open rebellion — the first in Spain since 1521. By Christmas the organization was complete and 182 Moorish villages around Granada began their revolt, while a task force endeavored to take Granada itself with the aid of the inhabitants of a large Morisco enclave in the heart of the city, the Albaicín. But the wealthy people of the Moorish quarter failed to join the rebellion, and the task force was obliged to withdraw.

The Morisco cause never recovered from this reverse: by March 1569 the Christian army under Mondéjar had recaptured all the villages in revolt, leaving only a few rebel units in the hills. However, just as success seemed near, Espinosa proposed a radical new policy: the deportation of all Moriscos from Granada. He also suggested that Mondéjar should be recalled, since he would be opposed to this policy and would be reluctant to carry it out. The marquis was therefore relieved of his command in favor of the king's bastard brother, Don John of Austria.

Don John was not a happy choice. Born in Regensburg in February 1547, he was the love child of the emperor Charles V (then aged forty-seven) and a local girl of eighteen or nineteen, Barbara Blomberg. The boy entered the imperial household in 1554 and went to Yuste with his father, although the emperor never let it be known that the child (who was always called Jerónimo) was his. The truth was revealed to Philip II only after his father's death; the young king was shocked, but behaved magnanimously and made his newly discovered brother welcome at court. In 1568 he made Don John captain-general of the Mediterranean fleet, and in 1569 supreme commander of the forces deployed against the Moriscos of Granada. Don John's inexperience was seen by the government as an advantage, for it meant that he was more likely to accept the draconian orders coming from Madrid. However, the tougher policy of deportation advocated by Espinosa naturally stiffened the resistance of the surviving rebels. Even the inhabitants of the Albaicín planned a revolt in June (although it misfired), while the main body of the insurgents, in their refuges high in the mountains of the Alpujarras, southeast of Granada, received numerous reinforcements. In October 1569 the king gave orders that the campaign was now to be waged without restraint — "with fire and blood" — by his soldiers, some of them recalled especially from Naples to defend Spain against its "fifth column." But little was achieved. The war became a stalemate and in March 1570 the king himself came south to Córdoba to superintend operations. Within a few weeks Philip decided to suspend the deportation of all the Moriscos, preferring instead a complicated plan for their redistribution throughout Castile. Reluctantly, he sent an emissary into the Alpujarras with orders to offer a free pardon to all who would surrender, and to begin negotiations with the rebel leaders for a settlement (although, characteristically, the emissary was instructed to act as if he were not authorized by the king!).

The king's change of policy came not a moment too soon. The spectacle of Spain's incapacity to crush a rebellion so close to her heart, despite heavy expenditure and large concentrations of troops, was welcome news to Philip II's enemies elsewhere. The prince of Orange, watching from his exile in faraway Dillenburg for another chance to invade the Netherlands, was impressed: "It is an example to us, in that the Moors are able to resist for so long even though they are people of no more substance than a flock of sheep. What, then, might the people of the Low Countries be able to do? . . . We shall see what will happen if the Moriscos can hold out until the Turks can send them some aid." The Turks were not unaware of their opportunity. In 1569 the king of Algiers, an Ottoman vassal, sent arms and ammunition to the rebels and launched attacks on the Spanish coast in order to distract Philip II's forces. In January 1570 Algerian troops seized the Spanish protectorate of Tunis. In April of the same year the sultan himself wrote to the Morisco leaders offering material assistance in their struggle against "the tyrannical and cursed unbelievers." He also ordered the king of Algiers to continue to send military supplies to the rebels. But it was too late: in May 1570 the Morisco commander-in-chief surrendered on terms. Although some of his followers in the mountains continued the struggle until hunger drove them out in the summer of 1571, the rebellion was over and the pacification now began.

The expulsion of all Moors from the city of Granada had been ordered in June 1569 and the Albaicín (formerly containing 25,000 Moriscos) was already three-quarters empty when, on 24 February 1571, Philip II signed a decree which ordered all Moriscos in the kingdom of Granada to abandon their lands. Those still in rebellion had their estates confiscated; those who were reconciled received compensation, but were still forced to leave their homelands. As the first batches of deportees were assembled, Don John was almost at a loss for words: "I do not know if one can find a more moving picture of human misery than seeing so many people setting out in such confusion, with women and children crying and so laden with burdens." A number of them never survived the journey. Some were drowned at sea as storms struck the galleys intended to carry them from Málaga to Seville; others perished in the snows of the bleak winter of 1570–1571 as they were force-marched northward, often manacled together to prevent escapes. Perhaps twenty percent of the total deportees, estimated at between 80,000 and 100,000 persons, may have perished en route. The survivors were distributed in colonies throughout Castile: 4,000 to Córdoba, 2,500 to Toledo (in addition to 400 Moorish slaves already there, taken prisoner in the war), 1,000 to Avila, and so on. Towns which had been free of the Moors for centuries (and were therefore politically "safe") suddenly saw an "albaicín" grow up in their midst. In the Alpujarras, a chain of forts was erected and garrisoned to defend the valleys against any surviving Morisco bandits in the hills and to avoid the risk of any future trouble in the terrain that had proved so difficult to subdue. No less than eighty-four forts were constructed in the kingdom of Granada. But preventive measures of this sort were only half of Philip II's solution to the Morisco problem. In March 1571 he created the Council for the Repopulation of Granada. This body was to survey and acquire the Moriscos' property and then redistribute it among new settlers, who were to be encouraged to migrate from overpopulated but "safe" areas in the north of Spain (like Galicia and Asturias). Eventually some 12,500 Christian families — or 60,000 people — were resettled in 259 Granadine communities.

The whole resettlement operation revealed the power, vision and amazing competence of Philip II and his government. No other Western statesman of the sixteenth century could have directed the movement of people on such a scale. And yet the operation was a failure. Many poor Christian communities in the north were abandoned or ruined when their more energetic settlers left for Granada. Many of the places resettled in Granada were abandoned after a few years, and the high lands were never recolonized. The Alpujarras region, for example, which had 5,848 families according to the census of 1561, had only 1,811 in 1587 — a loss of 69 percent. Even the city of Granada, which attracted the largest number of new settlers, saw its population decline from 11,624 families in 1561 to 8,737 families in 1587 — a loss of 25 percent. The kingdom of Granada as a whole lost around 85,000 people, also about 25 percent of its prewar population. It is true that the resettlement program removed forever the threat of an Islamic "fifth column" in the south of Spain, which had in the past cooperated with the Turkish fleet and the Barbary corsairs. But this new security had been purchased at a high price: the problem had become less intense only because it had been made more general. Now there were Moriscos everywhere, and everywhere they appeared to be a threat to Spanish security: in Valencia they were reputed to be breeding so fast that before long they would outnumber the Christians (a familiar slur used against poor immigrants); in Catalonia they took to banditry with new ferocity (and made close contacts with the French Protestants just across the border); in Andalusia a plot by the newly resettled Moriscos to seize Seville, Córdoba and Ecija in 1581 was only just foiled. But Philip II stood by his policy of integration. In 1582 he turned down a recommendation from his advisers that the Moriscos should be expelled; in 1592 he rejected a similar plea from the Cortes. Instead, in 1596, the king created a special Committee for the Religious Instruction of the Valencian Moriscos: each diocese in the kingdom of Valencia was to appoint twelve Arabic-speaking missionaries, led by "a friar who has been involved in the conversion of the Indians," to teach the Moriscos Christian doctrine. It was stressed that "in teaching them, no violence or rough methods are to be used; they are to be brought to the desired end by gentleness." The whole operation was to be superintended by two well-known figures: Fray José de Acosta, author of a celebrated history of the Indies, and the marquis of Denia, viceroy of Valencia, who was later to achieve fame as the duke of Lerma, Philip III's favorite. But in 1609 it was Lerma who ensured that the entire Moorish population of Spain was expelled. Philip II's attempt at assimilation, like all previous ones, had failed.

By a curious coincidence, just as the resettlement of a Moorish enclave in Christendom — Granada — was being effected at one end of the Mediterranean, the resettlement of a Christian island in the heart of the Ottoman empire — Cyprus — was taking place at the other. Every ten households in Anatolia were required, by the sultan's edict, to send one family to Cyprus, recently conquered from the Venetians. The attack on Cyprus, which began in the spring of 1570, was the principal reason for the sultan's failure to send aid to the Moriscos of Granada: even the Turks could not mount two major amphibious operations at once. Meanwhile, Venice strove to enlist aid from the other Christian powers of the Mediterranean to mount a relief expedition. Although Spain eventually signed a "Holy League" with Venice, Genoa, the papacy and other Italian princes, Philip II's aims were very different from those of his allies. The king's dearest wish was to regain the city of Tunis, captured by Algerian forces (under the sultan's suzerainty) in 1570. He was somewhat reluctant to fight alongside Venice, but the pope was prepared to be generous and conceded taxes on the Spanish Church worth over one million ducats a year. The sudden papal largesse, after so many years of extreme stinginess by the Roman curia toward Spain, caused some surprise among Philip's advisers. "His Holiness has demonstrated the truth of one of our Castilian proverbs: that the constipated die from diarrhea," exclaimed Cardinal Espinosa when he heard the news, and he counseled the king to join the league. Final signatures were exchanged in May 1571.

Philip remained highly suspicious of the Holy League, however. It would seem that he only agreed to join it because he believed that, as the most powerful partner, he would be able to dictate the policy of his allies. In particular he desired the campaign of 1571 to be directed toward the reconquest of Tunis, not toward the relief of Cyprus. When it became clear that it would not be so easy to get his own way, he seriously considered backing out. "To tell you the truth," he told Espinosa early in 1571, "I am not sorry that we have not yet finally joined the League." Carefully balancing prestige against profit, he continued:

> As the League is now, I do not believe it will do or achieve any good at all. It is impossible for me to fulfill what I have promised for this year, and in future years, and not even four times as much money as the pope has given me would suffice. . . . I have been much deceived in this; it is something to be looked at very carefully and in great detail, in order to see what we are obliged to do, for although we would not lose face by getting out of the League now, our prestige will certainly suffer if we do not provide what we promised.

The victory of Lepanto, however, on 7 October 1571, vindicated papal policy to the hilt: 127 Ottoman galleys and galiots were taken, thousands of highly trained Turkish soldiers and sailors were killed or captured by the combined Christian fleets under the command of Philip's brother Don John. It was a victory without precedent in the struggle against the Turks — the worst defeat suffered by a sultan since the battle of Ankara in 1402.

It is often claimed that King Philip was indifferent to the success of his fleet. Many commentators have been misled by his frosty rebuke to the excited messenger who brought him the news while he was at a service in the chapel of the Escorial: "Pull yourself together," he told the unfortunate man. "Wait until I have finished here and then we shall see." Even when he had heard the news in full, Philip merely asked the monks to sing an extra *Te Deum*. But against this apparent insouciance, there were signs of deep feelings of contentment. In 1572, for instance, the king pardoned a number of persons condemned for poaching in the royal parks "out of gratitude to Our Lord for the victory at sea and for the birth of a son" (Don Ferdinand, born in December 1571). These two events were also linked in Titian's massive painting *The Offering of Philip II,* which the king required to be as large as the same artist's picture of *Charles V at Mühlberg,* showing the emperor at his greatest victory. Titian was sent instructions and sketches, approved by the king, by Philip's court painter Alonso Sánchez Coello, and the picture emphasized — like the even more explicit Titian canvas *Spain Coming to the Aid of Religion* — the direct and special relationship between the king of Heaven and the king of Spain. Philip II knew he was doing God's work and he was proud of it.

Perhaps the principal area in which Philip felt himself to be God's chosen instrument was in the "taming of the New World." The crusade to convert the ignorant natives of America had gathered great momentum since the first serious attempt at evangelization by Fray Martín de Valencia and his twelve Franciscan "apostles," who had set sail for Mexico in 1524. By 1560 there were some four hundred Franciscan friars in America (serving eighty churches) and by 1570 the total number of Christian priests in the New World undoubtedly exceeded one thousand. They were, however, trying to minister to an impossibly large flock: perhaps 100,000 whites and 10,-000,000 Indians, many of them totally ignorant of Christian doctrine.

Much the same problems faced the secular authorities. The population of America was extremely large, and most people were unfamiliar with European norms of behavior and social organization. The Spaniards, in fact, never managed to cope with the Indians who had escaped Aztec and Inca control: Philip II's authority was confined largely to the areas which had been "civilized" in the fourteenth and fifteenth centuries and his ministers merely tried to continue and intensify the pre-Columbian policies of "civilization." But in the early years of Philip's reign there was trouble even within the areas conquered by Cortés and Pizarro. There was a revolt by the colonists of Peru in 1552–1554, and the viceroy who was sent to suppress it, the marquis of Cañete, spent over 300,000 ducats of public money on the maintenance of his household. The man sent out to replace him, the count of Nieva (1561–1564), spent a further 200,000. The count's extravagance and arbitrary rule reached such a pitch that the king was moved to administer the stinging rebuke: "You must live with more propriety than hitherto. I urge you earnestly to do this, and also to remember the dignity both of the office you hold and of the person you represent." In 1565 there was a rebellion in Mexico led by the descendants of Hernan Cortés. They planned to kill the principal officials of the central government and to seize all strategic centers, and only the ineptitude of the conspirators (who boasted of their plans before they were due to carry them out) saved the government from great embarrassment.

These political crises had repercussions all over the Spanish dominions in America. They interfered with frontier defense, so that there was an increase in attacks from the wild Araucanian tribes in Chile, the Inca survivors in Vilcabamba in Peru, and the "Red Indians" in northern Mexico. It was becoming clear that Spain's grip on the New World had become seriously weakened. In 1566 the king, advised by Cardinal Espinosa, decided to set up a committee of inquiry into the way in which America was administered. The committee was to be directed by Juan de Ovando, a member of the Council of the Inquisition and a protégé of Espinosa's, and during its five years of activity nearly a thousand matters requiring reform were uncovered. In Ovando's opinion, almost all the problems arose from two broad defects at the heart of the Spanish system: first, neither the Council of the Indies nor the administration in America was familiar with the laws actually in force; second, few members of the council really knew anything about the Indies or its problems (between 1524 and 1569 only six of the forty councillors appointed by the crown had actually been to America). The king accepted these findings and instructed Ovando, who was appointed president of the council, to take steps to remedy the shortcomings he had uncovered. At once the new president began work on codifying all the laws relating to the Indies (although the work was cut short by his death in 1575 and was not completed until 1680). To remedy the ignorance of the council, he had the office of "chronicler and cosmographer of the Indies" created (and he had his secretary, Juan López de Velasco, appointed to it) ; he sent the erudite Dr. Francisco Hernández to America with orders to collect flowers, plants and other articles of interest for the natural history of the Indies; and he had a questionnaire prepared and sent to every community in the Indies, seeking information about their origins, situation and condition. Ovando also supervised the appointment of new viceroys: Don Martín Enríquez for Mexico and Don Francisco de Toledo for Peru. Both were men of outstanding probity and capacity, both were thoroughly briefed by king and council before they left, and both were left in office for an unprecedented period (from May 1568 until 1580). In Mexico, Viceroy Enríquez organized an effective defense for the northern frontier, waging a "war of fire and blood" against the Red Indians after 1570. In Peru, Viceroy Toledo began a general inspection of the province. In 1572 he launched a major campaign against the "idolators" (that is, the Inca survivors) of Vilcabamba, and wiped them out, while from 1570 until 1575 there was a drive to extirpate survivals of the pre-Columbian religion elsewhere in Peru. Further south, Viceroy Toledo lent substantial financial and material aid to the settlers of Chile in their struggle against the Araucanian Indians. Finally, in July 1573, Ovando and the council in Madrid issued some important new regulations, which established norms and regulations for all future colonization in the New World.

The Ordinances of 1573, which were intended by Ovando to be the prelude to a new codification of all the existing laws on the Indies, represented the triumph of a new vision of Spain's destiny in the New World. The natives of America were expressly regarded as rational, with a natural right to life, liberty, private property and social organization. The new decrees were intended to be steps on the path of preparing the Indians for eventual Christian self-government. Indian slavery and serfdom were to be steadily reduced, and the natives were to be gradually concentrated in towns, built especially according to a standard cruciform plan laid down in the Ordinances. A major experiment in resettlement was carried out in Peru in 1569–1571 and in Mexico in 1598–1606 (the latter involving the movement of about fifty-six thousand Indian families), in the hope that the Indians could be "Europeanized" and given greater protection against exploitation by the Spanish ranchercolonists by organizing them into new European-style towns. The same desire lay behind the creation of the General Indian Court in the 1570's, where Indians could take cases of misgovernment and abuse (and they received legal aid for the purpose from state funds). The directives sent by the crown to the regional law courts always urged them to protect the natives from harm.

This impressive secular effort was accompanied by an intensification of religious activity. A surge of new missionaries went out from Spain in the 1560's and 1570's. Most of them were deployed in preaching to the people on the frontiers of Spanish America: in Chile and Paraguay in the south, in New Galicia and New Granada in the north, and in the Philippines. The conquest of the Pacific archipelago epitomized Spain's new outlook on conquest and colonization, and that attitude was itself epitomized more than a century later in the title of the history book written by Fray Gaspar de San Agustín: *The Conquest of the Philippines: The Temporal by the Arms of Philip II, the Prudent, the Spiritual by the Monks of the Augustinian Order* (Madrid 1698). The title page contained a map of the islands with, on one side, the king and a group of conquistadores and, on the other, a bishop and a group of friars.

The Philippines had been visited by Magellan in 1520 and by Loaisa in 1525–1528. There was another exploratory voyage in 1564–1565 under Admiral Miguel López de Legazpi, who was under personal instruction from the king to annex the islands to the Spanish crown peacefully and without bloodshed. This humane attitude was strikingly vindicated: Legazpi soon had most of the archipelago under control, with a minimum of fighting, and by 1590 some five hundred thousand Filipinos were under Spanish rule. There were 94 missionaries in the islands by 1586 and 267 by 1594; the first book printed in the Philippines was a manual on Christianity written in the main local language (the *Tagalog*, published in Manila in 1593) and it was soon followed by a Filipino printing of Bellarmine's *Dottrina Christiana* (Rome 1597). In Manila, as in the other American capital cities, the Spaniards founded law courts, schools and a university.

By the time of his death, Philip II controlled most of America (from 1580 he was ruler of the Portuguese empire too), and from the Río Grande in Mexico to the Bío-Bío in Chile, his authority was paramount. It was thanks to his firm and careful administrative control — to his zeal for "doing God's work" — that so much of America remained Spanish until the nineteenth century and Catholic to this day. The "taming of America" during the second half of the sixteenth century was unquestionably Philip II's greatest achievement.

SEVEN

Years of Failure, 1572–1579

IF CEMENTING Spain's control over the New World was Philip
II's greatest achievement, his inability to suppress the Dutch
Revolt was his greatest failure. The two problems were not un-
related. One of the critical reasons for the success of the Dutch
rebels was the support of England and France, and one of the
influences that led these two states to assist the Dutch was
Spain's ruthless destruction of all interlopers in America. In
1566 Philip II's forces butchered two colonies of French
Protestants who had settled in Florida: there were no Spaniards living in Florida at the time, but Spain viewed the entire
North American continent as her monopoly. In 1568 it was
the turn of an English expedition: Sir John Hawkins and his
men were attacked and annihilated by a Spanish fleet at San
Juan de Ulúa (off what is now Veracruz, Mexico). But there
was more to the Hispanophobia of France and England than
that. There was also Philip II's religion.

England and France had substantial populations of both
Protestants and Catholics in the 1560's, and it was far from
obvious which side would succeed in securing the upper hand.
England had been Catholic, at least in name, from 1554 until
April 1559, and Protestant, at least in name, thereafter; but

there remained a large Catholic minority. The French government was outwardly Catholic throughout; but the "first prince
of the blood" — the French king's nearest male relative — was
a Protestant, and the Protestant party went to war three times
in the 1560's — in 1562–1563, 1567–1568 and 1568–1570 — in
order to secure for itself some measure of toleration. In
1563, in 1567 and again in 1569 the French crown, supported
by the Catholic party, received military aid from Philip II: his
troops fought against the Protestants and helped to win several
victories. At the same time, Philip made contact with the
Catholics of the British Isles and began to plot the overthrow
of the Protestant Elizabeth in favor of her Catholic cousin,
Mary, Queen of Scots. In 1570 he decided to send massive assistance to the conspiracy organized by the Florentine adven-
turer Roberto Ridolfi, which was to place Mary on the English
throne. In July the Spanish Council of State agreed unanimously that the king had a divine mission to bring England
back to the Catholic Church and the duke of Alva, in the
Netherlands, was instructed (against his better judgment) to
send ten thousand of his best soldiers over to England to assist
the Catholic population to rebel. In fact, the Spanish invasion
never took place because in September 1571 the leading conspirators were arrested and revealed to the queen's ministers
the full extent of Spanish involvement.

These developments were fully exploited by William of
Orange and the other Netherlands rebels who had been in
exile since their defeat in 1568. Orange and his agents worked
hard to convince the French Protestants, the English, and
other anti-Spanish potentates like the elector palatine that
their best interests would be served by cooperating in a new
invasion of the Low Countries, which would reduce Spain's
ability to intervene in the affairs of northern Europe. There
were to be four simultaneous attacks: one by sea, by the French
Protestant fleet and the prince of Orange's own ships (popu-
larly known as the Sea Beggars) ; one from France by land by
the French Protestants under their leader, Gaspard de Coligny;

and two from Germany by the Netherlands exiles under Orange, with support from well-wishing German princes. It was hoped that England would lend aid as soon as the first attacks succeeded. And success was confidently expected since Alva's government in the Netherlands was extremely unpopular: his Spanish troops were brutal; his persecution of all who had been involved in the troubles of 1566–1567 made everyone fear possible reprisals; and his search for new sources of income to pay for the standing army of thirteen thousand troops had engendered bitter hostility and impoverishment. On top of all this, the year 1571 brought with it a succession of natural disasters: flooding, plague, harvest failure and, in the end, the worst winter in many years. The year 1572 was therefore an ideal time to challenge Alva's rule, and at first all went well: the Sea Beggars captured parts of Zealand in April, the French Protestants took Mons in Hainaut in May, Orange invaded in July. By August, large areas of the North Netherlands were in rebellion, and further aid began to flow in from France, Germany and England. Alva began to despair, but on 24 August his luck turned. In Paris the French government, which had no wish to become involved in open war with Spain, decided that it had to stop the dispatch of any further Protestant volunteers to the Netherlands. It therefore arranged for the assassination of the French Protestant leader, Coligny. The attempt failed, but before the day was over, government forces aided by the Paris Catholics had murdered not only Coligny but also a total of about six thousand Protestants in the city: the "massacre of Saint Bartholomew." French aid to William of Orange immediately ceased, and without the support of France, England also began to prevent further men and munitions from crossing the Channel. In September, Orange's army was defeated by Alva and Mons soon fell; in October and November all the rebellious towns of the northeast Netherlands were recovered by the Spanish army and in December they moved on to the provinces of Holland and Zealand, most of which had defected to Orange's side. There were only about thirty towns left in revolt: all that remained of the widespread Orangist gains of the summer.

And here Philip II's reign reached a watershed. The two rebel provinces were as difficult to take as the Alpujarras. In the place of mountains and Moriscos, there were lakes, rivers, well-fortified towns and determined Calvinists. The Spaniards, however, flushed with earlier victories, were confident. Even the French ambassador attached to Alva's army was impressed by the advantages in Spain's favor: "Since the people of Holland are not warlike and lack spirit, there is not a town there which will not ask to surrender when the duke's army approaches." He was right up to a point: early in December envoys from the town of Haarlem arrived at Alva's camp and offered to surrender in return for certain guarantees against reprisals. The Spaniards, however, rejected this: they insisted on unconditional surrender. The prince of Orange, now based in Holland, took advantage of the resulting delay and confusion in order to slip troops and leaders into Haarlem and, in the name of the town, they sent a defiant challenge to Alva. It was to take seven months, thousands of lives and millions of ducats before the Spaniards could make the garrison and citizens of Haarlem pay for their temerity (about twelve hundred people were eventually executed in cold blood) . And by then it was too late. The victorious Spanish army was restless and turbulent after its seven-month ordeal in the trenches, and as soon as Haarlem surrendered, the troops mutinied in protest against their conditions of service and refused to fight. The Dutch, for their part, observing the fate of those who surrendered, resolved to continue their resistance to the last man. The siege of Haarlem deprived Philip II of his only real chance of crushing the revolt of the Netherlands at a stroke.

For a considerable time, the king simply did not appreciate the full seriousness of the revolt of 1572. Things had seemed just as bad in 1568, but Alva had won total victory, and so the king provided large sums of money to pay for the mobilization of seventy thousand men in the Netherlands and waited impatiently for the results. Thanks to the massacre of Saint Bartholomew, victory seemed close in the autumn, but then came the stalemate in Holland. At the same time, a mounting volume of criticism of Alva's administration reached the court. It was asserted by responsible and trusted observers that the duke was greedy, cruel and corrupt; that his policies had made Spain odious to the Netherlands; that, in short, the duke himself had provoked the latest rebellion. By the beginning of 1573 the king had decided that Alva would have to go and he appointed as his successor one of his childhood playmates, a man with a reputation for moderation: Don Luis de Requesens. The new governor only arrived in Brussels to take up his office in November 1573, however, and by then the revolt seemed more deep-rooted than ever: the royal fleet had been disastrously defeated, the Spanish veterans had mutinied again, and a major siege of the little town of Alkmaar had proved a costly fiasco. More reverses soon followed. In 1574 two attempts to capture Leiden failed and there were two further mutinies by the troops, many of whom were owed many months, even years, of back pay.

The cost of the war in the Netherlands had become intolerable. Finance was fast becoming Philip II's principal problem and he was more and more obsessed by the need to raise money. He became testy when his advisers tried to tell him that

at the end, everything came to one thing — money and more and more money. They said that even though raising a large sum would cost me a great deal by way of interest, it would work out cheaper in the long run if we managed to succeed in bringing the war . . . to an end. . . . I told them that we would be very pleased to raise the money; and the reason why it is not forthcoming has nothing to do with the rate of interest we might have to pay but simply with the fact that we have no money.

The Lepanto campaign had cost Castile about 800,000 ducats (Spanish Italy paid a further 400,000). Subsequent campaigns in the Mediterranean achieved far less but cost far more, and they drained money away from Spain and away from the wars in the Low Countries, as the accompanying table shows.

THE COST OF PHILIP II'S IMPERIALISM, 1571–1577

MONEY RECEIVED FROM CASTILE
(IN DUCATS)

Year	By the Mediter- ranean Fleet	By the Army of Flanders
1571	793,000	119,000
1572	1,463,000	1,776,000
1573	1,102,000	1,813,000
1574	1,252,000	3,737,000
1575	711,000	2,518,000
1576	1,069,000	872,000
1577	673,000	857,000
TOTAL	7,063,000	11,692,000

The figures, recording only the money actually received by Philip's armed forces abroad, do not represent the full magnitude of the hemorrhage of public funds from Castile. There were also interest and transport charges to pay (and these averaged 20 percent and could sometimes reach 35 percent a year); there were other matters which required government funds (chief among them the salaries of civil servants and the cost of coastal defense); and there was also the interest to pay on the national debt (which normally consumed about half the crown's income). In April 1574, in a long, handwritten report, Philip's chief financial adviser (and former expert on the Indies), Juan de Ovando, laboriously calculated his master's total debts and liabilities at 74 million ducats — a sum equal to almost fourteen times the crown's annual revenue (a modest 5.5 million ducats).

The king scarcely needed Ovando's gloomy analysis to make him aware of his financial plight. Already in June 1573 he had set up a special secret committee, which he called the Committee of the Indies to disguise its real purpose from the outside world. Its true function was stated by the king as follows: "Firstly, we must provide enough money to meet immediate needs since there is so little available for the purpose, or, to put it better, nothing; secondly, we must see that short-term loans cease and do not consume everything as they are doing at present; the third point relates to the freeing of the crown's rents." The last point was the most important: how to redeem the revenues which had been mortgaged to the crown's creditors. After almost a year's discussion the committee came up with an answer: for the first problem, the Cortes of Castile was to be persuaded to triple the principal permanent tax, the *alcabala,* an excise on major foodstuffs; for the second and third problems, the committee recommended a "decree of bankruptcy." This device, which had already been used in 1557 and 1560, compulsorily converted the government's short-term debt at high interest into long-term debt at low interest. The committee put this solution to the king in July 1574.

Those who find the intricacies of sixteenth-century high finance confusing today may take consolation from the fact that Philip II and some of his advisers were equally perplexed. When, on one occasion, one of the abler members of the committee was absent, Juan de Ovando decided, just for fun, to say nothing at all; the rest of the committee were constrained to follow suit — none of them knew enough to make a proposal. The king was scarcely better off. He once observed to his secretary: "I have never been able to get this business of loans and interests into my head. I have never managed to understand it." On another occasion, when he received a memorandum on treasury matters from his secretary, the king had to confess:

> To be frank, I do not understand a word of this. I do not
> know what I should do. Should I send it to someone else for
> comment, and if so, who? Time is slipping away: tell me what
> you advise. If I see the author [of the memorandum] I do not
> believe I shall understand him, although perhaps if I had the
> papers in front of me it might not be too bad.

And so the bewildered king rambled on, laboring to understand why he had no money left and what he could do about
it. But some things were clearer than others. On the report of
July 1574, recommending that the king should repudiate all
his debts at once, Philip noted that he did not fully understand the proposals of his technical committee, but he did
realize that, after such action, no financier would have either
the desire or the money to advance further loans to the crown
and transfer the proceeds to the Netherlands or Italy, where
they were needed for the war. To repudiate his debts would
inevitably produce military collapse.

"I spend all my time thinking about Flanders," he told his
secretary, "because everything else depends upon it. We have
taken so long to provide money and the situation is so desperate that even if we succeed in making funds available I doubt
if we can save the Low Countries." And that, to Philip II, was
the most important thing.

The Committee of the Indies did not see things this way,
however: their prime responsibility was to solve the financial
situation at home, not to win the war in Flanders, and they
bombarded the king with more and more papers on the need
for an immediate decree repudiating all debts. Ovando sent a
particularly stinging letter in March 1575 speculating on how
much better off Philip might have been had he heeded the
advice tendered by his ministers almost a year before: "We
could have remedied the situation by adopting any of the
following schemes. We could have reformed the central tribunal of the exchequer; or we could have dealt with my

scheme for raising a large sum to free crown rents . . . ; or we could have resorted to 'the decree.' . . . Any of these measures would have sufficed to remedy the situation." Not surprisingly, the king came to hate the smug Ovando (who died in September 1575), but there was little that either man could do, either to save Spain from bankruptcy or to win her wars. After the mutinies and the military failures there was really no prospect of a Spanish victory in either the Netherlands or in the Mediterranean. "There would not be time or money enough in the world," Don Luis de Requesens wrote to the king in October 1574, "to reduce by force the twenty-four towns which have rebelled in Holland, if we are to spend as long in reducing each one of them as we have taken over similar ones so far." The only escape from the unfortunate stalemate in which Spain had become locked was to conclude peace: peace with the infidels in the Mediterranean, and peace with the heretics in the Netherlands. The king became morose and fatalistic. By March 1574 he was already convinced that only a miracle would restore the situation, and he instructed his principal clerical advisers to pray that "God will have mercy on us, because the cause is his; and [the thought of] this, and the damage that his religion is suffering, is what causes me most anguish in this matter." At first it seemed that the Lord of Battles had hearkened to his servant: a relief army raised for the rebels in Germany was crushingly defeated at Mook on 14 April. But the mutiny of the victorious Spaniards that followed dissipated all their advantage and in May the king confided to his private secretary that he considered "the loss of the Netherlands and the rest [of the monarchy] to be as certain as, in this situation, anything can be. . . . It is a terrible situation and it is getting worse every day." In June he returned to his despondent refrain: "I believe that everything is a waste of time, judging by what is happening in the Low Countries, and if they are lost the rest [of the monarchy] will not last long, even if we have enough money." He repeated in

July, "We must do everything we can to succor the Netherlands . . . because if we have no money, our position at the
conference table will prove even more difficult." But all hope
was vain. "We are running out of everything so fast," he
sighed, "that words fail me."

In this despondent mood, Philip could become depressed or
angry over even trivial matters. When he was called upon to
grant twelve commanderies in the military orders, he was dis-
mayed to find that there were 117 candidates to choose from:
"With many asking and little to give, most people will remain
discontented," he grumbled, "and for this and other reasons I
say that the position I hold is a foul one." On another occasion
he told his secretary: "I have not sent you anything, from
which you will see the problems I have these days. Really I do
not know how I survive." He felt "so tired and broken in
spirit" that he sometimes failed even to write to his secretaries!

There was no acceptable escape. Although Philip was prepared to make limited political concessions in the Netherlands
— the issue of a "General Pardon" and the restoration of much
confiscated property — he was not prepared either to change
the constitutional position or to grant religious toleration. He
even refused to punish the duke of Alva for his "excesses" in
the Netherlands, although a special committee was set up to
consider whether there was enough evidence against the duke
to justify a full investigation. The war was therefore allowed
to drag on, except for a brief hiatus in March and April 1575
while an abortive attempt was made to negotiate with the
Dutch.

Meanwhile, the Spanish army in the Netherlands, which cost
almost 700,000 ducats a month to maintain, continued its
financial demands on the Castilian treasury until in the
autumn of 1575 no more money was left and no more loans
were available. In September the king at last agreed to repudiate all his debts: in effect he declared himself bankrupt.
In the Netherlands, Governor General Requesens was horrified. He told his brother:

Even if the king found himself with ten millions in gold and wanted to send it all here, he has no way of doing so with this Bankruptcy Decree, because if the money were sent by sea in specie it would be lost, and it is impossible to send it by letters of exchange as hitherto because there is no merchant there [in Spain] who can issue them nor anyone here who can accept and pay them.

It was not long before the king himself recognized the truth of this. "I have not escaped from my necessity," he wrote to his secretary; "rather am I in greater need since I have no credit and cannot avail myself of anything except hard cash which cannot be collected quickly enough." There was nothing for the king and his ministers to do but be patient and see what effect the termination of the remittances from Spain would have. They did not have long to wait. In July and August 1576 the foreign troops in the army of Flanders mutinied; the rest soon deserted. In November the mutinous troops, some of them entitled to claim six years of pay-arrears, brutally sacked the city of Antwerp, the commercial capital of northern Europe: a thousand houses were destroyed and eight thousand people perished.

These events totally undermined Philip II's authority in the Netherlands. Within a matter of weeks his army disintegrated and his orders were only obeyed in Antwerp and a handful of other towns. In September, the representatives of the political elites of the various provinces — the States-General — began to assemble and to take decisions without reference to the king. In November they made a formal peace with Orange and the rebels (the "Pacification of Ghent") and began to negotiate with the king for concessions. Even Philip II was now ready to admit defeat:

If matters are in such a state that the States demand unilateral concessions [he wrote], it seems that, safeguarding religion and my authority as much as may be . . . we shall have to concede everything necessary to bring about a conclusion and save what we can. This is the ultimate solution to a problem like this, and we shall have to trust these people, in spite of all the risks involved.

At much the same time, the king decided to admit defeat in the Mediterranean. He had been thoroughly alarmed by the speed with which the sultan had replaced the losses sustained by his fleet at Lepanto: three hundred Turkish galleys had sailed to Tunis and captured it with ease in 1574. The great fleet, far larger than Philip II's, threatened Sicily and razed one or two Spanish fortresses. Next, in March 1576, one of the sultan's vassals conquered most of Morocco and turned it into an Ottoman protectorate. Never had Turkish power in the West seemed so imposing. But at just this moment the death of the Persian shah Tasmasp opened a period of anarchy in the areas to the east of the Ottoman empire which the sultan was anxious to exploit. Reliable reports of this new Turkish interest reached Philip II in the summer of 1576 and plans were put in hand to reduce the size of the Mediterranean fleet to one hundred galleys. At the same time a secret agent was dispatched to Constantinople to negotiate a truce. In March 1577, as his troops moved forward into Persia, the sultan agreed to a cease-fire in the Mediterranean and in 1580 a formal armistice was signed.

Philip II had therefore been forced to admit defeat in both of his principal endeavors of the previous decade, and the new policies of compliance were seen by many as humiliating. In May 1578, when a renewal of the truce with the sultan was required, there was a bitter wrangle at the Council of State over the propriety of such dealings with the archenemy of the Christian faith. The matter was reported to the king by the council's secretary, Antonio Pérez, who pointed out with some relish the poor performance and ill-considered advice of some of the councillors. The king could only agree. For some time he had been complaining about the lack of suitable ministers to serve him. "The pressure on me is growing, and my helpers are falling away," he complained. "It is a dreadful situation." Many of the king's first generation of advisers had died and the most prominent of the survivors, Cardinal Granvelle and the duke of Alva, were more or less out of favor. It was the absence of alternative councillors like Alva which, to some extent, aided the rise to prominence of Philip II's best-known minister, Antonio Pérez, and prepared the road to the most controversial and least defensible event in the king's reign: the murder of Juan de Escobedo.

EIGHT

Murder Most Foul?

ANTONIO PÉREZ WAS BORN in 1540, the illegitimate son of Gonzalo Pérez, a cleric of Jewish extraction who served as Philip II's personal secretary from 1541 until his death in 1566, and as secretary of the Council of State from 1556 onward. Although young, Antonio managed to succeed to some of his father's official duties, becoming secretary of state for the affairs of southern Europe, and it was in this capacity that he came into contact with the king's brother, Don John of Austria, after 1568.

Success had not improved Don John. His role in the victory of Lepanto in 1571 had made him into a hero and a figure of European renown. As such he became something of a problem for Philip: irascible and arrogant, Don John was ambitious for greater glory and for more tangible rewards. In particular he wanted some territory of his own. The king, however, was determined that he should have none, and it became the task of Antonio Pérez to control Don John's aspirations.

Over the years, a good working relationship was established. The secretary managed to procure additional funds for Don John's fleet and even persuaded the king to grant his brother viceregal powers over southern Italy; when Don John came to court, as he did from time to time, he stayed in the sumptuous country house of Pérez. But Pérez also kept the king informed of every step in his dealings with Don John, and he took care to ensure that the every move of the illustrious victor of Lepanto was watched by a corps of reliable officials who would report on untoward developments. At the end of 1574 Pérez had Don John's personal secretary removed and replaced by an old friend of his, Juan de Escobedo, secretary of the Council of Finance since 1566 and a relative of Ruy Gómez, the king's favorite. Even this was not enough to reassure Philip. He still feared that his brother might found a separate kingdom, whether in North Africa (where he conquered Tunis in 1573 only to lose it the next year) or in England (where the pope proposed to send him at the head of a Catholic army of invasion). In 1576, as a panacea for the king's worries, Pérez suggested that Don John could perhaps be made a cardinal, which would mean that if he did conquer a kingdom, he would have no legitimate offspring and so the territory would revert at his death to Philip II. The suggestion was never taken up, however, because in October 1576 the king decided that only the prestige and military skill of his brother could save the situation in the Netherlands. He therefore sent Don John, together with his secretary Escobedo, to the Low Countries with full powers to make concessions which would restore royal authority. Rather surprisingly, Don John succeeded: by May 1577 all the points at issue were, apparently, resolved. Don John was accepted as governor general by all the provinces of the Netherlands and made a triumphal entry into Brussels.

No sooner was this accomplished than Don John and Escobedo began to demand their recall. One proposal was that the two men should return to court and, together with Pérez, take control of the king's policies. Escobedo even suggested in one letter that Philip was getting too old for effective government so that for this reason, and in view of the extreme youth of the prince his son, it would be well that he [Philip] should have someone to share his burden; and in view of the wisdom, prudence and fidelity which His Highness [Don John] has displayed in these affairs, it seems that he is the person upon whom this position devolves and the person whom, as the Scriptures say, God has willed, in recompense for the piety of the king, to give him as a staff for his old age.

His old age! Philip was not quite fifty when this letter was written, and if he was shown it by Pérez (as Pérez claimed) he must have felt gravely slighted.

A second proposal made by Don John was that, with the Netherlands reconciled, he should lead an invasion of England (as the pope wanted) to dethrone Elizabeth. Philip showed no enthusiasm for this plan, and so in July 1577 Don John sent Escobedo back to Spain with instructions to persuade the king, via his friend Pérez, to provide the means for the invasion. But after Escobedo's departure the situation in the Low Countries changed dramatically. Don John's concessions did not content the Dutch. Under the influence of William of Orange, now the most powerful man in the Netherlands, Don John was faced with one new set of demands after another. In September 1577 he was presented with an ultimatum that required him to send home all his troops, to surrender all the towns loyal to him, and to retire to Luxemburg and ask the king to recall him.

This situation was too humiliating and, reluctantly, the king ordered two regiments of Spaniards to return to the Netherlands in order to protect Don John from further insults. The intention was (at first) not to make war again, merely to save his brother. In November the king told Pérez:

God grant that things will turn out as best suits His service, and if it is to be war in the Netherlands may He give us the means to wage it, for without His very special aid we can do little, especially with the business of the Mediterranean fleet. I was thinking that the preparations that have to be made now could serve for either purpose [for the Mediterranean or for the Netherlands].

As it happened God — and the miners of Peru — obliged with the dispatch of immediate assistance: on 18 August 1577 a fleet of fifty-five ships arrived at Seville from the Indies bearing over two million ducats for the king in bullion, a consignment larger than any previously received. And on 5 December Philip came to an agreement with his bankers whereby he agreed to honor the debts outstanding since the bankruptcy decree of 1575, in return for a new loan of five million ducats payable in Italy, by installments, in 1578 and 1579. This improvement in the king's financial position was sufficient to provide the means to maintain enough troops in the Netherlands to defeat the army of Orange and his friends at Gembloux in January 1578.

Don John's success, which appeared to presage the collapse of the Dutch Revolt, encouraged Escobedo (still at court) to press even harder for a decision on the English venture. This placed the king in a very difficult position, for if he refused Don John's demands outright he would alienate his victorious brother and jeopardize his position in the Netherlands; on the other hand he could not contemplate another attempt to invade England. There was simply not the money for it. Escobedo's importunities also placed Pérez in a difficult position. Over the years, the secretary had told Don John many things about the court, even about the king, which were confidential and secret; Escobedo, as Don John's confidential secretary, of course knew all about this. There was, for example, a letter from Pérez to Escobedo which served as a covering note to the suggestion by Philip that his brother might become a cardinal. Pérez said that Don John was to pay no attention to this and was also to disregard the harsh words in the accompanying letter, which were all added by the king; what mattered, said the secretary, were the parts written by

Pérez himself. If Don John were to do as he said, Pérez continued, "we shall save our cause and make sure of Our Man." "Our man" was Philip II. Curiously enough this letter, and others like it that made disparaging remarks about the king, appear to have been shown to their subject before dispatch. There is evidence that the king himself ordered Pérez to write them and then corrected the drafts before they were rewritten and signed, as if in private, by his secretary. Philip clearly suspected that his brother was up to no good, and Pérez's letters criticizing the king were meant to encourage Don John to write freely to the secretary and, perhaps, to let slip something damaging.

With the arrival of Escobedo at court, all this double-dealing assumed a new dimension. In the first place, it is clear that Philip II did not like his brother's secretary. In 1575, while he was at court on Don John's business, Escobedo had been irritating. "I am so fed up and tired [of his pestering] that I could not be more so," Philip complained to Mateo Vázquez. "We must get rid of him soon." It was the same during Escobedo's further residence at court in 1577, only this time his insistence extended beyond Don John's affairs to a desire to receive some royal reward for his long service and good conduct. Escobedo's eyes had become focused on the grant of a commandery, or at least a knighthood, in one of the prestigious military orders of Castile.

Escobedo was a short-tempered man — the king and Pérez, in their private correspondence, often referred to him as "the crosspatch" (*el verdinegro*) — and his patience began to fray when, after eight months at court, he still had achieved nothing either for his master or for himself. He rightly began to suspect that Pérez was not doing all he could to further his cause. He therefore began to make threats to Pérez about what would happen if the deadlock continued. What exactly these threats were we do not know. According to some versions, Escobedo found Pérez in bed with the princess of Eboli, widow of his former patron, Ruy Gómez, and threatened to tell the king; other versions of the story claim that Escobedo discovered that Pérez and the princess were selling state secrets to the enemies of Spain. These threats, whatever they were, clearly worried Pérez. Early in 1578 he began to urge the king to give in and grant Escobedo what he wanted — no doubt in order to avoid further embarrassment: "Escobedo is being tiresome about his knighthood. . . . I certainly think that it would be a good thing to give it to him, so that he does not worry Your Majesty to death." This ploy failed: the knighthood was not forthcoming and Pérez began to fear that Escobedo would discredit him with the king (either by telling lies or by telling the truth). Pérez therefore resolved to have Escobedo eliminated and at seven o'clock on the night of 31 March 1578 Escobedo was stabbed to death by a group of thugs as he returned to his lodgings only a few streets from the royal palace in Madrid.

The most remarkable fact about the murder of Escobedo was that nothing was done for months to establish who had killed him. Because he was a courtier and a royal secretary resident in Madrid, the crime came under the jurisdiction of the king's personal magistrates, the "magistrates of the household and court," and in marked contrast to their immediate action following other disorders near to the royal person, these officers did nothing. This fact did not go unnoticed. "I tremble with fear to see that there are people in the world who would dare to strike down secretaries of the king," wrote one minister, adding: "I am astonished to see that it was possible for such a thing to have happened in the court of the king of Spain." He, like many others, wondered why the crime went unpunished.

The answer was simple: Escobedo had been murdered at the king's command, and the deed had been arranged by Antonio Pérez. Although whole books have been written denying Philip's complicity in the murder, there seems to be little doubt about the matter. In the first place the king himself acknowledged responsibility. During the trial of Pérez he wrote to the judges: "He knows full well the proof I have that he had Escobedo killed and the reasons he told me existed for doing it." And the judges openly asked Pérez to state "the reasons which existed for His Majesty to consent to the death of Escobedo." Second, the king connived in the escape of the assassins hired by Pérez: the secretary's holograph notes, informing the king of his plans to spirit them away from Madrid, have survived. What is *not* clear is what, precisely, convinced the king that Escobedo had to die. One element, certainly, was the belief (which Pérez carefully fostered) that it was vital to the security of Philip's monarchy to eliminate Escobedo: if he returned to the Low Countries, the king feared, he would surely encourage Don John to fresh defiance; yet if Escobedo were arrested, Don John would realize that his designs had been discovered and might throw in his lot with the Dutch rebels. The only way out of this dilemma was therefore judicial murder. This was a standard technique of sixteenth-century statecraft. It had justified the murder of Gaspard de Coligny by the French crown in 1572, just before the massacre of Saint Bartholomew; it had justified the murder of David Rizzio by King Henry Darnley, and then the murder of Darnley by Bothwell and Mary, Queen of Scots, in 1566; and it was subsequently to justify the assassination of William of Orange in 1584. The evidence against Escobedo was overwhelming. There survives a copious correspondence about Don John's ambitious designs on England and his discontent with royal policy in the Netherlands. Pérez, for darker reasons of his own, may have helped to overcome any remaining scruples Philip might have had, but the king's mind was probably made up anyway.

Only full-hearted consent to Escobedo's murder can explain the king's reaction to the event. At first he did absolutely nothing (except to help the assassins escape from Madrid). He ignored the pleas of the dead man's family for action. In October 1578 he had his first chance to allay the rumors and speculation: Don John of Austria died of typhoid in the Netherlands, and the king now had nothing to lose by declaring the reasons which had led to the elimination of Escobedo. But he kept silent. Perhaps he felt that, given time, interest in the matter would abate and no further action would be necessary. He was wrong.

Philip II's court resembled a jungle in which only the fittest survived, and Antonio Pérez had made many enemies during his rise to power. The Escobedo affair provided a golden opportunity for these enemies to settle old scores, and in December 1578 the first blow was struck by Mateo Vázquez, Philip's chaplain as well as his secretary, who openly accused Pérez of murder and urged the king to arrest him. Gradually the enmity between Vázquez and Pérez spread until every member of the Spanish court was forced to take sides over the murder of Escobedo and the attempt to cover it up. Pérez became afraid to venture out of doors unless accompanied by an armed escort for fear of attack by his victim's family. Mateo Vázquez left court in protest against the king's inaction. The king's government was fast becoming paralyzed, just at the time when urgent and critical decisions were required on the best way to annex Portugal. It was an intolerable situation and a solution had to be found.

At first, the king decided to buy Pérez off, offering him a respectable diplomatic post abroad, honors at home or lucrative retirement. To his surprise, the secretary refused. The offers were improved, but without success. In March 1579 the king's go-between, no less a person than the president of the Council of Castile, reported: "We find ourselves in some confusion to discover that the man becomes more obstinate the more generous we are to him." But Pérez was not "obstinate," just realistic. He could see that any such move on his part would be construed by his enemies as an admission of guilt and, with Escobedo's heirs thirsting for justice, he could hardly imagine that there was much prospect of any long retirement.

After a year of subterfuge and secrecy, during which the king had brazenly sheltered from trial a man accused of murder, it was clear to everyone that if Pérez had not ordered the killing of Escobedo, Philip had. This was a truth the king also had to face. In March 1579 he went on his usual Easter retreat to "ask God to illuminate me and guide me." By the end of the month his mind was made up. On 30 March he wrote a letter to Cardinal Granvelle, now over sixty years old but the only experienced councillor not involved in the Pérez scandal. Granvelle was to come to Spain at once to take charge of the government. And until Granvelle could come, Philip struggled as best he could amidst his seething court. He kept away from Madrid, and his civil servants, as much as possible. The first time he visited the capital for more than a couple of days was in the middle of July, and by then he knew that Granvelle was coming. On 3 July the king wrote to Mateo Vázquez, asking him to return. On 9 July Vázquez agreed, but only on certain conditions: the king was to protect Vázquez against any enemies, and he was not to take advice from Antonio Pérez or his friends. The king accepted this ultimatum — the first open sign of the impending storm — and Vázquez returned to court. With Granvelle now nearing Madrid, the king made one final attempt to avert the inevitable change in policy: on 25 July he offered Pérez the post of ambassador to the republic of Venice. Pérez refused. On 26 July, a day of freak storms with hailstones larger than pigeons' eggs lashing his windows, Philip braced himself for action. He went to confession, received communion and called together his four leading courtiers (two pro- and two anti-Pérez) to warn them of his decision. Everyone was tense. On 28 July Granvelle arrived in Madrid. At 11 P.M. the same night, Pérez was arrested.

Still, however, the king refused to permit investigations into the death of Escobedo. Pérez was only kept under house arrest and even continued to transact government business while his assistants carried out their work as if nothing had happened. This only changed three years later, in 1582, when a government inquiry began into Pérez's tenure of his office of secretary. In June 1584 he was formally charged with accepting bribes, betraying certain state secrets, and making errors in the decipherment of state papers, but in the event Pérez was only condemned by the government's inspectors to a fine and loss of office. He was not disgraced, scarcely even discredited. Eventually his wife was granted a pension in respect of her husband's years of service, and even in the 1640's Pérez's daughter was still receiving a government pension.

However, something else happened in 1584 which was far more damaging to Pérez: one of the men he had hired to murder Escobedo turned king's evidence, confessed his guilt, and accused the secretary of responsibility. (The man was partly influenced by bribes from Escobedo's heirs, who had managed to track him down; but even more he was moved by fear that he himself would be eliminated — his three accomplices in the murder had all disappeared in mysterious circumstances.) In January 1585 Pérez was formally arrested, and although he tried to take sanctuary in a nearby church, he was removed and imprisoned in Turégano castle near Segovia. He almost escaped from there and was moved back to Madrid the following year. Gradually a case was being built up against him, and Pérez was interrogated intensively over the winter of 1589–1590. On 23 February 1590 he was put to the torture and made to confess to the murder of Escobedo, asserting, in his defense, that he had acted on the king's orders. But here lay the catch, for Pérez could not prove his statement: his papers, including the memoranda exchanged between him and the king, had been seized. He was condemned to death for the murder on 1 July 1590.

Whether the king, after so many years, would have allowed the execution of Pérez is an academic question, for on 19 April the secretary escaped from his prison, and although still weak after the torture, he managed to ride the two hundred miles from Madrid to Zaragoza, where he had managed to secrete copies of his correspondence with the king concerning the murder of Escobedo. From that moment onward he began a bitter defiance of Philip, which lasted as long as Philip lived.

One of the most vexing questions of the whole Pérez affair has been the reason for Philip's change of heart in 1589. If he was convinced that Pérez's role in the death of Escobedo was culpable, why did he not proceed against him in 1579, or at least in 1584, when the confessions of one of the actual murderers was to hand? At any point after that he could have ordered a secret trial followed by a summary execution for treason. Yet that policy was not chosen until 1590, although the king had no more of a case against Pérez in 1590 than in 1584 and in some ways he had less, for in September 1589 Escobedo's heir expressly pardoned Pérez for his part in the death. And yet the sudden rigor against the secretary after 1589 clearly originated with the king. Why did his attitude change? Why did he suddenly find the "cover-up" for Pérez intolerable?

The king appears to have been moved, not by anything Pérez did, but by changes in the political situation. Up to 1588 and the dispatch of the Spanish Armada, "God was a Spaniard" and all went well for the policies of Philip II. The disasters of 1588–1589 clearly shook the king's confidence, and caused him to search his conscience for any failing that might have offended God. His role in the death of Escobedo was an obvious possibility. Perhaps he had been maneuvered by Pérez into blessing a private vendetta? Perhaps Pérez had deceived him: perhaps his brother and his brother's servant had been blameless, and God had resolved to punish Philip for the murder of an innocent man? We can never be sure that these (or any other) thoughts carried any weight with the king. We can no longer penetrate the obscurity that surrounds the whole affair, and for two reasons: first, much of the crucial evidence was never written down. As Philip wrote tantalizingly to Pérez on one occasion: "I am afraid of what Escobedo may do in this matter, but in due course let us talk about it, for it is something to speak about rather than to write about." Second, many of the secrets consigned to paper were subsequently destroyed. In 1576 and again in 1579 Pérez deliberately burned a large number of his letters to and from Don John, and he did everything in his power to ensure that Don John did the same. All that survives are the copies made by

Pérez in a special book. The copies may be authentic and accurate — and no one at the time, not even the king, suggested. that they were not — in which case Philip II was deeply involved in compassing the death of Escobedo. On the other hand, Pérez may have interpolated passages, or even invented whole documents: it would have been very easy (only he and the king would know since Escobedo and Don John both died in 1578) and it would have been very advantageous (since Pérez's defense throughout was that he had only acted on the king's orders). Whatever the truth may be, there are no extant original papers which prove beyond all doubt that Philip did — or did not — suspect Escobedo and Don John of treasonable designs. Pérez's unauthenticated copies would not be accepted as evidence in any modern court of law. As Fernand Braudel has written: "In this mysterious matter no one will ever have the last word."

NINE

Years of Triumph, 1579–1588

CARDINAL GRANVELLE ARRIVED at the court of Spain at a critical moment in Philip II's long reign. In the Low Countries the king's nephew Alexander Farnese, prince of Parma (only son of Philip's sister Margaret) had first managed to divide the opponents of Philip II in the Netherlands, reconciling the French-speaking and Catholic provinces of Hainaut, Walloon Flanders, Namur and Artois with the king (Treaty of Arras, May 1579), and had then inflicted a major defeat on the rest of the "rebels" by taking the stronghold of Maastricht (June 1579). Further military and diplomatic successes followed. In the Mediterranean, the truce of 1577 with the sultan was renewed in 1578 and held good throughout the 1580's.

In Portugal, another of the king's nephews, Sebastian I (son of his sister Joanna) had died childless at the battle of Alcazarquivir in Morocco (4 August 1578), leaving a childless cleric of sixty-seven years, Cardinal Henry, to rule the kingdom and its vast overseas empire. This, in turn, left Philip II as the closest male relative, entitled to succeed to the Portuguese throne as soon as the aged king-cardinal died. Almost immediately Philip took steps to establish his right of succession. The news of the disaster at Alcazarquivir arrived at the Escorial, where the king was, on 13 August (only nine days after the event). Philip locked himself away for a day to meditate and then left for Madrid, departing through the gardens secretly "to see to all that has been made advisable by the fate which has befallen the king of Portugal." The king's advisers, spiritual as well as political, were unanimous in their opinion: Philip's title to succeed was valid, and the union of Spain and Portugal was desirable. To support his claim they adduced three justifications: first, it would promote greater security and prosperity in both the neighboring kingdoms; second, it would strengthen the Catholic Church; third, it would enable the Catholic states to beat off more effectively the Protestant challenge. These reasons were accepted by Philip II entirely — so much so that he included them in his testament of 1594, together with an injunction that Castile and Portugal were to remain forever joined — and almost at once a "peace offensive" was begun to win over influential sections of the Portuguese population to the idea of a Spanish succession. In March 1579 a special "Portuguese committee" was established to coordinate the effort. There was no time to lose. As Philip II observed: "The health of King Henry is so undermined that he may die at any moment." The first converts were the Portuguese Jesuits, and some of the other "militant" religious orders, who saw clearly that Philip of Spain offered the best chance of furthering their cause. The merchants of Lisbon, Setúbal and Oporto were similarly impressed by the possible advantages of Luso-Spanish cooperation in the Far East. And the support of many noble families was purchased with money provided by Philip II to ransom those unfortunate aristocrats — some eight hundred in number — who had been taken prisoner at the battle of Alcazarquivir.

Philip II met with little opposition at first. All the other claimants to the throne suffered from grave handicaps: the duke of Savoy and the prince of Parma lacked the resources to challenge Philip's title (in the words of an English observer, "Their parts are least in the pudding"). The duke of Braganza was unambitious and reluctant to alienate Philip. Of the serious candidates, Braganza's son and the illegitimate grandson of Manuel I, Dom Antonio, were both in prison in Morocco, whence the former was ransomed by Philip II and subsequently held in Seville, while Dom Antonio only escaped in November 1579, when Philip's "peace offensive" was already within an ace of success. In January 1580, Cardinal Henry summoned the Portuguese Cortes to decide on the succession question. He himself favored Philip II, as did most of the clergy and the nobility, but before the third estate's consent could be secured (it was split between Dom Antonio and Braganza), Henry died and the succession question became a matter for open dispute.

This was a setback for Philip: he had very much hoped that Portugal would be delivered to him by constitutional means and without the use of force. With the death of the cardinal-king on 31 January, the situation was transformed: no sooner had the news arrived in Madrid than Philip, at Granvelle's insistence, issued orders for the mobilization of troops throughout Castile (4–5 February 1580). The duke of Medina Sidonia, whose estates were along the Portuguese frontier, raised 4,000 infantry and 450 cavalry almost at once and even inland towns like Valladolid offered to raise soldiers at their own expense. Valladolid's 400 men, together with a further two infantry companies and a company of light cavalry recruited by royal captains at the king's cost, were eventually sent in October to Galicia, where an army was collected under the count of Benavente. In the south were Medina Sidonia's troops, and in the center a large force under the duke of Alva (appointed captain-general at Granvelle's suggestion). Granvelle also argued that the king must go to Portugal himself (no doubt he remembered all too well the consequences of Philip's failure to go to the Netherlands in the 1560's). He argued that there was no time to lose, because some Portuguese leaders, directed by Dom Antonio, were preparing to oppose a Spanish invasion and were trying to secure foreign support for their cause. But the king was a reluctant convert to the use of force. His ambassador in Portugal, Don Cristóbal de Moura, assured him that the Portuguese Cortes would eventually agree to a Spanish succession, given time and money. Hoping that formal recognition of his claim would be forthcoming, the king delayed his departure to the Portuguese frontier until after Easter, and even then he traveled but slowly, arriving at the frontier stronghold of Badajoz only on 27 May. Still he delayed: Moura continued to assure him that the Cortes was on the point of granting him recognition. But at last Philip's patience ran out. The Cortes continued to procrastinate, wishing to discuss Philip's title when the king believed that only unquestioning recognition of his divine right to rule was required. On 13 June he reviewed his army at Badajoz — 20,000 Italian, German and Spanish veteran infantry, 1,500 cavalry and 136 pieces of artillery — and two weeks later he ordered them to cross the frontier into Portugal.

It was already almost too late. On 18 June, Dom Antonio had himself proclaimed king by a splinter group of the Cortes, and on the following day the town of Santarem declared for him, followed a little later by Lisbon and Setúbal. There were promises of aid for the insurgents from France. Invasion and armed conflict were now the only means left to Philip, and he did not shrink from using them: as usual he was implacable once his authority had been openly challenged. He appeared unmoved when first Setúbal and then Lisbon were brutally sacked by his troops: both had resisted when commanded to surrender. In August the forces of Dom Antonio were crushed in a brief battle outside Lisbon, the "pretender" fled to the north, but was defeated again in October. Portugal was entirely under Philip's control, and old scores began to be settled. The king ordered that all his vassals who were convicted of involvement in the troubles should be executed, whether they were Portuguese, Spaniards or Italians; foreigners should be condemned to the galleys. It was the "Council of Troubles" all over again and, as with the Netherlands repression, the "big fish" escaped: Dom Antonio managed to get out of Portugal on a Dutch ship, and in 1582, aided by a French Huguenot fleet, he tried to overrun the Azores Islands, which lay on Spain's vital trade route to the Indies (Terceira, one of the largest, had declared for him in 1580 and had defied Spain ever since). Dom Antonio was beaten off by a large Spanish fleet. Another French fleet was sent in 1583, and again it was defeated; and this time all the adherents of Dom Antonio in the archipelago were compelled to submit. The conquest of Portugal and her empire was at last complete and Philip, who was solemnly accepted by the Portuguese Cortes as their king in April 1581, was again free to turn his attention to other matters. In April 1583 he returned to Madrid, after a residence of over two years in Lisbon.

The view from Madrid was not displeasing to King Philip. Spain was peaceful and prosperous. The Mediterranean was still peaceful (the truce with the sultan was renewed again in February 1581, this time for three years). Above all, the fruits of the new policies in Spanish America were beginning to appear. In cash terms alone, the improvement was impressive: in Peru, Don Francisco de Toledo, viceroy between 1568 and 1580, had increased crown revenues from about 100,000 to over 1 million ducats annually. The total treasure registered at Seville from the New World rose from 30 million ducats in the 1560's and 35 million in the 1570's to 64 million in the 1580's and 83 million in the 1590's. At the same time, the peaceful extension of Spanish domination in the Philippines completed Philip II's chain of communication around the world. The Prudent King now possessed an empire upon which the sun indeed never set.

However, developments in northwestern Europe were soon to challenge the Iberian seaborne empires. In 1577–1580 Sir Francis Drake and a small English fleet sailed around the world, plundering Spanish shipping all along the way. In 1581, a few months after Philip was recognized as king of Portugal, the States-General of the Netherlands declared him deposed as prince and lord of the Low Countries. In his place they chose Francis, duke of Anjou, brother of the French king Henry III. In February 1582 Anjou arrived in Antwerp and was crowned — by William of Orange — as duke of Brabant; on the same day it was announced that the duke was engaged to be married to Queen Elizabeth of England. The new Dutch-French-English axis against Spain soon began to lend support to Spain's enemies in other areas. In 1582 and 1583 they provided the leader of the Portuguese opposition, Dom Antonio, with ships and munitions for his two assaults on the Azores.

Philip II decided that this invidious situation could not be allowed to continue. Soon after he left Portugal for good, in the spring of 1583, he determined to intensify his war effort against the Dutch. His principal financial adviser was informed that "the present necessity [in the Low Countries] is so great that it would be of the greatest importance to be able to provide at once some four or five hundred thousand ducats; and for the future it would be very good to arrange a provision by months, from 150,000 to 200,000 ducats per month." In the weeks which followed, vast convoys of gold and silver were exported from Spain to Lombardy; there they were either remitted in gold or by letters of exchange to the army of Flanders. In 1584 and 1585 the provisions from Spain even arrived in advance and, thanks to this, the troops of Philip II overran almost the whole South Netherlands, ending with the capture of Antwerp, after one year's siege, on 17 August 1585. The victorious prince of Parma was confident that the remaining provinces in rebellion would now offer to negotiate, rather than withstand the rigors of a siege in their turn. He pointed out to his master the lack of leadership within the republic — Orange and Anjou had both died in the summer of 1584 — and the patent divisions between the towns of Holland and Zealand, which alone were willing to continue the struggle, and the other "rebel" provinces, which desired some form of settlement.

However, no settlement was forthcoming. On 20 August

1585, at Queen Elizabeth's palace of Nonsuch the English government solemnly undertook to provide military aid and political advisers to the Dutch. In the event over 6,000 foot and 1,000 horse were sent over; the queen paid one-quarter of the republic's military budget; and her favorite, Leicester, became governor general for the States. In addition, the English government dispatched a fleet of twenty-five warships to the Caribbean under Sir Francis Drake with the express purpose of harassing Spanish shipping and destroying Spanish property in the West Indies. The fleet sacked Vigo in Spain before crossing the Atlantic to capture and ransom Santo Domingo and sack Cartagena in the Caribbean.

The news of this astonishing development — which meant war between Spain and England for the first time since the fourteenth century — arrived while Philip II was in Aragon, following the sumptuous wedding of his daughter Catalina to the duke of Savoy. He did not return to Castile until March 1586, but already wheels had been set in motion. In August 1583 the commander of the victorious Azores fleet, the marquis of Santa Cruz, had argued in favor of a direct attack upon England, a course also favored by the pope. The marquis pointed out that Dom Antonio's fleet had included a number of English ships (in fact there were eleven). Although the king turned this project down, preferring instead to concentrate his resources on the conquest of the Netherlands, his attention was again drawn to England's naval policy when, in May 1585, he ordered the arrest of all ships in Spanish ports carrying Dutch goods: many of them were English. And he was also painfully aware of the growing tide of English piracy in Spanish-American waters. But the king still resisted pressure from the pope to launch a direct attack on England. Even the Spanish ambassador in Rome, the count of Olivares, suggested in July 1585 that if Antwerp fell to Spain "Your Majesty might instruct your ministers to consider whether it would be better to prefer the conquest of England to that of Holland and Zealand, bearing in mind the greater facility with which the former could be carried out." But the king was unmoved. The war in the Netherlands, he pointed out, cost two million ducats a year and had drained his treasury. He firmly restated his priorities: England would only be attacked after the reconquest of Holland and Zealand.

Such was Philip's view in August 1585. Within five months it had totally changed. In January 1586 the king asked the marquis of Santa Cruz to prepare a detailed plan for an invasion of England, and he wrote to the pope stating that he had allowed himself to be persuaded by His Holiness's entreaties to mount an attack on Elizabeth before completing the reconquest of the Netherlands. He now wanted the papacy to agree to contribute money to the enterprise. Paradoxically, the pope, Sixtus V, at once became skeptical: he argued that Philip II was motivated only by greed, considerations of global strategy, and revenge — not by religious motives at all; and that therefore the papacy should not be asked to pay for something that Spain needed to do anyway. Philip was stung by this taunt, but it was undoubtedly true. He did his best to justify himself, pointing out to the pope that there were cheaper ways to defend the Low Countries and the Indies than by sending the Armada: "I have no reason to allow myself to be ambitious for more kingdoms and estates, nor to win prestige, because Our Lord, in his goodness, has given me so much of both that I am content," he claimed. But the dating of the policy change gives the lie: his letter of January 1586 accepting the pope's invasion plan followed the arrival of news of Nonsuch and Drake's attack on Vigo; and the decision to adopt Santa Cruz's detailed project came just after news arrived in March of Drake's sacking of Santo Domingo. The king was in favor of a direct attack on England, which would compel Elizabeth to withdraw her forces both from the Indies and from the Netherlands. But the problem was the cost. Santa Cruz had originally asked for a fleet of 560 ships and 94,000 men — a ridiculously large figure: far more than the Christian forces at Lepanto or the army and navy that had conquered Portugal — and this estimate was gradually scaled down. The underlying plan, however, remained intact: the invasion fleet, it was recognized, would have to be so large that it could overwhelm all possible English opposition. It had to be "invincible" — too big to be defeated.

The strain of this change of policy and of implementing such a mammoth operation left its mark on Philip II's government. "There is," a French observer noted in 1586, "less decision and less speed . . . so that it seems as if the excellent order which there used to be in the government of this monarchy is aging along with the king." Nothing could have been further from the truth! The French resident, M. de Longlée, was notoriously ill informed and unreliable. He failed to discover that the king's daughter Catalina was going to marry the duke of Savoy until just before it happened; he could not afford to pay spies and had to rely for news on conversations with other ambassadors; and his master even forbade him to send express couriers at one point, in order to economize. There was, however, an important change in Philip's style of government at this time which perhaps gave Longlée the impression that the administration was "aging."

In October 1585, when the king and his indefatigable secretary Mateo Vázquez both fell ill at Monzón in Aragon, Philip accepted the advice of his chaplain that a formal committee should be created to sift through the incoming administrative papers and recommend the decision that the king should take. At first the committee was composed of Don Juan de Zúñiga, Don Cristóbal de Moura, Don Juan de Idiáquez and the count of Chinchón, with Vázquez as secretary. Zúñiga, son of the stern governor of Philip's first household and an experienced minister in his own right, was the most important of these councillors, but he died in November 1586 and thereafter the four survivors were given special responsibility for a particular area of business. Vázquez continued to deal with Castilian affairs (handling papers from the councils of the Orders, the Indies, Castile and War and the Committee of

Works) ; Idiáquez dealt with foreign affairs; Moura handled finance and Portuguese matters; Chinchón was responsible for Aragon and Italy. Each minister received the papers from "his" councils, made a précis in the margin, added his own recommendation, and sent it to the king. The royal reply would then be drafted by Vázquez, and the king would either correct the minute and write it out himself, or he would return it to Vázquez for a fair copy which he could sign. Occasionally the secretary was authorized to reply in his own name. The committee, which became known as the Junta de Noche (the Committee of the Night), met virtually every evening and dealt with all the papers brought by the courier that day. When the royal household was on the move the four ministers "got into the same coach and there dealt with the matters of greatest urgency, the secretary reading out the papers and noting the decisions on them in pencil (in order not to damage the original)." They tried to complete their business before supper, so that the king could see everything the same night, and when they failed to do this, Philip complained: "This packet arrived late today, and it is already almost time for Mass and giving audiences, so I have not been able to reply before now. It would be best to send me papers earlier, so that I can reply at once."

This new system of government faced its first real test in the preparation of the "Invincible Armada." In January 1587 the government began to estimate the cost of the enterprise and to think of ways of raising the necessary funds. The total cost was worked out at seven million ducats, an unprecedented sum. The king accepted the estimate and urged upon his advisers the paramount need for two things: secrecy — "given the importance of the matter and the danger which we can see may result from any slight carelessness, even by those who keep secrets well" — and speed. "Be quick," he told his secretary, "so that between tomorrow and Saturday I can be sent the decision which I asked for the other day, because time is passing us by very fast and time lost is never regained." Money, secrecy and speed, however, were not the only problems. Santa Cruz's strategy, with its emphasis on unbeatable size, placed an enormous strain on Spain's industrial capacity: it was simply not possible for her metallurgical and munitions industries to produce all the powder, shot, small arms, and military equipment required for the great fleet. Nor was it easy to build or commandeer enough ships, to collect enough food, to accumulate enough barrels and water jars. "The singeing of the King of Spain's beard" by Drake in April 1587, when considerable quantities of provisions and munitions gathered at Cádiz were destroyed, did not help; but the problem was more deep-seated. Philip II's Spain was never capable of fitting out a truly "invincible" fleet. As events were to show, the Armada which actually left the peninsula in July 1588 was not, in fact, large enough to withstand any adversary: the 130 ships and 33,000 men assembled, although a remarkable demonstration of Spanish power, were not sufficient to guarantee success.

It was mainly this realization that led Philip II to make a crucial change to the original plan. Although as late as the spring of 1587 he still favored a direct attack on England, during the course of the summer it became clear that it would simply not be possible to assemble all the men and munitions required for the invasion. The king therefore decided to employ some 17,000 of his veteran troops already in the Netherlands for the enterprise. They were already recruited, trained and equipped, and, he believed, if the Armada from Spain could reach the coast of Flanders, the veterans could be escorted across the Channel to the coast of Kent. Once they were safely on English soil, the objectives were clear and simple.´ The invading army, commanded by the redoubtable Parma, was to occupy Kent, take London by storm (preferably with Elizabeth and her ministers still in it) and hope that the enemies of the Tudor régime in the north, in the west and in Ireland would rise in rebellion and aid the invaders to master the kingdom. But Philip realized that success on this scale was somewhat unlikely. He therefore devised an alternative plan.

If there was no native rising, or if London could not be taken, Parma was to use his presence on English soil to force Elizabeth to make three important concessions. In descending order of importance, these were toleration of Roman Catholic worship in England, the surrender to Spain of all Dutch towns held by English troops (especially Flushing, which commanded the sea approaches to Antwerp), and perhaps the payment of a war indemnity.

Philip was convinced that these goals were attainable, provided the fleet and the troops in the Netherlands could be brought together. He noted in September 1587 that "although the forces we now have both there and here are insufficient on their own, together — if we can get them together — they will win." Philip was probably right. His soldiers were far superior in experience, discipline and skill to those of Queen Elizabeth; their commanders were also better. There were no properly fortified obstacles between the Kent coast and London, and in any case the Armada carried a train of forty-eight great siege guns mounted on mobile field carriages. Finally, the English government had no overall strategy of defense (some wished to spread the troops out along the coast and "answer" the enemy "at the sea side"; others wanted to withdraw all but a skeleton force inland in order to make a stand at Canterbury and there "staye the enemy from speedy passage to London or the harte of the realme"); and such forces as it had were deployed in the wrong place (in Essex around Tilbury instead of in Kent around Margate).

The invasion project, even when modified by the king in 1587, was thus no crackbrained scheme. If the fleet from Spain and the army from Flanders had managed to join their forces, the Armada might well have proved "invincible." But the first problem was still how to get the great fleet to sea: the new plan did not mean that the ships assembled in Lisbon harbor could set sail at once. On the contrary, its state of readiness appeared to be deteriorating. The king was puzzled and frustrated, and in January 1588 he sent a special investigator to

Lisbon to find out what was wrong. The answer was simple: Santa Cruz was ill, trying to direct the fleet's preparations from his sickbed. He died on 9 February. Swiftly the king decided that the new commander-in-chief was to be the duke of Medina Sidonia, who had amply demonstrated his capacity to organize and outfit naval and military expeditions during the Portugal campaign. The appointment proved an outstanding success: the duke arrived in Lisbon in mid-March and took the fleet to sea by the end of May. But almost at once, his ships were driven into Corunna harbor, considerably damaged, by storms. The commander claimed that this proved that the enterprise was not feasible and should be called off — the setback, he suggested, might even be a sign from God that the venture was doomed. The king replied in characteristic vein, taking up with relish the argument about divine favor. In the first place, he reasoned, if the Armada were disbanded, the English would argue that God was against Spain; second, "if this were an unjust war, one could take this storm as a sign from Our Lord to cease offending him; but being as just as it is, one cannot believe that He will disband it, but will rather grant it more favor than we could wish." These moral arguments were of course augmented by logistical ones: the English had no allies and their forces were inferior to Spain's; the fleet could be in the Channel within a week; from Corunna, the Armada could play no part in bringing the English to negotiate and, worse, it might be subjected to an English blockade. The position was clear to the king and Medina Sidonia was told in no uncertain terms what should be done: "I have dedicated this enterprise to God. . . . Get on, then, and do your part."

At first things went according to plan. Medina Sidonia and his 130 ships sailed into the Channel in late July and reached Calais, only a few miles from Parma's waiting army, on 7 August. The sea was calm, the breeze was fresh, and the English had failed to break the Armada's formation. But God was not for Spain that day.

The story of the disaster that followed is well known — the

fireships, which broke up the fleet; the Dutch navy, which prevented Parma's forces from putting to sea; the desperate decision to sail back to Spain by the northabout route. Perhaps forty ships were destroyed off the coasts of Scotland and Ireland and perhaps fifteen thousand of those aboard died, many of them cut down like cattle by the English garrisons when they landed, exhausted, in Ireland. But it was a long time before all this became known in Spain. In Burgos, which had always maintained a close watch, for commercial reasons, on developments in the north, news arrived on 18 August that the fleet had beaten off English attacks. Then there was silence, which most people feared meant that something had gone wrong. Sure enough, on 9 September reports arrived of the defeat in the Channel and then, on 26 September, a letter arrived from Medina Sidonia, at Santander, asking the town to send beds, food and supplies for the sick survivors who had managed to make port (thirty mules, laden with provisions, left the next day). It was only as the weeks passed and no more ships arrived that the full scale of the disaster became apparent. It was, in the words of one of the monks of the Escorial, a misfortune "worthy to be wept over forever . . . because it lost us respect and the good reputation among warlike people which we used to have. . . . The feeling it caused in all of Spain was extraordinary. . . . Almost the whole of Spain went into mourning. . . . People talked about nothing else."

Philip II was not immune to this general feeling of despair. On 13 October 1588, when it was clear that most of his fleet had been lost, he sent out a circular letter to all bishops asking for special services to be held in all churches to thank God that not everything had been destroyed; he also asked that prayers should be said "entrusting to Our Lord most sincerely all my deeds, so that His Divine Majesty may guide and direct them to whatever end may be to His greatest service, exaltation of His church, and benefit and preservation of Christendom, which is what I desire." His public utterances were philosophical ("I sent the fleet against men, not against wind and water," he is said to have remarked on one occasion) or devout ("God be praised for everything") but in private he was shocked that God had allowed such a thing. When the first rumors arrived at court that something terrible had happened, they were passed on by the faithful Vázquez, who drew an infelicitous comparison between the Armada and the disastrous fate of the second crusade of Louis IX of France in 1270: "When we consider the fate of King Louis of France, a Saint, and on such a saintly expedition, with his army dying of plague, defeated and captured, we cannot fail to fear greatly for the Armada." The king was horrified at the suggestion: "I hope that God has not permitted so much evil, for everything has been done for his service," he snapped back.

This was not humbug. The king genuinely believed that the invasion of England was an enterprise that was entitled to divine favor, and he was convinced that if problems arose, divine assistance would be forthcoming to overcome them. But there had been other motives for sending the fleet in 1588: after all, there had been religious justification for overthrowing "the English Jezebel" since 1559 but, except in 1569–1571, the king had refused to lend open support to those who wished to depose her. The "crusade" was only authorized after political considerations appeared to make it imperative — that is, after Drake's expedition to the Indies and Leicester's arrival in the Netherlands. And after that, Philip was caught in a logistical trap. Once the Armada plan was decided upon and became known abroad, it had to be followed through. Even though it might not be necessary for Spain to defeat the English fleet and dethrone Elizabeth, it had to be clearly established that Spain *could* do these things if she chose. It was therefore essential for the Armada to put to sea. This explains the choice of Medina Sidonia as commander: what Philip required was not a fighting admiral but rather an efficient quartermaster who would ensure that the vast fleet was able to sail. This aspect of royal policy — that there was only one thing worse than sending the Armada to defeat and that was not sending it at all — emerged clearly in the letter sent by the king to Medina Sidonia in July, after the fleet had been driven into Corunna by storms: "If the fleet remains in Corunna," Philip argued, "it will do nothing to enhance our prestige in any peace negotiations, if there are any; rather, it would be likely to encourage the enemy to more hostilities, thinking we are weak. . . . Even if our purpose were solely to make peace, this could not be done on honorable terms without the fleet proceeding and joining the duke of Parma, clearing from its path whatever might cross it." Therefore, "to leave our fleet bottled up and ineffective would be a disgrace . . . by which we would lose both advantage and reputation."

There seems no doubt that the king was correct in his appraisal. The success of the Armada in reaching the Channel, and the knowledge that Philip II still had the resources to send further expeditions in subsequent years, drove the Tudor government into a most costly program of fortifications and troop training. Carisbrooke, Pendennis and many other places were given new defenses, at vast public cost, lest another Spanish fleet should descend on them. The fear of Spanish power lasted long into the seventeenth century: Englishmen found that their country had become "the beleaguered isle." Although there can be no doubt that the Armada was a military failure — and was seen as such by both Spaniards and others at the time — one should not overlook this *psychological* success. One must not deduce from the defeat of the Armada that the entire machinery of Spanish government was ineffective and outdated. It was not. On the contrary, contemporaries admired the advanced techniques of government employed by Philip II, for only through those was he able to create and control the Armada, a feat far beyond the capacity of other rulers of the time.

Lord Howard, commander of the English navy sent to stop the Armada, "never supposed that they [the Spaniards] could ever have found, gathered and joined so great a force of puissant ships together, and so well appointed them with cannon, culverin and other great pieces of brass ordnance." Writing some twenty-five years after the event, Sir Walter Raleigh still cherished no patriotic illusions: Queen Elizabeth's troops were "of no such force, as to encounter an Armie like unto that, wherewith it was intended that the Prince of *Parma* should have landed in *England*." In spite of the defeat of the Armada, Philip II was, and appeared to be, the most powerful mortal in Christendom, if not in the world, ruling an empire which stretched from Antwerp in the north to Angola in the south, and from Spain and Italy, through Mexico, Peru and Brazil, to the Philippines and the East Indies. The lines written by Shakespeare a year or two after Philip's death could have applied to the king of Spain just as well as to Julius Caesar:

> *Why, man, he doth bestride the narrow world*
> *Like a Colossus, and we petty men*
> *Walk under his huge legs . . .*

TEN

"The Most Potent Monarch of Christendome"

THE KING OF SPAIN, wrote an admiring Englishman, is "the most potent Monarch of Christendome, who in his own hands holds the Mines of the Wars' sinews — money — and hath now got a command so wide, that out of his Dominions the *Sunne* can neither rise nor set." This was particularly true during the 1580's, when the power of Philip II was at its zenith. Gone were the uncertainties and the hesitations of policy: the conquest of Portugal, the recovery of the South Netherlands and the taming of America had seen to that. Gone, too, was the personal diffidence and embarrassment. The pale face that looks out at us from the portraits of this period is confident, calm and resolute. The king was going bald, his remaining hair and his beard were entirely white, and his teeth were almost all gone; but his steel-gray eyes were still clear and stern, and his presence struck fear into many men who came to visit him. But as the 1590's advanced, the commanding presence began to crumble. In the last portrait of him, the court painter, Pantoja de la Cruz, has placed the monarch in front of a somber background. His eyes are tired and melancholy, the lips down-turned and parted, the hair sparse and silver. His invalid chair waits in the background.

This aging of the king, from the youthful gallant painted by Titian to the chronic invalid of Pantoja, was also noted by that astute body of men "paid by their country to lie abroad," the ambassadorial corps at Philip's court. Scores of them wrote down, for the benefit of their masters, their impressions of the king and his world, and of the changes that were taking place. As early as 1584 the French resident at the court of Spain thought that he could detect that "the king begins to age. . . . His face is not as fair, showing that his spirit must be borne down by cares, making him more melancholy than he used to be." Two years later, he returned to the same theme: "The news coming from the Indies and the Netherlands has caused the king's countenance to age and become more pensive." Other ambassadors concurred. Although Philip remained, even in his sixties, a man of regal bearing and dignified appearance ("He neither says anything nor does anything except with the decorum and majesty proper to a king," wrote a Venetian envoy in 1593), it was noted that he was sleeping more and doing less. There was also a hardening of the king's control over his emotions. Several people noted that neither the Armada nor the reverses in the Netherlands after 1590 had caused the king to lose his almost reptilian composure — but there was a hint of reproach implicit in their descriptions of his equanimity. It seemed to some that disaster and distress had left the king indifferent and insensitive. A sort of "hardening of the arteries" appeared to have taken place.

One of the few features of his surroundings that seems to have kept the king from becoming totally inhuman was the love of his family, something he only discovered late in life, in his fifties. Anne of Austria, who married Philip in 1570, supervised the upbringing of her stepdaughters Isabella (born in 1566) and Catalina (born in 1567), and she bore her husband seven children herself (two of them stillborn) during their ten years of married life. The birth of their first child on 4 December 1571 was a great event: it was the first son Philip had sired since the birth of Don Carlos a quarter of a century before.

When, four days later, the Venetian ambassadors came to present their official congratulations to the proud father, they found him wearing a black silk jacket and silver-colored velvet breeches and hose, with a cloak of damask trimmed with fur. A special painting was commissioned from Titian (*The Offering of Philip II*) and prisoners were freed in thanksgiving.

Philip's joy at the birth of his other three sons, 1573, 1575 and 1578, was scarcely less, and his sorrow at their death or illness was poignant and real. Nevertheless one can detect a curious indifference in his attitude toward children while they were still young, an indifference shared by his contemporaries. It is true that he bought dolls for his infant daughters and toy soldiers for his sons. It is also true that he encouraged his young daughters to keep birds in a gilded cage in their room, just as he had done himself forty years before, and that he took them with him into the countryside, sometimes to hunt and sometimes simply to admire the beauty of nature. Like all fathers, Philip II knew that his children had a sweet tooth and he sent them "candies" and special preserves from Portugal while he resided there in 1581–1582, but he never seems to have coddled his children or played with them while they were babies. Perhaps, again like his contemporaries, he felt that it was not worth becoming emotionally attached to such vulnerable beings. In Europe at large during the sixteenth century, only half of all children born survived to maturity; of Philip II's eleven children, only four reached their teens. Of course the death of the rest saddened the king, but not as much as we might expect. Thus in July 1575, at the height of the financial crisis that preceded the decree of bankruptcy, the king's second son, Carlos Lorenzo, died, causing his mother to give premature birth to her third child, Diego, the following day. At the same time the eldest boy, Ferdinand, fell seriously ill with dysentery and his doctors disagreed and despaired over the remedy. The king gave advice on the best food for his ailing son (omelets) and asked for frequent reports on his eating and sleeping. Thus far, the model father. But the underlying fatalism appeared the next day when the doctors reported that the child, aged four, would not eat the omelets prescribed, and asked the king to come in person to encourage the boy to take them. The king refused: "At his age, I do not think he will have much respect for me in matters of food. If they want him to eat through fear, he will be more afraid of his governess. He is not old enough . . . to benefit by my going to see him." (The prince was at the country house of Galapagar, only fifteen miles from Madrid.) In the event, Ferdinand did recover, but only to die, aged seven, in 1578.

The death of Philip II's next son, Diego, from smallpox in November 1582, was much harder to bear because it left the king, a widower of fifty-five, with only one sickly son (the future Philip III) to succeed him. "It is a dreadful blow," he wrote, "coming so soon after all the others; but I praise God for all it has pleased Him to perform, submitting myself to His divine will and praying that He will be content with this sacrifice." Then he ordered: "Let prayers be said continuously in the church of Our Lady at Zaragoza for the life and health of the children who remain to me," he ordered, "so that in all possible ways we may seek to placate the wrath which God must so justly hold against us. . . . I hope that the Lord will be satisfied with what is done, but if not, His will be done in all things." But this stoical acceptance of the death of his children was no longer possible once they were grown up. Thus in 1597, when news arrived of the death of Catalina, one of his beloved daughters by Elizabeth de Valois, Philip broke down. He wept and raged, he howled and shouted in a manner never seen before, railing against the ill fortune which had brought him so many personal sorrows. Such was his grief that one of the monks at the Escorial noted in his journal that the death of Catalina "deprived the king — who was then seventy years old — of many days of life and health." Catalina and her elder sister, Isabella, who remained with the king to the end, were the two people whom Philip loved most dearly, and he spent a great deal of time with them. He regularly played cards and dice with them for money (the accounts of the girls' household contain frequent entries concerning money issued "to play with the king our lord"). When he returned from Portugal in the spring of 1583 he began to take his meals with his daughters. After 1585, when Catalina left Spain to become duchess of Savoy, the king often ate alone with Isabella, and she sat beside him as he worked, drying ink and passing him papers.

This personal contact was absent between December 1580 and March 1583, while Philip was in Portugal; yet, curiously, it is precisely these years which have provided posterity with the most intimate glimpses into his private life. Every Monday during his absence he wrote a letter to his teen-age daughters in his own hand. Thirty-four of them have survived in the archives of Turin, where they were left by Catalina: clearly she had taken them with her when she left Spain in 1585 and she had treasured them ever since. A further ninety-three letters written by the king to Catalina alone have also survived, running from 14 June 1585 (the day after she set sail for Italy) to September 1596 (a year before her death). All had been kept by Philip's devoted daughter. The king, by contrast, destroyed his children's letters when he had replied to them — and he made no secret of the fact: "I have decided not to reply to your other letters because they were already old. Instead I burned them so that I should not be burdened with too many papers. I do not believe that there was anything in them to which I should have replied, but if there was you can write to me about it again." This was perhaps a little insensitive — many fathers exiled from their children would have chosen to keep the fruits of their youthful endeavor — but the king meant well. In June 1588 he revealed that he had been counting the days since Catalina left his side: "Yesterday," he wrote to her, "was the third anniversary of your embarkation. I have not seen you since then, which has given me little comfort, and I know very well that you *would* bring me comfort because of the love you have for me and the love I have for you." This passage followed a long discussion of the merits of giving birth to children lying in bed rather than sitting up in a special chair — Catalina had experienced difficulty in giving birth to her third child, "and I who have seen it all [childbirth] can give you this good advice" — but most letters were taken up with trivia. In 1582, for example, he reported in detail the safe arrival of a galleon from the East Indies:

> I only know that the ship carried an elephant, which has been sent to your brother [Prince Diego] by the viceroy whom I sent to the Indies . . . who has already arrived there, and he arrived at a good time too because the one who was there already — I mean the viceroy who was there already — was dead. Tell your brother about the elephant, and tell him that I have a book in Portuguese to send him to help him to learn to read the language. It would be very good if he knew how to speak it already. Don Antonio de Castro [a Portuguese courtier who had just returned from Madrid] has come back very pleased with the words the prince said to him in Portuguese — which was very good if he really did say them! This is already a very long letter for someone who is convalescent and weak. God keep you as I desire: your loving father.

The same solicitude for family health was present in almost every letter. In this one, it was the king himself who had been ill (with "gout" and stomach cramps), and he described self-pityingly his medicines: a syrup every morning ("which tastes awful because it contains rhubarb") washed down with ghastly drafts prepared from liverwort. In another letter Philip described how he had almost fallen into the sea while getting out of a boat, but landed heavily on his leg instead so that he had difficulty in walking. In other letters he inquired about the illnesses of his children. Had Catalina been left with any scars after her smallpox? Why did Isabella's nose bleed so often? (The king thought it would stop when the girl began to menstruate, "which seems to be rather overdue," he opined.) This constant concern with illness and bodily functions might seem a trifle morbid to us, but it was fully justified: in October

1580 Queen Anne had died of influenza, and Philip himself had been at death's door; of the five children whom the king had left behind at his departure for Portugal in 1580, only three were left alive at his return in 1583. By 1587 he had laid seventeen members of his own family to rest in the vaults of the Escorial.

Inevitably a lot of space in the letters to his daughters was taken up with news of what the king had been doing, what the children's favorite courtiers had been doing, and what the weather was like. There was also a considerable amount of thinking aloud (as in the king's notes to his secretaries) :

> I hear that your young brother [the future Philip III] has just cut a tooth. It seems to me that it has taken its time, because he is now three years old — today is the anniversary of his baptism, as you will remember, although I am uncertain whether it is two or three years ago. I think it is three. He must be handsome, as you say. I am also uncertain how old your other brother [Diego] will be on his next birthday in July. I think six years old. Let me know the truth, and God keep you and them as I desire.

Sometimes he wrote the same piece of news more than once, and had to apologize when his daughters pointed it out to him: "I have just seen the letter in which you say that I have already described to you the windows my sister has in her chapel, and I have written about it again in this letter; so in all I have mentioned it three times. You can tell from this how my poor head must be, with so many things to worry it."

But there was also a more serious side to the letters: making sure of good behavior. The king encouraged his family to go regularly to church and could not conceal his delight when, for example, he discovered that he and his daughters "had the idea of going to a Franciscan monastery on the same day, you in Madrid and me here." Later the same year, he sent a special rosary for his young son Diego, then aged six, "so that he can start reciting it" and a colored Agnus Dei from the Indies "for your baby sister [Maria, aged a year and a half] to use in whatever way seems best to you." In matters of religion, above all, the king felt it was important to set a good example. Thus on Christmas Day, 1581, he described how he had only got to bed at 3 A.M. the previous night "because the Midnight Mass only ended a little before that. I heard it, and also matins, from a window in my room which opens into the chapel." Few letters failed to mention which services Philip had attended and where he had attended them.

Not only religious education was dealt with in these letters. The king sent his daughters treasures from overseas, unusual fruits, and even rare flowers for them to see. He told them to encourage young Prince Diego to dance, and he studied with pleasure a letter and a picture of a horse done by the prince "which seemed to me better done than he usually manages." He promised to send a picture book as a reward. Later he sent his son some letters of the alphabet to color in, and announced that he had more to send when they were required. "But make sure," he warned his daughters, "that he colors them in little by little, so as not to get bored; and also see that sometimes he copies them, so that in this way he will learn still more and will (I hope) learn to write neatly. Until he does this, it is better for him not to write at all, because he will learn better how to put the letters together when he has someone to show him properly."

The king was also anxious that his children should grow up to love music. There was a lute in the household from their earliest years, and both the daughters learned to play it. His son Philip III could play the viol so well that at the age of fourteen he began giving lessons to one of his grooms. Although it has been stated (by Luis Cabrera de Córdoba, a member of the royal household) that the king himself never sang or played, he certainly possessed a fine ear for music and a large collection of musical instruments (the inventory compiled after his death included ten clavichords, sixteen bagpipes and thirteen vihuelas — a sort of lute — "used to teach the child choristers to play, so that they eventually got broken"). He also took a keen personal interest in his music, both secular and liturgical. Under his direction, 219 *cantorales* (hymnbooks) were made and illuminated at the Escorial between 1572 and 1586, so that each chorister would have his own copy and thus (he hoped) avoid singing the wrong note. Philip opposed bitterly the attempts of the papacy, on the advice of Palestrina, to introduce new musical chants into church services in place of the traditional plainsong, and he opposed it on the grounds of artistic merit: he preferred plainsong, and he wished to retain the right to hear it if he chose. The king felt equally strongly about bells. Despite the undisguised distaste of his Spanish monks, Philip installed two carillons of Flemish bells in the towers of the Escorial. One had nineteen bells, the other had forty, and they were operated by a single keyboard whenever the king chose (but the glockenspiel was silent after his death). Philip II also patronized promising musical composers and performers — notably Tomás Luis Vitoria (1548–1611), an outstanding and prolific composer and the chaplain of Philip's sister Maria; Antonio de Cabezón (1500–1566) and his family, all gifted organists and composers of the royal chapel; and Philippe Rogier (1560–1598), one of the many distinguished singer-composers who came to his court from the Netherlands to form part of his Flemish choir (the Capilla Flamenca).

All these musicians, of whom there were perhaps 150 at any one time, formed part of the royal household, the enormous body of fifteen hundred or so salaried officials who constituted the permanent entourage of the king and his family. These ranged from the duke of Alva (who from 1548 until his death in 1582 ruled the household with absolute authority as the king's *mayordomo mayor*) down to the stable grooms and the twenty or so boys who kept the king's hunting dogs. Moreover, when the court traveled outside Madrid (where the king normally spent the winter), all sorts of additional servants and officials appeared, either to serve the royal family or the leading ministers. In 1591 it was reckoned that for the five months (December to April) of every year that were normally spent in the Madrid palace, the household required 135 fanegas of grain a month, but for the rest of the year, 239 fanegas a month (an increase of 77 percent). This meant a total grain consumption of 2,400 fanegas (about 3,600 bushels) over the whole year, at a cost of 3,600 ducats. (A further 7,500 ducats were needed for the hay and oats consumed in the royal stables). The size of the household was a major embarrassment when the king decided to visit one of his country houses, whether close like Toledo or Aranjuez, or more distant like Valladolid or Valencia. In May 1560, for example, when the court moved from Madrid to Aranjuez for a week, more than four thousand people were involved in the move. Each principal member of the household had his own portable kitchen (although the food was provided at the king's expense) and this population of displaced courtiers was forced to live in tents while the royal party enjoyed the palace gardens by the Tagus.

Inevitably, mass movements on this scale were inconvenient, and they gave rise to serious administrative problems, which sometimes involved even the king. Thus in 1565, when Philip had gone to his new palace of El Bosque, near Segovia, he brought only a small entourage with him because his doctors told him (correctly, for once) that too many people would cause disease to spread. The king took this advice to heart and warned the duke of Alva, as head of the household, to control strictly the number of people in attendance and what they did. He singled out fish as a medical risk. Trout, he ordered, were to be eaten only at table: "if people eat them outside, the evil smell will also be a health risk." The king's attention to detail had not abated a quarter of a century later. In September 1590 there was a lot of illness among the courtiers at the Escorial, and one of them asked that 250 pounds of fruit and two loads of ice (from the special "ice wells" created by the king high in the Guadarrama mountains) should be brought daily to the sick. The king disagreed: "I think the doctors should rather stop fruit and snow being taken by some of the sick . . . and we can avoid bringing snow in some winter months, because I do not take drinks with ice, and it does more harm than good to everyone else at that time of year." Decisions like these could be taken only by the king. Likewise, only he could choose who to appoint to household office: even menial cooks and porters had to be chosen by the king from lists of up to twenty applicants submitted to him by his secretaries. The household was a tiresome, time-consuming and uncongenial burden for the king, and it is small wonder that from time to time he liked to escape from its cloying embrace.

Yet however large or small the king's entourage, one category of courtier was always included: the dwarfs, jesters and buffoons of the royal family. The letters written by Philip to his daughters while he was in Portugal are full of references to people like Magdalena Ruiz, a mentally retarded dwarf to whom the king's daughters were devoted. In the Prado Museum there is a painting of Isabella with her hand on the head of her faithful dwarf, who had been her servant since 1568 (when the princess was two) and died at the Escorial in 1605. She had epileptic seizures, she was heavily addicted to alcohol, and she was capable of staging tantrums in front of the king himself. "Magdalena is very cross with me," Philip told his daughters in one letter, "and she has gone off saying she wants to leave." She was a favorite with the crowds, who always chanted, "Whip her, whip her," whenever she appeared in public, in an attempt to provoke or frighten her. Magdalena could always be relied on to do the wrong thing — to fall over; to overeat (especially strawberries) and be sick; to be seasick before anyone else — but that was all part of her charm. The king filled several pages of his letters to his children with accounts of her deeds and defects, sometimes told with an obvious smirk, it is true, as one might describe the slapstick of a circus clown or the antics of a dog, but the tone was more often one of affection and sympathy. There was no shortage of clowns, either, at the court of Spain, and in all, we know of three professional buffoons (some of them also conjurers or jugglers), ten dwarfs and ten simpletons maintained at court during Philip's reign.

But despite the diversions provided by the jesters and buffoons, for most people life at court was not particularly pleasant. It was expensive, demanding and often tedious. Most courtiers were obsessed by the twin problems of boredom and promotion, obsessions that were neatly reflected in a special game for courtiers, first published in 1587: *The Courtier's Philosophy* of Alonso de Barros, dedicated to Mateo Vázquez. The game was played on a board with dice and tokens, and it combined elements from Monopoly and Snakes and Ladders. The board was divided into sixty-three squares, to represent the years of a man's life, some of the squares representing hazards to his progress, others bonuses. Those who landed on square 15, entitled "the step of hope," paid the "bank" and advanced to square 26, "the house of the favorite." By contrast, those who landed on square 32, "the well of forgetfulness," lost a turn and had to pay all the other players to remind the favorite of their existence. Those who landed on square 40, "change of ministers," were sent back to square 10, "the house of adulation"; and those who landed on square 43, "your patron dies," had to go back to the start. As Lord Burleigh said of the Elizabethan court: a man without friends at court is like a workman without tools.

Another chance reflection of the underlying realities of court life comes from a fragment of a court betting book, which has survived from August 1572. The book, kept by the *corredor* or "banker," was double-entry, with a double page for each punter: his winnings were entered on the right, his losses on the left. There were two heavy gamblers — one of whom owed over six hundred ducats at the end of the month, and another (referred to only as "The Judge") who owed even more at one stage but won it all back in some daring bets — but there were several smaller operators, including courtiers of rank and distinction. Unfortunately, the subject of the bets is never stated, but the prevalence of feverish gambling among the people of early modern Europe is well known: they might bet for or against anything. It is the volume of transactions that is surprising, with most of the ten courtiers recorded in the fragment (only nine surviving folios from a book of three hundred or more) making a bet, on the average, once every two days. Small wonder that many men were ruined by their residence in the royal palace.

Life at court was not always so wild and disordered, however. The betting and the gaming were always more prominent during the winter months at Madrid; the summers at the Escorial were more relaxed and the number of persons at court was smaller. The great gray granite pile of the Escorial, which is today the best-known monument to Philip II, was built on a spot chosen by him on the southern slopes of the Guadarrama mountains, three thousand feet above sea level and about thirty miles northwest of Madrid. It was begun in 1563 and completed in 1584. The king, who paid for the entire cost of construction (5.5 million ducats), intended it to serve a number of purposes. To begin with, it was to be one more royal monastic foundation, like the Parral at Segovia or Saint Jerome at Granada or Our Lady at Guadalupe, all founded by Philip's predecessors. Like these three, the monastery was to be staffed by members of the Hieronymite order, for whom the royal family had particular respect (according to Philip II's deed of gift). The monks were to give perpetual thanks for the victory of Saint Quentin — won by Philip II's forces on Saint Lawrence's day (10 August 1557); to pray for the souls of Philip's deceased relatives; and to beg for God's special help in governing his kingdoms. But there was more to the Escorial than that. From the first, the king intended it to be a royal mausoleum and there were regular funeral processions to the monastery whenever a member of the royal family died. Philip had the remains of his father brought there from Yuste in 1568 and he wanted to bring "the Catholic Kings," his great-grandparents, from Granada, but the bodies were too far decomposed (instead he had special lead sarcophagi made for them, so that their mortal remains would be better protected). But San Lorenzo el Real, as the monastery was to be called, was to cater to the living as well as to the dead. The king founded a seminary and a school there, and he encouraged the monks to take an interest in scholarship. He also donated his books, maps and antiquities to the monastery, and he toyed with the idea of creating an astronomical observatory there too. A small scientific laboratory already existed, with retorts and an enormous still for producing the "essences" the king used for medicines and perfumes. The still, known as the Philosopher's Tower, could produce two hundred pounds of distilled water a day. These refinements, unusual perhaps for a monastery, stemmed from Philip's final purpose in founding the Escorial: he wanted to live there. He wished to emulate his father, who had spent his last years living in a small palace attached to the Hieronymite monastery of Yuste. The religious order was the same; the situation of the royal apartments, with special views of the high altar in the church, was the same; even the gardens at both palace-monasteries were laid out by the same monk, Fray Marcos de Cardona. The "palace" was one of the first parts of the monastery to be completed, and the king began to reside there for ever longer periods from 1566 onward, watching the work proceed on the monks' quarters and on the great cathedral. When everything was finished, in September 1584, the king wept openly with emotion.

Perhaps the king had good reason for his tears, for not everything had gone according to plan with the construction. There had been delays, two serious fires, and the building had been struck by lightning. There had even been a mutiny among the workmen in May 1577, when a couple of their compatriots were imprisoned for brawling. A column of fifty laborers marched to the prison, with pipes and drums playing, to release their friends. The authorities were scandalized, comparing their behavior to the mutinies of the army of Flanders: "Anyone who heard about what has happened here would think it happened in the Netherlands," wrote one appalled observer. The king, who came to the monastery especially to appease the troubles, was generous (he needed his builders) and only the ringleaders were punished. But at other times, court discipline was enforced more sternly.

The *alcaldes de casa y corte* (magistrates of the royal household and court) dealt swiftly and ruthlessly with any courtier who stepped out of line. When, for example, at 11 P.M. on the night of 22 May 1577 the strains of a love sóng were heard beneath the tower of the Madrid palace where the queen's ladies-in-waiting slept, some palace guards emerged to find Don Luis Carillo and a friend serenading their ladies with vihuelas. The guards told them to stop and refused to accept the bribes offered to purchase their compliance. Frustrated, Carillo put his hand to his sword — a fatal mistake, because resisting the officers of the law was always punished severely, and Don Luis (although a nephew of the head of the queen's household) was hauled off to spend the night in prison and was fined. More serious crimes were dealt with more severely, with the important exception that noblemen tended to escape relatively lightly. In 1583, for example, Don Alonso Gutiérrez, a royal councillor, was murdered at court. It was found that the deed had been done by four servants of the count of Melgar, on the express order of their master. The four were promptly sentenced by the court magistrates to death, to loss of half their goods, and to a fine of 800 ducats for legal costs; but Melgar was only fined 1,000 ducats and sentenced to four years' exile from the court — a fairly lenient punishment for cold-blooded murder. Much the same thing happened after the rape of a lady-in-waiting to Joanna, the king's sister, by Don Gonzalo Chacón, brother of the count of Montalbán, in August 1572. The passionate Don Gonzalo took refuge in a monastery in Seville and was hidden there by one of the friars. Eventually, he was caught, and the unfortunate friar was taken to Madrid for trial. The king ordered him to be brought in for a personal reprimand before sentence. "Friar, who taught you to disobey your king, and who persuaded you to harbor such a villain?" demanded Philip. The friar raised his eyes with great humility and replied, "Charity." The king was taken aback and muttered twice, "Charity? Charity?" Then, after a pause, he turned to the waiting magistrate and said, "Send this man back to his convent at once, in a dignified way, for if charity moved him, what else can we do with him?" This sympathetic story, narrated by Porreño, ends with the magistrate's respectful wonderment at the king's magnanimity: he had expected to receive an order to carry out a harsh sentence on the friar. Therefore, "from that time onward, the alcalde venerated and revered the king more than ever, knowing him to be so just, pious and clement." Don Gonzalo, too, according to Porreño, was let off with exile and an obligation to marry his ravished victim. But this "happily ever after" scenario was reserved for the wellborn. Porreño strangely forgets to say that in June 1575, after almost three years in prison, three of the court lackeys who had helped to arrange the gratification of Don Gonzalo's passions were sentenced to death, and ten more were condemned to exile or a term on the galleys!

Crimes of violence committed at the court were, of course, made especially serious by the proximity of the royal family. During Philip's lifetime, several monarchs were assassinated — Antony, king of Navarre, in 1563; Henry Darnley, king of Scotland, in 1566; Henry III, king of France, in 1589. Henry IV, king of France and Navarre, was to follow in 1610 (after nineteen lucky escapes in previous years). There were innumerable attempts on the life of Elizabeth of England, and at least two are known against Philip II, both by Frenchmen, in 1571 and 1583. The king was an easy target. Although after the assassination of Henry III of France Philip was more careful, appearing in public less often and traveling in a closed coach, he had spent much of his life in the open, among his subjects. In the funeral oration given for Philip at the Escorial, Fray Francisco Terrones drew attention to the king's implicit trust in his subjects: "How secure and confident he felt, sleeping beside the street, next to low windows containing only glass. He used to go out in these fields alone, without an escort, and he gave audiences alone and unarmed."

There are many touching examples of the mutual love and respect that bound Philip II to his subjects. In 1585–1586, for example, when he visited his three Aragonese kingdoms, at every town the king got out of his carriage, mounted his horse, and rode, alone, at the head of the procession. At his entry into the city of Valencia, on 20 January 1586, the upper windows of all the houses along the royal route were full of young women and girls, "whom His Majesty saluted with great courtesy, raising his hat whenever he saw especially pretty ones." On his journey to Portugal five years before, there had been similar touching scenes. At Campomayor a woman in the street greeted the king as he rode by with the words "God bless you, Sire: we want to see you become just like us" and she gave him a jar of cool water to drink. The king was touched by this spontaneous display of affection, and seemed so happy for the rest of the day that his retinue confessed "that they had never seen him so pleased." The king was not afraid of his subjects, and he was never afraid to do as they did. In 1585, on Ash Wednesday, he happened to be in Zaragoza walking through the streets with his entourage when he met a religious procession coming the other way. At once the king moved aside into the crowd and fell to his knees, bareheaded, and remained there in the midst of his subjects in silent respect. Even at the age of sixty-five, in 1592, on his last great progress, Philip still publicly went to church every day and in Valladolid he took his children to some public lectures at the university, where he sat with them among the students.

Philip had the common touch, and so did his family. When, in 1570, Anne of Austria was making her way to Segovia for her marriage to the king, she spent the night before her wedding in the village of Valverde. After the singing and dancing that normally greeted the arrival of royalty, the local people began to come, shyly, to offer the queen-to-be bed linen, wine glasses, cutlery and other small items useful to a newlywed about to set up house. It was the local custom, and Anne had been born not far away, at Cigales. She was delighted, according to a chronicle of her progress to Segovia, "for truly, the minds of people of even the highest station are often relaxed by laying aside for a short space of time their majesty and grandeur and descending to simplicity and ordinary life."

This informality is a far cry from the frosty, formal and aloof monarch described in the various reports of foreign ambassadors at the court of Spain. But they did not lie. It was simply that Philip II reserved protocol and ceremony for those who liked it: the grandees, the courtiers and the ambassadors themselves. The king himself could not stand their way of life for long. Sometimes he exploded with rage at the petty vanity of his ministers: "When I gave orders for them [a committee on finance] to meet, it was so that they could devote themselves to business and not to questions of precedence. . . . Now is not the moment to discuss precedence or to waste time over trivial matters when there are others of such great importance," he wrote in 1577. But at other times the king preferred escape to anger, and he would rise before dawn, mount his horse, and ride off almost alone to one of his secluded palaces, leaving strict orders behind him that no courtier, minister or ambassador should follow. One day in 1565 he wrote to his secretary: "It seems to me that the weather is so good today that it should not be wasted, so I plan to go to the Pardo palace this afternoon and tomorrow to the Escorial. . . . Do not tell anyone about the Escorial until after I have gone."

It is true that Philip did insist on strict respect and deference for the office he held — but only at certain times and in certain places. When he visited Córdoba Cathedral in 1570, for example, he found that the embalmed corpse of his ancestor Alfonso VIII (1158–1214) lacked the staff it had once held. When he discovered that the staff had been broken, and that the canons had not dared to replace it, the king was delighted and, removing his hat out of respect, placed his own stick in the corpse's hand, observing that "only a king should give his stick to another." But Philip never insisted on this sort of respect for himself as a person. In 1585 he happily agreed that thenceforth he should be addressed simply as "Sir" (Señor), not by the elaborate style of his predecessors, "Sacred Catholic Royal Majesty," and on all occasions he tried to reduce formality. A nervous local magistrate who asked the king's secretary in 1589 whether he should kneel, bow or walk backward in the royal presence was informed by the king himself that he need only remove his hat. Although Philip sometimes wore his splendid robes of state — for instance, at his coronation as king of Portugal at Tomar in April 1581 — even then he did so unwillingly (or so he told his daughters, to whom he had no need to conceal his feelings). Of course his clothes were always clean — he made almost a fetish of personal cleanliness — and he had a new suit of clothes made every month. But the clothes were normally plain and simple. Even when he set out to meet his future son-in-law, the duke of Savoy, at Zaragoza in March 1585, he was "dressed in black without any pomp, wearing his insignia of the Golden Fleece." That is how he appears in the famous portrait in the Pardo palace by Sánchez Coello, painted at about this time. A little later, when the duke met his bride-to-be for the first time, everyone was refulgently dressed "except the king, who looked very ordinary, dressed in black just like the citizens." That is, very probably, precisely how Philip II would have wished to appear to his subjects. As the Venetian ambassador Soranzo observed just after Philip's death: "He abhorred vanity in all things," and it was one of his most likable traits. But the last years of his reign were to rob him of some of his dignity, and of some of his popularity too.

ELEVEN

Toward the Grave, 1589–1598

THE TOTAL COST of the Armada had been in the region of ten million ducats. On top of this, there was the cost of the war in the Netherlands (over two million a year) and the subsidies to the French Catholic leaders (three million ducats were sent from Spain between 1585 and 1590). Even with the increased income from the Indies, the cost of imperialism was growing too great for Castile to bear. In 1589 the Cortes were cajoled into voting a new tax known as the *millones*, worth eight million ducats, but collection was spread over almost a decade and even then the whole sum was not equal to the cost of the Armada. Castile, however, could afford no more. Even before the imposition of the millones, the average peasant farmer of Castile was forced to surrender half his income in taxes, tithes and seigneurial dues. Taxation had increased far faster even than prices during the reign of Philip II, especially after about 1575: taxes appear to have increased little during the reign of Charles V, but between 1556 and 1570 they rose by around 50 percent and between 1570 and the end of the century they grew by a further 90 percent.

Yet even tax increases on this scale were not sufficient to finance Philip II's imperialism, and government borrowing increased rapidly. The figures in the table below, which were prepared by the Castilian treasury, speak for themselves.

PUBLIC FINANCE IN CASTILE, 1560–1598
(in millions of ducats)

Year	Estimated Income	National Debt	Debt Interest
1560	3.1	25.5	1.6
1575	5.5	40.0	2.7
1598	9.7	85.0	4.6

In the course of his reign, therefore, Philip II's revenues tripled, but the size of the public debt almost quadrupled. In almost every year debt interest absorbed half or rather more than half of the crown's available income, leaving insufficient funds to meet its military and other needs, and making further borrowing unavoidable. The Spanish government became chronically incapable of balancing its budget, and the recurrent deficit steadily increased the size of the debt.

At a time of rapidly rising prices and economic growth, of course, such a situation need not have been disastrous, particularly if the government's excess expenditure had led to additional demand for Spanish goods and additional jobs for Spanish workers. Alas, it did not. The Spanish economy could not produce in sufficient quantity the munitions, the equipment and the other goods required for the war effort. And although thousands of Spaniards were recruited and sent abroad on military service, their wages (paid for by the Castilian taxpayer) were spent in Italy, France or the Netherlands and rarely returned to refuel the Spanish economy. The capital tied up in the public debt was money lost to private investment, and even the interest payments were often pocketed by foreign financiers who remitted their profits abroad, above all to Genoa.

Capital starvation and overtaxation were two of the reasons for Spain's economic crisis in the 1590's, and both were the direct result of Philip II's imperialism. There was a third cause, however, over which the king had no control: a run of harvest failures, which afflicted the whole of Western Europe. All the evidence points to a climatic change in the last decade of the sixteenth century, probably connected with a temporary decline in solar energy, which reduced the average summer temperature and delayed and diminished harvests (whether grain, grapes or olives) everywhere. In the towns of Old Castile, all three problems — shortage of capital, overtaxation and poor harvests — became acute from 1595 onward. In the first few months of the year, the town council of Palencia (to take one town as an example) was preoccupied with a 40 percent increase in its tax obligations and with its inability to raise the additional sums required; but beginning in October all other business was eclipsed by the need to import grain and wine from outside in order to supplement the disastrously bad local harvest. Although the harvest of 1596 was better, there was another failure in 1597 and in the winter of 1597–1598 heavy frosts killed off all the vines and damaged the seed corn. The 1598 harvest, or what remained of it, was finally destroyed by "a hailstorm which struck the countryside around this city with the worst force ever seen." Gradually Palencia filled up with starving country people, attracted by the meager rations doled out by the town granary, until in August it was resolved to expel all immigrants and to bar the gates against further refugees. In September it was reported that there were crowds of poor people dying of hunger at the city gates but, with scarcely enough grain to feed the citizens, the town council had to maintain their prohibition on further entry. Their prudence was reinforced by the rumors of plague spreading southward from the Cantabrican coast, striking down emaciated victims in thousands as it advanced. Perhaps 600,000 died in Castile during the great plague of 1598–1599: almost 10 percent of the total population. In Palencia, in place of the 10,700 inhabitants listed in the census of 1589, there were only 5,100 ten years later, a drop of over one-half in a decade. In Valladolid, a town of around 36,000 people, the town government opened a "black list" of all places known to be affected by the plague, but this and the other measures taken to keep the disease under control (measures which included turning the public brothel into an extra hospital) failed to protect the population from a terrible sacrifice: in 1599 alone 6,600 citizens of Valladolid are thought to have perished — almost one-fifth of the total number of inhabitants. Segovia with a population of 28,000 lost 12,000 people during the plague. And Segovia, Valladolid and Palencia were by no means isolated cases: the whole of Spain seems to have passed through a severe population crisis in the last years of the sixteenth century.

The king could not fail to be aware of these serious developments. He still moved around his kingdoms — in 1592 he made a tour of Old Castile and saw the decline of Burgos, Valladolid and the rest for himself — and he received letters from his ministers drawing attention to the desolation and depopulation of Spain. In February 1591, for example, Secretary Mateo Vázquez wrote to his master complaining that in Castile

> the population is failing, and in such a way that many reliable people who have come from various parts of this kingdom are saying that it is a marvel to meet anyone in the smaller villages. In this way agriculture will very soon fail. . . . It is to be feared that everything here will collapse at once, through lack of funds. . . . If God had intended Your Majesty to heal all the lame who come to you for cure, He would have given you the power to do so; and if He had wished to oblige Your Majesty to remedy all the troubles of the world, He would have given you the money and the strength to do it.

The pessimism of Vázquez, who was a dying man, already bedridden (he died on 5 May), was shared by the king. In a note written at this time, Philip had sympathized with his secretary's illness, and added: "Do not allow yourself to be drawn into melancholy, which is a very bad thing, although the times we live in bring it with them, and so does what is happening in the world. I cannot escape this altogether because I am greatly grieved when I look at the present state of Christendom." Nevertheless, amid his sorrows, the king felt that the way of retrenchment and reduced overseas commitments (advocated by Vázquez and others) was not the correct one. "I know you mean well," he told his secretary (and chaplain), "but these are not matters which can be abandoned." The king's foreign commitments could not be dropped because "the religious issue involved takes priority over everything." This was to be the king's constant refrain in the 1590's.

On 1 August 1589 a Catholic fanatic murdered Henry III, the last Valois king of France. His acknowledged heir was the leader of the French Protestant party, Henry of Navarre, who at once had himself proclaimed King Henry IV. Philip decided that a Protestant triumph in France would jeopardize the security of his entire monarchy — as his erstwhile secretary Antonio Pérez once observed: "The heart of the Spanish empire is France" — and he therefore increased his support of the French Catholics. Some three million ducats were paid in direct subsidies to the Catholic leaders; there were major military expeditions from the Netherlands in 1592–1593, in 1595–1596, and in 1597, and one from Lombardy in 1595; and Spanish garrisons were maintained at Philip's expense in the principal Catholic areas (Brittany, Languedoc, Franche-Comté, Savoy and Paris). Even this was not enough to achieve a Catholic victory, although it did compel Henry of Navarre to embrace the Catholic faith in order to win more support. Henry announced his conversion in July 1593, was crowned with papal blessing in February 1594, and entered Paris in triumph the following month. Spain fought on until May 1598, but failed to achieve any further successes — indeed, all her gains in the war had to be restored at the Peace of Vervins.

The nine years of war in France were costly not only in terms of money. The funds allocated to the support of the French Catholics were badly needed elsewhere. In the Netherlands, the troops of the Dutch Republic reconquered the provinces of Friesland, Groningen, Overijssel, and most of Gelderland, while the Spanish army was campaigning in France. In the New World, the policies of expansion desired by the government had to be abandoned for lack of funds. On the northern frontier of Mexico the "war of blood and sword" against the "Red Indians" had to be abandoned in the 1590's. In Chile, where the war against the Araucanian Indians was called by one Spanish chronicler "the Flanders of the Indies," the war effort (carried out, in fact, by troops commanded by a Flanders veteran, Don Alonso de Sotomayor) merely provoked a massive Indian rising in 1598 which wiped out the gains of the previous few years. The trade between the Iberian peninsula and the New World also suffered. Over one hundred English privateers constantly preyed upon Spanish and Portuguese shipping, and from time to time there were larger English expeditions which seized places in America (Recife in 1595; Puerto Rico in 1598) and stopped all transatlantic trade. The total volume of prizes taken by the English probably varied between a half-million and one million ducats annually; the value of those taken by the Dutch was probably rather more, and from 1594 onward there were also direct trading voyages by Dutch and English merchants, first to the Caribbean, then to West Africa, and finally to the East Indies.

Such a succession of reverses gave rise to a wave of unrest in Spain, exacerbated by the economic recession. In Castile, the trouble began at Avila, where in October 1591 several broadsheets were put up complaining of the high taxes and the king's policy of keeping the nobles out of government. The magistrates acted swiftly to preserve order, and they were supported by the king, who immediately sent a special judge to discover who was responsible. The judge worked fast: in February 1592 Don Diego de Braçamonte, a member of one of the most illustrious families in the city, was condemned to death and executed. Others were sentenced to the galleys or to fines. The king was firm, not only because he had always been firm in cases involving opposition to his authority, but because he was aware of the general discontent latent in Castile and wished to set an example. In Avila itself, the citizens showed their sympathy with Braçamonte by wearing mourning after his death. In Madrid there were also riots in 1591 and there was further unrest in Toledo and Seville. Some government ministers began to fear a general rising "because the Castilians will not be content to blow bubbles with their discontent at the taxes and tributes which have been laid upon them these last few years." The clearest manifestation of this discontent among the taxpayers was the intransigence of the Cortes of Castile. Throughout the reign of Philip II, the Cortes was normally a timid, docile assembly of thirty-six oligarchs (two from each of the eighteen "voting towns" of Castile). In 1590, as previously noted, they had voted the "millones" to pay for the Armada. In 1592 they were called back to vote more money for the wars with France, England and the Dutch, but this time there was a solid core of deputies, led by those from Burgos and Seville, who refused: they opposed every crown proposal for raising money with arguments about the depopulation and impoverishment of the countryside. They even presented memorials criticizing the king's expensive foreign policy: one deputy suggested that the war in the Netherlands alone had cost Castile 115 million ducats, and that this was too much. According to one crown adviser: "Almost all the deputies are in favor of begging Your Majesty most insistently that, before anything else, you will order a reduction in war expenditure, both in the Netherlands and elsewhere." On 6 May 1593, the antiwar feeling reached its height and one deputy went so far as to say that "although the wars with the Dutch, England and France are holy and just, we must beg Your Majesty that they may cease." This parliamentary opposition exasperated the king. He ordered his ministers to rebuke the deputies for daring to criticize his foreign policy and to remind them that "they should and must put their trust in me, and in the love I have for these kingdoms, and in the long experience I have in governing them, that I shall always do what is in their best interests. Speak to them at length in this vein . . . and advise them that they are never, for any reason, to discuss coming to me with a similar suggestion again."

In the course of time, some deputies were won over by government bribes and promises, while others were intimidated by summary arrests and house searches. The king even harnessed the support of "higher powers" to bolster his fiscal demands: in July 1593 he informed his secretary that it was "necessary that the theologians of Madrid should be forewarned, so that if the deputies of the Cortes should turn to them for advice, they may include in their opinions a full account of my case." Letters were also to be sent to inform the theologians of the various "voting towns" of the need to find some remedy for the present emergency. It was all to no avail. The Cortes continued to refuse their consent to further taxes. Only the English attack on Cádiz in June 1596, which the king tried to blame in part on the deputies' unpatriotic meanness, produced a change of heart: the deputies at last agreed to vote taxes worth 1.5 million ducats annually for a period of eleven years.

Philip was faced by "parliamentary opposition" in other areas during the 1590's. Although Lombardy and Naples remained quiet, the former ravaged by the war with France and the latter still cowed by the repression that followed a revolt in 1585, there were serious political crises in Sicily and Aragon. In the former, where famine made the situation especially volatile, the nobles in the Sicilian parliament refused to consent to any further tax. They were, however, not supported by either the clergy or the commons, and after some negotiations and threats (which included moving a cavalry regiment to the outskirts of the capital) the leaders of the movement were isolated and arrested. The "revolt" was over in a matter of weeks.

The troubles in Aragon were far more serious. Tension in the province had been rising for at least ten years, centered around three separate disputes. The first concerned the county of Ribagorza, the largest baronial fief in the kingdom, containing over two hundred communities stretched along the French border. From the 1550's the crown made repeated attempts to wrest control of the fief from the counts, whose title to ownership was dubious. In this the king was supported by most of the count's vassals, who bitterly resented the tyrannical rule of their feudal lord; but the counts managed to hold their own against both crown and vassals in the various legal tribunals of Aragon until 1594, when the last count was dispossessed. The second dispute, which came to a head in the 1580's, also involved the county of Ribagorza, which had a large Morisco population (most of Aragon's seventy thousand Moriscos — about one-fifth of the kingdom's total inhabitants — lived on baronial estates). There was a tradition of violent relations between these Moriscos, mostly settled farmers, and the old Christian sheep ranchers who lived in the higher land to the north — the Muntanyeses, or "people from the mountains." In 1585 one of the sheep owners was murdered in the Morisco town of Codo. This led to an escalating series of "incidents," which culminated in the sack of Codo in 1588 by an army of mountain people, aided by a highly organized bandit gang led by Don Lupercio Latrás. Seven hundred Moriscos died at Codo, and the government felt obliged to intervene. An army of three thousand men was sent against Latrás, who escaped abroad and returned with promises of aid from Queen Elizabeth of England and with the active support of more bandits from the French side of the Pyrenees. He appealed to the courts of Aragon for a fair hearing of his case, for he was a vassal of the count of Ribagorza and had been driven into banditry by the tyranny of his lord. In 1590, however, Latrás was captured by the king's officers and was summarily executed, without reference to Aragon or its laws, and about forty Aragonese who had aided him were also executed. To these two disputes (Ribagorza and the Muntanyeses) was quickly added the third. Philip II seems to have decided in 1589 that the government of Aragon was getting out of hand and needed to be changed. With the French frontier so close, and with French reinforcements coming south to aid Latrás, the need for action appeared to be urgent. There was also the growing bandit problem to consider. The adverse economic climate ruined many smallholders, especially those living on poor soil. In the kingdoms of Aragon, many of these people were Moriscos and, for them, banditry might easily seem the only refuge from starvation. The bandits of the 1580's and 1590's were not only more numerous, they were also better armed: the spread of the flintlock musket, so much more reliable than the matchlock, had an impact similar to that of the repeater rifle in the nineteenth-century American West. The bandits were now equal — and often superior — in numbers and equipment to the forces of the government. In 1587 one gang managed to capture an entire convoy of royal silver as it traveled from Madrid to Barcelona; in 1588 another gang defeated a regular siege of their stronghold by Philip II's troops. Royal authority in Aragon was becoming seriously compromised.

The king resolved that one way of tightening his grip on Aragon was to appoint an energetic viceroy who was not born in the province. There was some doubt, however, about whether this was legal: the Aragonese claimed that the viceroy had to be a native. The king therefore started a formal lawsuit before the supreme court of Aragon to establish whether he had the right to appoint anyone he chose to be viceroy. The king's action may seem innocuous today, but in 1590 it appeared to be yet another threat to the country's traditional "privileges" — which, it must be remembered, constituted the citizen's best defense against arbitrary rule in early modern times. Taking together the drive against Ribagorza, the summary execution of Latrás and his friends, and the new tough policy against the bandits, the crown appeared to have undertaken a full-scale campaign against the "privileges," and a concerted opposition began to emerge, led by the soon-to-be-dispossessed count of Ribagorza (usually known by his other title of duke of Villahermosa). It was at this point, on 20 April 1590, that Antonio Pérez arrived in Aragon.

The secretary's father was Aragonese, and he knew his rights under the kingdom's constitution. Pérez placed himself in the prison of the supreme court and claimed, as had Latrás before him, that he was the victim of wrongful persecution. He had with him a volume of copies of the memoranda he had exchanged with the king concerning the death of Escobedo, and these he made public in his defense. The contents were enough to discredit the king thoroughly, and they were profoundly embarrassing. They made Philip II look a fool. It was in a rather ham-fisted attempt to silence Pérez that in 1591 the king's lawyers denounced the secretary for heresy, on preposterously inadequate evidence, so that he could be moved from the more or less open confinement of the supreme-court prison to the more secure cells of the Inquisition in Zaragoza. The Inquisition could be counted on to be cooperative and Pérez was moved on 24 May 1591. Immediately Zaragoza was convulsed by riots: here was further proof that the liberties of the kingdom were threatened, and the pro-Pérez rioters were led by those who had been involved in the unrest of the 1580's — Ribagorza and his aristocratic friends. A league of seventeen nobles was formed to defend the "privileges," and the Inquisition was compelled to return Pérez to the supreme court. Zaragoza was, in effect, in rebellion.

Alarmist reports began to reach Madrid about the risks inherent in this situation: "If there is not action at once, with a strong hand and a rapid punishment, Aragon will be like the Netherlands," wrote one loyalist. "If His Majesty does not provide a remedy at once, we will have another Netherlands," warned another. The king took these predictions very seriously. In June he issued orders to mobilize an army in Castile for possible use against Aragon. It was ready in August, and at the end of the month he ordered his troops to move up to the frontier of the kingdom, but not to cross. From this position of strength the king ordered Pérez to be handed back to the Inquisition in Zaragoza before 24 September. The authorities prepared to obey, but on that day, as the secretary was led from the prison of the supreme court toward that of the Holy Office, another riot broke out in the city. Thirty people were killed, more were wounded, and Pérez escaped from his captors. Zaragoza was now in open defiance and its leaders tried to secure support from Catalonia. Philip now had nothing to lose by sending in the troops and the order to invade was given on 29 September. Within a month, an army of fourteen thousand men invaded Aragon and after a campaign lasting only four days they entered Zaragoza in triumph.

The "pacification" was quickly carried out. The leading nobles, including Ribagorza, were arrested and died in prison; their humbler henchmen were executed. Pérez escaped to France, where he tried to secure aid for his cause from Philip's Protestant enemies. When that failed he took up his pen and gave the world its earliest picture of the Prudent King at work: the *Relaciones,* printed for the first time in 1591 and reissued in 1598. But this too failed to secure Pérez any real satisfaction and he died in poverty, in Paris, in 1611.

Aragon fared better than Pérez. As with Portugal in 1580, where the king had also faced open rebellion, Philip chose to maintain the status quo and not to use his victory to "create a new world" as he had so fatefully attempted in the Netherlands after 1567. Instead, he merely pushed a number of measures through the Cortes of the kingdom, thereby increasing his power: he secured recognition of his right to appoint a "foreigner" as viceroy, and the Cortes agreed that measures required only majority approval, not unanimity, before they could become law. There were also some changes to the legal system which made it less easy for a person suspected of treason to shelter behind the "privileges" as Pérez had done. And, in 1594, a citadel was constructed in Zaragoza, the Moriscos were ordered to surrender their arms, and the county of

Ribagorza was finally united to the crown domain. Philip had crushed his last rebellion, making a personal journey to the pacified province in 1592 to make sure that order was properly restored (another lesson learned from the Dutch Revolt). Philip, however, was now twenty-five years older than when he had sent the duke of Alva to the Low Countries. He was tired and weak and the journey to Aragon, which involved 549 miles of traveling, almost killed him.

At the age of sixty-five the king was no longer as strong as he had been. He suffered an attack of fever and "flux" (probably dysentery) early in November 1592, and although he was able to enter Aragon in his accustomed manner, alone and on horseback, the effort exhausted him. When at length he returned to Madrid on New Year's Eve, 1592, the people of the capital fell silent as their pale sovereign trundled past, slumped in the back of his carriage, looking almost dead. From then onward he began to restrict his activities. The king reduced his traveling to a minimum. He spent his winters in Madrid and his summers in the Escorial, with a visit to Aranjuez (to see his gardens) in May and a visit to the Pardo (to hunt) in November. He was in Toledo from June to August 1596, but otherwise he kept to his restricted routine. Traveling was now painful because his various ailments were all becoming more serious: arthritis ("gout") now kept him confined most of the time to a chair; his attacks of fever, almost certainly malarial, were becoming more frequent; and there were the normal symptoms of old age — the loss of teeth, poor digestion, the need for more sleep, and a general slowing down of his mental and physical processes. In February 1591 he complained that he was sent so many papers that "they do not leave me time to deal with all the things there are to do." More and more state papers were lying on Philip's desk unattended. For example, in September 1589, the general of the Hieronymite order (to which the Escorial monastery belonged) wrote to Mateo Vázquez to complain that an earlier letter to the king had not been answered. The king was contrite: "The blame for the delay is mine, because with the pressure of business I have not yet been able to see it or order a reply. You had better tell the general this: that one cannot always do what one wants." The situation deteriorated yet further after the death of Vázquez in May 1591. In July of that year a secretary complained that the king had not replied to several important papers which had been sent to him some days before. The king replied apologetically: "I am very sorry that the pressure of business should be such that it does not leave me time to see to these things, or many others that I should do, but I cannot manage any more. However I shall do everything possible." An attempt to change the governmental system was therefore made, placing a new institution at the top: the Junta Grande (the Grand Committee). It was a fairly large body, containing the presidents of most of Philip's advisory councils, and it was called upon to review the memoranda prepared by most of these bodies and to add a recommendation. The dossier was then sent to the Junta de Noche for a final recommendation, which the king could see and approve. In this way a two-page consulta might be reduced to a single line and twenty consultas might be covered in a double page of foolscap. It was obviously saving the king's time, but the new system did not last long.

During the journey to Aragon in 1592 all power reverted to the Junta de Noche, and as the king's health deteriorated, more and more executive decisions came to be taken by this body. Philip began to worry that its members — Idiáquez, Chinchón and Moura — might become too powerful. In September 1593 he therefore abolished the committee and replaced it with another, which he called the Junta de Gobierno (the Governing Committee). The new body contained the three veterans of the old Committee of the Night, together with the king's nephew, the archduke Albert (who had been viceroy of Portugal since 1582). The committee was to meet for three hours a day in the presence of the prince, later Philip III, and their decision was taken to the king by Moura, the senior councillor and the grand chamberlain. The committee was beginning to act like a modern cabinet, with Philip II reduced by illness almost to playing the role of a constitutional monarch and the councils relegated to the duties of modern ministerial departments providing data on problems and possible solutions to them. Even the audiences Philip had always given were delegated to the archduke. Only the papal nuncio retained inviolate the right to speak to the king in person. Then in August 1595 Albert was appointed captain-general of the army of Flanders and left Madrid for the Low Countries. His duties were gradually taken over by Prince Philip, the heir apparent, a youth of seventeen, and the old king began to withdraw from affairs, commenting less and less on the papers referred to him. After early September 1597 he rarely signed official papers: this task, too, was performed by his son.

The king's health was failing, and everyone could see it. In May 1595 he was struck down by fever for over thirty days, and "the doctors say that his body is so withered and feeble that it is almost impossible that a human being in such a state could live for long." After this illness, the king spent most of the rest of his life in the sixteenth-century equivalent of a wheelchair. It was a sort of couch, with movable positions from vertical to horizontal, seven feet long and two and a half feet wide, with a horsehair mattress. The king sat, ate and slept in it, wearing loose garments that did not put pressure on his arthritic joints. The only problem with this chair was its great weight: it could not be easily moved. There was a disaster in August 1596. While the king was eating in a village cottage on the way to the Escorial, a sudden storm broke. Water poured down and before long the room where the king lay in his chair became flooded. The water came up to the king's waist, but the chair was too heavy to move and the "Monarch of the World" was too weak and sore to get out, so he had to wait, soaking wet, until the rain stopped and the flood subsided. It was after this humiliation that the portable invalid-chair now on display at the Escorial was made and Philip spent almost all the last three years of his life permanently confined either to his bed or to one of his special chairs. It seems clear that the king's concentration and intellect also deteriorated. He spent far longer asleep, and was prevented from attending to any official papers for long periods by serious illness (March–April 1596; January–March 1597; almost all of 1598). The court began to prepare itself for the inevitable death, realizing that (as one experienced courtier put it) "when he goes, we shall find ourselves on another stage, and all the characters on the stage will be different." But Philip was not prepared to relinquish his worldly power, as his father had done, before his time. He had governed for forty years but he was not willing to contemplate abdication. Even on 5 August 1598, barely six weeks before his death, he found the strength to sign some papers himself, and he was still prepared to initiate new policies and make sure that they were carried through. In the words of the Venetian ambassador: "So far from resigning while alive, His Majesty does all he can to rule after he is dead."

A small but revealing example of this tenacity concerns the expulsion of the Jews from Spanish Lombardy. Philip II had always been anti-Semitic, perhaps influenced by his first teacher and confessor, Juan Martínez de Silíceo, who as archbishop of Toledo passed the first anti-Jewish statute on "purity of blood" (stipulating that only those who could prove they had no Jewish blood in their veins could hold church offices in Castile). The statute was passed in 1548 and was confirmed by the king in 1556. In his confirmation the king expressed the view that "all the heresies which have existed in Germany and France . . . have been sown by the descendants of Jews." The king, therefore, heartily approved of his father's action in expelling the Jews from Naples (in 1544) and desired to follow his example with the nine hundred or so Jews living in Lombardy. In December 1590 he at last gave orders for this to be carried out, but there were many in Lombardy who were reluctant to obey and they managed to place one obstacle after another in the king's path. In October 1596, the king signed a letter to his lieutenant in Milan which commanded the expulsion "most straightly and without further delay or objection and without awaiting any further orders from me." He added in his own hand the threatening postscript: "If this is not done at once, it will be necessary to send someone from here to do it." It might be thought that such a warning, sent in duplicate, might terrify the king's servants into immediate action. It did not, any more than the original order of December 1590, reiterated in June 1595 and May 1596. In January 1597, the king had to write again, repeating the threat to send a special minister and adding that if there was not immediate execution "we shall seek out and punish whoever has caused these delays." This time the expulsion was carried out — the remaining seventy-two Jewish families were forced to leave — but the incident demonstrates the king's continued grasp on affairs even in 1597, as well as the difficulties he could experience in making himself obeyed.

Another area in which the aged king made unusual efforts to have his own way concerned town planning. He spent the months of June and July 1596 at Toledo, where he noted that part of the commercial center of the city, the Plaza de Zocodover, had been destroyed by fire. The king issued orders that it should be rebuilt "for the greater beauty of the city," given "how much it offends the eye in its present state." An overall plan for the rebuilding was drawn up and the king ordained that no one was to rebuild except according to the plan. "If the owners of the houses in the square do not wish to rebuild according to the plan, and there are other people who are willing to do so, let the present owners be forced and encouraged to sell, receiving for the property the just price." The king defended this foretaste of modern town and country planning with a characteristic flash of enlightened despotism: "Because it is my will, and because it accords with reason and justice that it should be done since it is to beautify such a principal and important city."

However the king's main concern in his last years was neither the expulsion of the Jews nor the rebuilding of Toledo, important though he considered them both to be. He earnestly desired to make an end to the wars he had begun in northern Europe. Although his efforts to interest Queen Elizabeth in a settlement were fruitless, talks with France began at the end of 1597. Henry IV needed peace in order to consolidate his position and to revitalize the French economy after almost forty years of civil war, and peace was concluded at Vervins on 2 May 1598. The settlement was seen by some as another "Spanish peace" because it restored the situation as it had been laid down in the Peace of Cateau-Cambrésis. But was the situation the same? France in 1598 was far stronger than France in 1559 and for her the new peace, in view of the forty years of turmoil and civil chaos which had preceded it, was a considerable victory. The war of Saluzzo (1600–1601), in which Henry IV easily defeated and dictated ignominious terms to one of Spain's most important allies, the duke of Savoy (who, it will be recalled, was also Philip II's son-in-law), demonstrated beyond all doubt that France was once more a power to be reckoned with.

Peace between Spain and France was indispensable, however, to the achievement of Philip II's dearest wish: a settlement in the Low Countries. By 1597 he had come to realize that total victory was no longer possible, and that some form of negotiated agreement was unavoidable. In 1594 he had considered making the Netherlands into a separate, semi-independent state governed by his nephew, the archduke Ernest of Austria, who would marry the king's beloved daughter Isabella. But in February 1595 Ernest had died. The king's thoughts now turned to Ernest's brother Albert. After almost three years of thought, the details were made final and the king informed the Netherlands that, after his death, he would be succeeded there by his daughter Isabella, who was to marry Albert. On 6 May 1598 the final act of cession was signed and Prince Philip (soon to be Philip III) was made to sign away his rights to the Low Countries in favor of his sister (although ultimately Spain and the Netherlands were to remain connected: Philip III was to succeed if Isabella predeceased him without issue; if she had a child it was to marry back into the Spanish ruling house; if Philip III died without issue, Isabella was to return to Spain and govern the whole of her father's empire). In August 1598 Albert assumed the sovereign power in the Netherlands in Isabella's name and in April 1599, in Valencia, they married. The longed-for settlement with the Dutch "rebels" was signed ten years later. Even from the grave, Philip II's influence lived on.

With the cession of the Netherlands to Isabella in May 1598, Philip II considered that his work was done. Turning his thoughts increasingly to the afterlife, he began to compose two final papers of advice for his son. They were very different from those Charles V had given to him in 1543. The first was a Spanish translation of the last advice given by Saint Louis of France to his son, also known as Philip III (of France), in 1270. The second was a discourse on the government of his inheritance. Although it was full of the familiar platitudes about the need to defend the Church, maintain justice and protect the poor from oppression, there were one or two more noteworthy pieces of advice: the prince must always remain in Spain, because of the trade with the Indies and the need to intimidate England; there must be a fixed seat of government, and even within Spain there should be no excessive traveling about the country because it placed a heavy burden on the people who lived along the way. Philip advised his son to pay special attention to keeping up his prestige abroad and to maintaining in his armies the same mixture of foreign and native troops that had proved itself capable of defending the empire so well. The king also defended himself against the charge of being slow to transact business. Some of the trouble lay with negligent ministers, he admitted, but far more was caused by lack of money (especially in wartime), which delayed action, and by the long distances that separated his various domains. In the more elegant language of Fernand Braudel, Philip II's government "had to respond to the workings of the first economic and political system that spanned the known world. This was one reason why the pulses of Spain beat at a slower pace than others." Philip II himself was perhaps the first to acknowledge this.

In the spring of 1598 the king's constitution at last began to fail him. Dropsy set in; fever and arthritis combined to sap his vitality; a blood infection caused his skin to erupt in boils and sores. He was too ill to go to Aranjuez as usual in May, but in June he managed to go to the Escorial. It was his last journey. After a short period of relative recovery, on 22 July he was forced to lie flat on a bed in his tiny study in the Escorial and there he remained for fifty-three days, unable to move and unable to bear being touched, his body a mass of sores. Although only semiconscious through pain and fever for much of the time, and although sleeping a good deal, the king still suffered greatly. Some things were particularly unpleasant for a man who was unusually strict about personal cleanliness, as his sensitive valet, Jehan Lhermite, remarked:

> He was forced to be incontinent which, without any doubt, was for him one of the worst torments imaginable, seeing that he himself was one of the cleanest, neatest and most fastidious men the world has ever seen. . . . He could not tolerate a single mark on the walls or floors of his rooms. . . . The evil smell that emanated from the said sores was another source of torment, and certainly not the least, on account of his great fastidiousness and cleanliness.

Amid these distressing conditions, which impressed on him the mortality even of kings, Philip II made his final preparations for death. He had by his side Charles V's scourge (which still bore traces of the emperor's blood) ; he also had the crucifix which both his father and mother had held as they died; he had his coffin brought to his bedside; and he was surrounded by the priceless holy relics he had collected all his life. In his lucid moments he invited his favorite preacher, Francisco Terrones, to instruct him, alone, by his bedside (Terrones never forgot these terrifying occasions, face to face and alone with his earthly master), and with Terrones and the Escorial monks he made arrangements for his own funeral "down to details such as which door of the church his coffin was to go in and go out, so that it seemed that he was preparing to go to a great celebration rather than to his death."

According to his confessor, he had always prayed that he would be fully conscious during his last moments of life. When he awoke from his last coma in the early hours of 13 September, realizing that death was near and that his prayer had been granted, he smiled and seemed elated. He grasped his parents' crucifix firmly and, with his eyes wide open, he felt his life gradually ebb away. "He died slowly," wrote one of the monks at his bedside, "so that with only a faint motion, giving two or three small gasps, his saintly spirit left him." The children of the Escorial seminary, his seminary, had just begun to sing Mass.

There was no attempt to hide the news. Later the same morning the town council of El Escorial, a community "made" by the late king, were told that Philip II was dead and they at once voted themselves six ducats apiece in order to buy a decent suit of mourning in his honor. In Madrid, where the news arrived later the same day, the magistrates ordered "that all people of every degree and quality shall don mourning for the king our lord, who is in glory, within three days. Women will put on black bonnets and shall wear no dresses of silk. Those who cannot afford to wear mourning or a *caperuza* [a special pointed hat], shall wear a hat without trimmings as a sign of sorrow." The news gradually spread: to Palencia, where on 25 September the magistrates received notification of the king's death and resolved that everyone should go into mourning, the poor who could not afford a hat being required to wear something black on their heads; to the Low Countries, where the news arrived on 10 October and a special memorial service was held on 29 December, the fortieth anniversary of the service held for the late king's father, Charles V. There were innumerable funeral orations extolling the virtues of Philip II; there were also many criticisms. The king had passed from history into the realm of myth and legend.

TWELVE

Epilogue: Philip II in Myth and Legend

"No character was ever drawn by different historians in more opposite colors than that of Philip," wrote Robert Watson, principal of St. Andrews University, in his best-selling biography of the king first published in 1777. And the opposite colors were revealed even before Philip's death, for although the king refused to allow any "official history" of his reign to be written, there were others who were only too happy to write an "unofficial" one. The first, and in many ways the best (or worst), was the *Apology* of William of Orange, published in 1581. In August of the preceding year, Orange was declared an outlaw by the king, and a price of 25,000 crowns was placed on his head. The edict of outlawry, which was drawn up under the personal supervision of Cardinal Granvelle, Orange's old enemy, not only blamed the prince for disloyalty, rebellion and treason; it also made offensive references to the prince's personal life; for instance, to his divorce of Anna of Saxony and remarriage while Anna was kept in close confinement, accused of madness. This was certainly unseemly and, given Philip II's similar personal misfortunes, rather imprudent: Orange could not afford to let such a slur go unanswered. So the prince and his advisers spent much of September and

October 1580 composing a reply which not only justified the prince's political career in detail, but also turned all the personal smears back against their initiator. The *Apology* charged the king with adultery, with incest, with murdering his son Don Carlos and his wife Elizabeth de Valois, as well as with the more conventional crimes of tyranny, duplicity and deceit. It was an elegant piece of propaganda. It was short (only about fifteen thousand words) and it was soon a best seller: editions in French (five), Dutch (two) and Latin, German and English (one each) came out in 1581 alone. More were to follow. It formed one of the three main sources on which almost every subsequent biography of Philip II written by Protestant writers was to draw. Robert Watson even printed extracts in his *History*.

The second basic source for Protestant biographies of the king was the collection of documents and commentary published by Antonio Pérez: the *Relaciones*. There was an anonymous first edition in 1591, and a definitive, extended one in 1598. Both were printed in France. Later came volumes of "aphorisms," selections from the "letters," and even selections from the "aphorisms." Pérez observed in 1595 that writing had become "my business and my spirit's recreation." The picture of Philip II that emerged from the pen of Pérez was one of a petty, vindictive and rather obtuse tyrant. The published documents, with their rambling royal comments, were cleverly calculated to denigrate the king as well as to rehabilitate his ex-secretary. The information Pérez made public, with its apparent authenticity, condemned the king out of his own mouth and quickly made its way into other studies of Philip II's life and times. The *Relaciones* were quoted explicitly, for example, in Pierre Matthieu's *Histoire de France* published at Paris in 1606. Matthieu, and many other authors, also drew upon the numerous (and mostly unfavorable) anecdotes about Philip collected by the French courtier and man of letters Pierre de la Bourdeille, lord of Brantôme (1540–1614), whose *Lives of the Great Men of His Day,* although only published in the 1660's, circulated widely in manuscript during his lifetime. Although Brantôme seems to have used both Orange's *Apology* and Pérez's *Relaciones* to a considerable degree, he also added new material of his own, collected during his residence at the court of Spain in 1564–1565, where he visited the queen, Elizabeth de Valois. The eventual publication of Brantôme's biography in 1661 seems to have sparked off a flurry of revived interest in Philip II. First came a study of Don Carlos by the abbot Saint Réal (Amsterdam 1673); then there was a play on the same subject by Thomas Otway (London 1676), and a new biography of the king by Gregorio de Leti (Cologne 1679). All three were fanciful compilations — Leti once acknowledged to a friend that he thought that fiction could be more entertaining than fact when it came to writing history.

The popularity of such blatantly hostile portraits is easily explained. Spain and her rulers had seldom been popular with the outside world. In the fifteenth century a "Black Legend" grew up in Italy, which characterized the Spaniard as always cruel, proud and lascivious (and frequently "tainted" with Jewish or Moorish blood as well). As Spanish power penetrated deeper into Europe, the Black Legend spread with it. *"Non placet Hispania,"* wrote Erasmus — "I don't like Spain." And his reason was simple: there were too many Jews. "The Jews abound in Italy, but in Spain there are hardly any Christians," he wrote on one occasion. And where Erasmus was content to scoff, others were more vitriolic in their attacks, making the conquering Spaniards out to be inferior in moral fiber, cultural achievement and religious commitment. The persecution of Protestantism by the Habsburgs merely intensified the campaign against Spain. Atrocities committed by the Spanish armies at Antwerp in 1576 or by the Spanish colonists in America were immediately used to reinforce the Black Legend, and these and all other "crimes" were inevitably laid at the door of Philip II by his Protestant biographers. Those who read with relish Fray Bartolomé de las Casas's famous book *A Very Short Account of the Destruction of the Indies* would also enjoy the anecdotes of Orange, Brantôme and Watson. Just as almost every edition of Las Casas until the nineteenth century was published in a Protestant country (of 139 editions, forty-six were Dutch, thirty-seven French and thirteen English) so until 1800 almost every biography of Philip II was written outside Spain by a believer in the Black Legend. Surprisingly enough, even the first Catholic assessments of Philip II were far from favorable. The "Anatomy of Spain," an anonymous tract written in 1598, popularized many hoary myths about the king: that before he married the princess of Portugal in 1543 he had two children by a court lady, Doña Isabel Osorio (since he was only just sixteen at the time of his first marriage this seems somewhat improbable) ; that during the 1560's he got another lady, Doña Eufrasia de Guzmán, pregnant, forced the prince of Asculi to marry her, and then had the prince poisoned. There was also more detail on Don Carlos and the death of Escobedo (Pérez's book was specifically mentioned) , and there were vivid descriptions of the (unpunished) atrocities committed by Philip's troops in Portugal, the Netherlands and the Indies. The "Anatomy of Spain" aimed to point out the "cost" of Philip II to the world. Its closing words execrated "this perfidious Philip, great hypocrite, incestuous king, accursed murderer, unjust usurper, detestable tyrant and monster" — but it was never published. The first condemnation of the king which circulated widely in Spain, albeit again only in manuscript, was also written just after his death. Its author was Iñigo Ibáñez de Santa Cruz, a secretary of the duke of Lerma, principal adviser to the new monarch. Ibáñez hoped to find favor with Philip III, who was thought to be hostile to his father, but in fact he was dismissed from office and tried for treason. In any case, his criticisms were superficial and trivial: the late king's foreign policy was condemned as too expensive, his personal habits were ridiculed as "petty and effeminate" (a circumstance ascribed to the fact that Philip was born under the sign of Venus) .

As time passed, however, criticisms of Philip by Spaniards

stopped. His reign came to be seen, in retrospect, as a golden age to which later generations wanted to return. As early as 1621 the chief minister of Philip IV announced that it was the young king's intention to "restore everything to the state it was during the reign of Philip II." A "Philip II cult" grew up, starting with the funeral orations for the king, many of which were printed, offering sympathetic portraits of the monarch full of personal details. They were followed by more formal eulogies, such as that of the late king's doctor, Cristóbal Pérez de Herrera, of which 750 copies were printed in 1604, and Diego Ruiz de Ledesma's *Brief Life,* first published at Milan in 1607 and at Barcelona in 1608. The best known — and best — of this genre of anecdotal biography was Balthasar Porreño's *Deeds and Sayings of King Philip II,* first published at Cuenca in 1621 and frequently thereafter (1628, 1639 [twice], 1663, 1666 and so on). Porreño got a good deal of his information from his uncle, Francisco de Mora, who had been Philip's chief architect, and his stories soon passed into all the standard histories. Even Robert Watson of St. Andrews possessed a copy of Porreño (which is still in the university library there, complete with his annotations).

By the time Porreño wrote, there were already several official or semiofficial histories of Philip's reign in print: Antonio de Herrera's *History of the World* (covering only the years 1554 to 1598), which was based on official documents; Cesare Campana's *Life of Philip II,* which was little more than an abridged Italian translation of Herrera; Lorenzo van der Hammen's *Philip the Prudent,* which was anecdotal, like Porreño's work, and, best known of all, Luis Cabrera de Córdoba's *History of King Philip II,* which combined a narrative of events with an attempt to explain the motives that underlay individual decisions.

Cabrera's is incomparably the best history of Philip II written by a contemporary. It is judicious, perceptive and accurate, thanks to the author's personal knowledge of court life and his habit of keeping full notes on events. As he himself admitted: "When [the king] sent me out to see the world, it was to study it — which I did, keeping a diary of what happened, as if I were destined to write this History, which I could not have done without the aid of my papers." Unfortunately, Cabrera was only allowed to publish the first half of his narrative, which went up to Philip's return from Portugal in 1583. He was refused permission to print the rest because his account of the troubles of Aragon was found objectionable by the Aragonese Cortes, and the manuscript (which found its way into the library of Cardinal Mazarin) was only published in 1876. It was the same with many other studies of the king written by those who actually knew him: the *Memoirs* of Fray Juan de San Jerónimo were not published until the 1840's; the diary (or *Passetemps*) of Jehan Lhermite, not until the 1890's; the history of Fray Jerónimo de Sepúlveda not until the 1920's. The only other detailed evaluation of the king written by a Spaniard who knew him well appeared in Fray José de Sigüenza's *History of the Order of Saint Jerome*, part III, published in 1605, which described the Escorial in detail, and also its founder. Toward the end, Sigüenza provided a moving testimony to the love which the late king had inspired. In reporting his death, the monk noted: "All of us who were present shed a great number of tears at his passing, but they were few in comparison with our loss. And many have not yet dried their eyes, nor will they cease to weep until their life ends."

This, then, was the position until the nineteenth century: only a few biographies of the king contained authentic material, and the only documents available for study were those printed by Pérez and Herrera. But despite this, there was no shortage of works produced that included a cameo of Philip: he appeared as a dramatis persona in a large number of Spanish plays (among them, twelve works by Lope de Vega), and even in the eighteenth century Schiller's *Don Carlos* (1787) and Alfieri's *Filippo* (1783) showed that public interest was still considerable. The unparalleled power of Philip II, coupled with his personal tragedies, created a dramatic character who continued to fascinate posterity.

The opening of the various national archives in the early nineteenth century released documents to the public which made the Prudent King yet more enigmatic and interesting than before. First came the ambassadorial reports, especially those of the Venetians, heavily used by Ranke in the 1820's and then published by E. Albèri in the 1860's. The French printed the correspondence of their ambassadors to Spain a little later. Other primary sources were soon published. Apart from the court chronicles, a number of diaries kept by members of the king's entourage on the major progresses of the reign were printed or reprinted: Calvete de Estrella on the journey to the Netherlands in 1548, Andrés Muñoz on the English voyage of 1554, Enrique Cock on the progresses of 1585 and 1592. At the same time the great Belgian archivist-historian, Louis Prosper Gachard, began his work at Simancas, collecting and publishing in abstract form the correspondence of Philip II on Netherlands affairs. Many of the same documents, and many more, were published in extenso in the 112 volumes of the *Colección de documentos inéditos para la historia de España,* which began publication in 1846 and has formed a staple of every book on Spanish history ever since. Both were central to the celebrated history of J. L. Motley, *The Rise of the Dutch Republic* (1856).

Motley's picture was extremely influential and it has left its mark, either directly or indirectly, on most subsequent studies, particularly those written in English. The recent verdict of Charles Wilson (to take one example), that Philip II was "a man with Hitlerian ambitions but with the mind of a medieval monk," owes a good deal to the work of Motley. Motley's portrait of the king has been influential for a number of reasons. First, it was based extensively on "the secret, never published correspondence" of major historical figures, which gave Motley's readers the pleasure of sitting "invisible at the most secret councils," both of Philip II and of his enemies. The deep appeal this intimacy offered was reinforced by the emotive force of Motley's prose: there was a passionate intensity in all his writing. Philip II was openly presented as the incarnation of Evil, "the common enemy of Christendom," a man whose "malignity and duplicity" were almost "superhuman," a man who lacked "a single virtue" and who was prevented from possessing every vice only because no human can "attain perfection, even in evil." The intelligent use of original documents to support this passionate partiality made Motley's strictures particularly telling; but matters were not left here. Motley was a "romantic historian," whose history was conceived as a drama built around a heroic theme in which the reader was to be directly involved as a participant. Motley agreed with Macaulay that history and drama differed more in conception than in execution, and he devoted much attention to characterization and to minor anecdotal or circumstantial detail, in order both to make readers identify with the historical figures involved and to give them the illusion of participation. Motley's great strength lies in his characterization of forty or so historical figures in his narrative, and none of his sketches is more memorable or lifelike than that of Philip II. The details are legion, unforgettable and grotesque, like the description of Philip receiving a formal visit from the corpse of his half-brother, Don John, which was brought from the Netherlands to Madrid in three sections but then had to be stuffed, wired together and dressed formally for the royal interview. It is with concrete examples such as this, drawn from authentic and contemporary sources, that Motley creates a picture of tyranny in action that can never be completely erased from the reader's memory.

And where is the modern student of the Prudent King after all these biographies — scores of them, in all languages from Icelandic to Turkish? Was Philip II the heroic figure perceived by his Catholic contemporaries: a ruler whose power was almost boundless and whose ways were inscrutable? Or was he the *debil con poder* as discerned by one recent historian, Gregorio Marañón: the weak man with supreme authority, a person of mediocre intelligence afraid that he could never live up to the example of his father? Obviously, the present biography has eschewed the "heroic" thesis, but to some extent this was inevitable. "Archives and documents are the memory of time past," Philip II once wrote, and given the volume of his surviving papers, it is not surprising that he appears less inscrutable and less godlike than once he did. During his fifty-five years in power, over forty of them as supreme ruler, responsible for the largest empire the world had ever seen, he was involved in many tragedies and many crises. Because he preferred to write down his thoughts at such moments, he often appears uncertain, hesitant and indecisive.

However, the later sixteenth century was an era of hesitant and indecisive rulers. It was a time of unusual political complexity thanks to the struggle between the resurgent Roman Church and its Protestant critics. Religion played a crucial part in the only successful rebellion against Charles V — the revolt of Germany in 1552 — and in the only successful rebellion against Philip II — the revolt of the Netherlands in 1572. Protestantism had rapidly become a major political problem. By 1570 almost half the people of Europe had repudiated the authority of the pope. Although there was to be a strong recovery by the Catholic Church over the next half-century, the Reformers had succeeded in creating fundamental divisions that ran across political frontiers and engendered double loyalties. In the Netherlands' wars, which lasted for almost eighty years, Germans fought Germans, English fought English, and Netherlanders fought Netherlanders because the participants in the struggle were united by religion, not nationality. The same happened in the French "wars of religion" and in the Thirty Years' War. All these conflicts destroyed the tentative balance of power which had grown up in Europe in the first half of the sixteenth century, for after the 1550's no Protestant power (such as England) could consent to a permanent alliance with a Catholic state (such as France or Spain). European politics were rendered unstable; the earlier formulas, practices and alliances no longer worked. Religious intransigence ruled out compromise, it prevented consistency and, until the intensity of religious feeling declined in the mid-seventeenth century, it created an international polity in which no politician could succeed for long. Neither opportunist inconsistency, as displayed by Elizabeth of England or Catherine de' Medici, nor painful adherence to principle, as attempted by Philip II, could make headway against the exceptional fluidity of international relations. It has been noted, with some surprise, that the Prudent King had no "blueprint," no set of fixed objectives for his foreign policy; this was surely because, given the extreme uncertainties of politics in the later sixteenth century, no blueprint could conceivably have worked. None of the political leaders of the time could claim outright successes. None of them achieved exactly what they wanted.

And yet Philip II seems to have achieved less of what he wanted than most. By the side of the "taming of America" and the conquest of Portugal and the Philippines, which were outstanding successes, one must set the revolt of the Netherlands, the exhaustion of Spain, the loss of almost all North Africa to Islam, the defeat of the Spanish Armada, and the triumph of Henry IV in France. All these failures came about in much the same way: an ambitious and intransigent policy was adopted, became increasingly impracticable, and yet was not altered until the cause was already lost. There could have been peace with the sultan in 1559, which would have safeguarded the western Mediterranean as a "Christian lake," but the king deliberately broke off the talks; and when a settlement was eventually reached, in 1577, Moslem power in the West was far greater, extending to Morocco, the Sudan and the Atlantic coast of West Africa. Likewise, in the Netherlands a compromise with the "rebels" in 1575, 1577, 1579 or even 1589 would have preserved Philip's inheritance intact and Spanish preponderance would have been made unshakable. The Habsburg empire with the Netherlands included would have been as invincible in the seventeenth century as the British empire would have been in the nineteenth, had the American colonies remained part of it.

Philip II's failure to overcome the problems facing him in the Netherlands and in the Mediterranean was very much a personal one. The explanation lies largely in his own psychology. In 1574 an English agent in the Netherlands observed that "the pride of the Spanish government and the cause of religion" constituted "the chief hindrance to a good accord." Philip had been brought up to believe that one should never negotiate with heretics (or Moslems); he also believed that one should not deal with rebels. Instead, he aimed to achieve outright victory and then dictate his own terms (which, as the aftermath of the Aragon revolt in 1591 showed, might be extremely lenient). Although several more sophisticated justifications were advanced to explain Philip's aversion to compromise, underneath them all there lay a sort of idealism. Philip II was not a "weak man with supreme power"; he was a man of rigid principle with supreme power. It was only when the course dictated by his principles seemed impossible (as in the case of the Dutch Revolt), or when his principles broke down (as in the case of Escobedo and Pérez), that the king showed real weakness: without them, he was simply at a loss. Perhaps his religious zeal caused him to elevate his principles beyond the level of common sense, but this scarcely makes him a weak man, merely an inflexible one. However, his adherence to principle was not only reinforced by religion: there was also a deep-seated fear of *appearing* weak. The king seems to have been deeply afraid of changing his mind in public. Once he had made a decision he could seldom be persuaded to alter it. He even seems to have hardened himself against possible alternatives, becoming less objective in his evaluation of information, "reinterpreting" it in a partial and biased way that made it support his original design. His behavior during the Armada campaign of 1588 offers a clear example of this: the king and Medina Sidonia viewed the same events in a totally different light, both twisting the facts to suit their prior interpretations.

It has been claimed that the distance separating the king from the outposts of his empire explains this strange intransigence. Philip, it is sometimes suggested, feared to countermand an order lest it should create confusion or chaos at the distant scene of action. But this cannot be the complete explanation, for the king's handling of the Antonio Pérez affair, on his own doorstep, displayed exactly the same reluctance to change course until the very last moment. Equally unconvincing is the excuse that Philip refused to abandon certain policies when they ran into difficulties because he believed they were God's work: precisely the same tenacity appeared in other matters that did not directly involve God's service. Religion merely reinforced the king's personality.

However, psychological speculation about "cognitive dissonance" and the like can only take the historian a certain way. To say that Philip II was ruled by his heart as well as by his head is only to make him like other men, and like other "great" men. Whenever we know as much about a statesman's inner thoughts as we know about Philip of Spain's private world, we find similar evidence of uncertainty, hesitation and inflexibility. Winston S. Churchill and John F. Kennedy, to take two recent examples, appeared to be formidably resolute and inspired leaders while they were in power, but subsequent research into their papers and the publication of the memoirs of their close associates, and especially of their medical advisers, have exploded many myths and legends. Both men are revealed to have had poor health: Churchill with a heart condition that could leave him comatose at cabinet meetings; Kennedy permanently dependent on pain-killing drugs. Both men appear by turns as obstinate and petty, indecisive yet afraid of strong men. Both relied heavily on unofficial advisers who were totally dependent upon them. Kennedy, at least, was plagued by family problems and Churchill, like Philip II, could not resist meddling with the minutiae of government: he "concerned himself with every triviality from the size of the jam ration to the spelling of foreign place names." Yet for all their failings, large and small, to their contemporaries both men indubitably appeared as great and inspiring leaders.

The historian must certainly try to penetrate beneath the confidence and euphoria that people in power are usually able to project to their public. But he must also guard against the temptation to accord undue importance to a few moments of hopeless anguish and a few wrong decisions. What is important is not to crow over the errors and condemn them, but to understand how they came to be made. Men in action are still men.

The king's celebrated contemporary, Martín González de Cellorigo, wrote in 1600 that Spain had become a "republic of bewitched beings who live outside the natural order"; but Philip II was not a member of that society. He was, even though a king, very much a "natural" being. We may condemn, praise or pity him as we wish but, thanks to the survival of his personal papers, it is possible for every one of us to enter his private world and understand him. And therein lies the secret of his continuing fascination and charm.

Source References

Abbreviations Used in the References

AA	Archivo de la Casa de los Duques de Alba, Madrid
Addl. MS	Additional Manuscript
AGPM	Archivo General del Palacio Real, Madrid, Sección Administrativa
AGS	Archivo General de Simancas
AHN	Archivo Histórico Nacional, Madrid
AMAE *MDFD*	Archives du Ministère des Affaires Etrangères, Mémoires et Documents: Fonds Divers
BL	British Library (formerly British Museum Library), Department of Western Manuscripts
BPM	Biblioteca de Palacio, Palacio de Oriente, Madrid
CMC	Contaduría Mayor de Cuentas
CO. DO. IN.	*Colección de documentos inéditos para la historia de España*
CSR	Casas y Sitios Reales
HS	Archivo de la Casa de la Condesa Viuda de Heredía Spínola, Madrid
IVdeDJ	Instituto de Valencia de Don Juan, Madrid

PAGE

6   J. M. March, *Niñez y juventud de Felipe II*, II (Madrid 1942), 31: instruction of Charles V to his son, 6 May 1543.

8   Ibid., I, 46, and II, 29–30.

9   Ibid., I, 236–237, Zúñiga to Charles, 25 Feb. 1540.

11   John Elder in 1554, quoted by C. Bratli, *Philippe II* (Paris 1912), 221.

14   AGS *CSR* 36 fol. 1, pp. 220–224, about the books purchased.

17   L. P. Gachard in *Biographie Nationale de Belgique*, III (Brussels 1872), col. 666.

18   From the instruction printed in March, *Niñez*, II, 12–34.

21   BL *Egerton MS* 2148/16v, Journal of Sir T. Hoby.

21   March, *Niñez*, I, 323–326, Charles to Zúñiga, 17 Feb. 1545.

24   Escorial, MS I.III.30, fol. 134, "Raggionamento" of Philip II.

24   E. Spivakovsky, *Felipe II, epistolario familiar* (Madrid 1975), king to Catalina, 27 Aug. 1586.

28   AGS *Estado* 1049/107, king to the viceroy of Naples, 13 Feb. 1559, minute.

28   BPM MS II-2291, unfol., G. Pérez to Granvelle, 16 Apr. 1560.

28   Gachard, *Correspondance de Philippe II sur les affaires des Pays-Bas*, I (Brussels 1848), 358: Pérez to Armenteros, 30 June 1565.

PAGE

30 AGS *Estado* 148/181, Chinchón to the governor of Lombardy, 12 Dec. 1566.

30 IVdeDJ 81/1251, Requesens to Zúñiga, Nov. 1572.

30 AMAE *MDFD Espagne*, 239/126–35, king to President Covarrubias.

31 IVdeDJ 61/130, king to P. de Hoyo, Apr. 1567.

31 BL *Addl. MS* 28,699/114, king to Vázquez, 2 May 1577.

31 IVdeDJ 44/127, king to Vázquez, 16 Apr. 1575.

31 IVdeDJ 53/carpeta 6/51, king to Vázquez, 15 May 1577.

32 HS 144/1, Vázquez to the king (undated, but sent on 19 Apr. 1573).

32 IVdeDJ 51/162, king to Vázquez, 11 Apr. 1578.

33 BL *Egerton MS* 329/8–10, "Estilo que guarda el Rey."

34 IVdeDJ 21/576, king to Vázquez, 21 July 1575.

34 E. Schäfer, *El consejo real y supremo de las Indias*, I (Seville 1935), 149–150.

35 Duke of Maura, *El designio de Felipe II* (Madrid 1957), 38: king to Medina Sidonia, 29 Oct. 1578.

35 E. Spivakovsky, *Felipe II: epistolario familiar*, 48–49: king to Catalina, 18 June 1585.

35 BL *Egerton MS* 330/8–8v, "Copia de carta que escriuió . . . D Luis Manrique."

36 IVdeDJ 53/carpeta 5/15, Vázquez to the king and reply, 27 Jan. 1576 ("de las audiencias me queda poco en la cabeça").

38 IVdeDJ 61/1, king to P. de Hoyo, undated (= 1562).

39 AGPM 1/166v–7, order of 17 May 1553.

41 AGPM 7/66v, order of 19 Mar. 1588 (about an "abestruz bravo" [ostrich] attacking a gardener).

41 IVdeDJ 61/105, king to Hoyo, 10 Feb. 1566.

42 AGS *CSR* 275/2, fols. 60, 74, 87–88, about poaching in 1569.

43 IVdeDJ 61/19, 131 and 85–86, Hoyo to the king and reply 22 May 1562, undated 1564 and Aug. 1565.

44 HS 146/100, Hoyo to the king and reply, Nov. 1566.

44 IVdeDJ 61/85–6, Hoyo to the king and reply, Aug. 1565.

44 AGS *CSR* 247/1, fol. 126, J. B. de Toledo to Hoyo, 13 Aug. 1565.

49 F. Pérez Mínguez, ed., *Revindicación histórica del siglo XVI* (Madrid 1928), 437: Hoyo to the king and reply, Feb. 1567.

51 R. Taylor, "Architecture and Magic: Considerations on the *Idea* of the Escorial," in D. Fraser et al., eds., *Essays in the History of Architecture Presented to Rudolf Wittkower* (London 1967), 86.

52 A. Heredía Herrera, *Catálogo de las consultas del consejo de Indias*, I (Madrid 1972), 403: consulta of 28 Sep. 1582.

53 Quoted by H. G. Koenigsberger, "The Statecraft of Philip II," *European Studies Review*, I (1971), 11.

55 IVdeDJ 51/175, Vázquez to the king and reply, 29 Dec. 1577.

56 IVdeDJ 51/105, Vázquez to the king, 22 Aug. 1583.

PAGE

57 AGS *Estado* 547/3, king to Alva, 14 Sep. 1571, minute.

58 Quoted in Pérez Mínguez, *Revindicación*, 157.

59 IVdeDJ 21/586, king to the Council of Castile, 14 Dec. 1575, minute.

60 AGPM 3/164v–6 and 274, orders of 22 Dec. 1569 and 18 Oct. 1571.

63 BPM MS II-2320/124, Granvelle to J. Vázquez de Molina, 21 July 1559.

68 AGS *Estado* 527/5, Philip II, note of 24 Mar. 1565 (this dating has been established by Dr. David Lagomarsino, who also helped me to interpret this difficult but crucial document).

68 A. González Palencia, *Gonzalo Pérez*, II (Madrid 1946), 487: king to Pérez, 24 Mar. 1565.

68 AGS *Estado* 527/5: "es la una y m[e] estoy durmyendo todo."

70 AGS *Estado* 146/147, Pérez to the king and reply, (10) Apr. 1565.

72 "Relation," quoted in C. Bratli, *Philippe II*, 199, n. 354.

82 Duchess of Berwick y Alba, *Documentos escogidos del archivo de la casa de Alba* (Madrid 1891), 99–103: Don Diego de Córdoba to the duke, 1 Feb. 1571.

83 A. González de Amezúa y Mayo, *Isabel de Valois*, II (Madrid 1949), 59 and n. 161.

86 Ibid., II, 533 n.: king to Catherine, 28 June 1569.

87 Ibid., II, 530 n.: king to his ambassador in France, 2 Apr. 1569.

89 Quoted in F. Pérez Mínguez, *Psicología de Felipe II* (Madrid 1925), 106.

89 IVdeDJ 61/78, Hoyo to the king and reply, Oct. 1564.

90 L. P. Gachard, *La Bibliothèque Nationale à Paris*, II (Brussels 1877), 247: Fourquevaux to Catherine de' Medici, 24 Aug. 1567.

91 *CO. DO. IN.*, XCVII, 460: Zúñiga to Rodrigo Manuel, 28 Apr. 1568.

91 J. Lynch, *Spain under the Habsburgs*, I (Oxford 1965), 179: king to Pope Pius V, 9 May 1568.

91 Gachard, *Bibliothèque Nationale*, II, 257: Fourquevaux to Charles IX, 6 Apr. 1568.

92 Pérez Mínguez, *Psicología*, 120–121: count of Lerma (the prince's keeper) to his brother, St. Francis Borgia, 1 Oct. 1568.

94 IVdeDJ 38/70, Espinosa to the king and reply, undated (= 1569): "cierto yo no estoy bueno para el mundo que agora corre; que conozco yo muy bien que havría menester otra condición no tan buena como dios me la ha dado, que solo para my es ruín."

100 IVdeDJ 51/189, Vázquez to the king and reply, 20 Apr. 1586.

100 AHN *Inquisición libro* 284/156–8, consulta of 30 July 1578.

100 BL *Egerton MS* 1506/21, inquisitor general to the king and reply, 16 July 1574. However, a little later (fols. 21–22) the king condemned certain "disorders" which characterized the Valencian inquisition and refused to accept any excuses because "I saw it with my own eyes" (*"Yo lo vi por mis ojos"*).

106 G. Groen van Prinsterer, *Archives ou correspondance inédite de la maison d'Orange-Nassau*, 1st ser., III (Leiden 1836), 362: Orange to Count John, 20 Feb. 1570.

PAGE

107 B. Vincent, "L'expulsion des morisques du royaume de Grenade et leur repartition en Castille, 1570–1," *Mélanges de la Casa de Velásquez*, VI (1970), 220: Don John to the king, 5 Nov. 1570.

109 IVdeDJ 45/177, consulta of the Junta de Gobierno, 11 July 1596.

110 IVdeDJ 21/43, Espinosa to the king with reply, undated (= Jan. 1571).

112 I. Sánchez Bella, "El gobierno del Peru, 1556–64," *Anuario de estudios americanos*, XVII (1958), 496: king to Nieva, 27 Feb. 1563.

120 L. Didier, *Lettres et négociations de Claude de Mondoucet*, I (Paris 1891), 106–110: Mondoucet to Charles IX, 25 Nov. 1572.

121 A. W. Lovett, *Philip II and Mateo Vázquez de Leca* (Geneva 1977), 26–27: Espinosa to the king and reply, undated (= 1570).

123 Quoted by A. W. Lovett, "Juan de Ovando and the Council of Finance," *The Historical Journal*, XV (1972), 8.

123 J. Gentil da Silva, "Philippe II," *Annales: Economies, Sociétés, Civilizations*, XIV (1959), 736–737: royal note dated 11 Feb. 1580.

124 BL *Addl. MS* 28,699/103, king to Vázquez, 22 Apr. 1577.

124 Lovett, *Philip II*, 50: king to Vázquez, 4 July 1574.

124 Lovett, "Juan de Ovando," 18.

125 *Nueva CO. DO. IN.*, V, 368: Requesens to the king, 6 Oct. 1574.

125 BL *Addl. MS* 1506/18–19, king to Quiroga, 16 Mar. 1574.

125 Documents quoted in Parker, *Dutch Revolt*, ch. 3, n. 50.

126 IVdeDJ 44/116–17, Vázquez to the king and reply, 28 Feb. and 3 Mar. 1575: "Por esto y otras cosas digo yo que es muy ruín oficio el myo."

126 IVdeDJ 44/119, Vázquez to the king, 10 Mar. 1575: "Cierto yo no sé como vibo."

127 IVdeDJ 67/121, Requesens to Juan de Zúñiga, 30 Oct. 1575.

127 IVdeDJ 60/138–43, king to Antonio Pérez, 23 Mar. 1576.

127 Gachard, *Correspondance de Philippe II sur les affaires des Pays-Bas*, IV (Brussels 1861), 425–426: king to Don John, Oct. 1576.

128 IVdeDJ 44/145, Vázquez to the king and reply, 29 Nov. 1575.

132 J. H. Mariéjol, *Master of the Armada: The Life and Reign of Philip II* (London 1933), 218: Escobedo to Pérez, 7 Feb. 1577.

132 IVdeDJ 60/18, royal apostil on Pérez letter, Nov. 1576.

134 *CO. DO. IN.*, XV, 547, quoted in G. Marañón, *Antonio Pérez*, I (Madrid 1951), 266, n. 31.

134 IVdeDJ 38/62, king to Vázquez, 25 June 1575.

135 BL *Addl. MS* 28,262/546, Pérez to the king, undated (= 1578).

135 G. Muro, *Vida de la princesa de Eboli* (Madrid 1877), appendix, 20: E. de Ibarra to Vázquez, Apr. 1578.

135 Marañón, *Antonio Pérez*, I, 349, 351, 365–366: documents from the trial of Pérez.

137 Muro, *Vida*, appendix, 30: Pazos to the king and reply, 7 Mar. 1579.

PAGE
138   Muro, *Vida*, appendix, 47: the "treaty" with Vázquez.
140   BL *Addl. MS* 28,262/599–601, Pérez to the king and reply, undated
      (= 1577 or 1578).
147   IVdeDJ 68/306, H. de Vega to the king and reply, 8 June 1583.
148   AGS *Estado* 946/103, Olivares to the king, 28 July 1585.
149   Ibid., 947/102, king to Olivares, 2 Jan. 1586.
150   A. Mousset, *Un résident de France en Espagne au temps de la
      Ligue* (Paris 1908), 48: M. de Longlée to Henry III, 19 June
      1586.
151   IVdeDJ 45/386, Junta de Noche to the king and reply, 1 Dec. 1588.
151   IVdeDJ 99/99–101, king to Vázquez, 31 Jan. and 3 Feb. 1587.
153   English "strategists" quoted in G. Parker, "If the Armada Had
      Landed," *History*, 61 (1976), 365.
154   E. Herrera Oria, *La Armada Invencible* (Valladolid 1929), 210–
      214: king to Medina Sidonia, 1 July 1588.
155   J. de Sepúlveda, "Historia," in *Documentos para la historia del
      monasterio de San Lorenzo El Real de El Escorial*, IV, 59.
155   Duke of Maura, *El designio de Felipe II* (Madrid 1957), 278–279.
156   IVdeDJ 51/190, Vázquez to the king and reply, 4 Sep. 1588.
157   Herrera Oria, *Armada Invencible*, 210–214.
157   Lord Howard, quoted by C. Martin, *Full Fathom Five* (London
      1975), 231.
158   W. Raleigh, *History of the World*, I (London 1614), 306.
158   W. Shakespeare, *Julius Caesar*, I, ii.
159   Owen Feltham, *A Brief Character of the Low-Countries* (London
      1652), 84–85.
160   A. Mousset, *Un résident de France en Espagne*, 48: Longlée to
      Henry III, 20 June 1584 and 19 June 1586.
160   E. Albèri, *Le relazioni degli ambasciatori veneti al senato durante
      il secolo XVI*, 1st ser., V (Florence 1861), 420–425 ("Relation"
      of T. Contarini, Apr. 1593).
161   IVdeDJ 51/170, Vázquez to the king and reply, 20 July 1575.
161   IVdeDJ 21/576, Vázquez to the king, 21 July 1575.
162   E. Grierson, *King of Two Worlds* (London 1974), 166 (king to
      Granvelle).
162   IVdeDJ 7/6, king to Vázquez, 23 Nov. 1582.
162   J. de Sepúlveda, "Historia," *Documentos . . . Escorial*, IV, 181–
      183.
163   L. P. Gachard, *Lettres de Philippe II à ses filles* (Paris 1884), 184:
      letter of 30 July 1582.
163   E. Spivakovsky, *Felipe II, epistolario familiar* (Madrid 1975), 94–
      96: letter of 14 June 1588.
164   Gachard, *Lettres*, 184.
164   Ibid., 95 and 111: letters of 26 June and 21 Aug. 1581.
165   Ibid., 87: letter of 1 May 1581 (of course the king got both ages
      right).

PAGE

165 Ibid., 175–176: letter of 4 June 1582.

166 Ibid., 197–198: letter of 1 Oct. 1582.

168 AA 5/49, king to Alva, undated (= Apr. 1566).

168 IVdeDJ 7/95, king to Vázquez, 24 Sep. 1590.

169 Gachard, *Lettres*, 122–123: letter of 23 Oct. 1581.

170 A. de Barros, *Filosofía cortesana* (Madrid 1587) — the "courtier's game."

170 AGS *CSR* 36/3: an untitled gathering of folios numbered 270v–278v (the court betting book).

173 B. Porreño, *Dichos y hechos del rey Phelipe II* (Antwerp 1666), 49–51, and IVdeDJ 45/24, bundle of papers concerning Chacón's rape.

174 F. González Olmedo, *Don Francisco Terrones* (Madrid 1946), xlii.

175 E. Cock, *Relación del viaje hecho por Felipe II en 1585* (Madrid 1876), 226, 252; I. Velásquez, *La entrada que en el reino de Portugal hizo la SCRM de Don Phelipe* (Lisbon 1583), fol. 79.

176 *Relación verdadera del recibimiento que hizo la ciudad de Segovia* (Alcalá 1572), fol. C–C2v.

176 A. W. Lovett, *Philip II and Mateo Vázquez* (Geneva 1977), 99: royal apostil of 5 June 1577.

176 BL *Addl. MS* 28,350/173, king to Hoyo, 4 Feb. 1565.

180 Details from Archivo Municipal de Palencia, "Libro de Acuerdos 1595–1600" (on the poor harvests).

181 IVdeDJ 51/1, Vázquez to the king, 8 Feb. 1591; IVdeDJ 45/452, Vázquez to the king, 5 Feb. 1591.

184 José, marquis of Pidal, *Historia de las alteraciones de Aragón*, II (Madrid 1862), 44: letter of the count of Chinchón.

184 *Actas de las Cortes de Castilla*, XVI (Madrid 1890), 166–170: J. Vázquez de Salazar to the king, 28 Apr. and 6 May 1593.

185 Ibid., 195–197: king to J. Vázquez, 23 July 1593.

188 Pidal, *Alteraciones de Aragón*, II, 48n: Fray Antonio Labata and the count of Morata to the government.

190 IVdeDJ 21/740, notes by the king and Vázquez on a letter from the general, 12 Sep. 1589.

191 IVdeDJ 21/374, J. Gassol to the king and reply, 8 July 1591.

193 J. H. Elliott, in *New Cambridge Modern History*, IV (Cambridge 1970), 435: duke of Feria to T. Fitzherbert, 28 Feb. 1597.

193 *Calendar of State Papers Venetian*, IX, 338–339: Soranzo to doge and senate, 31 Aug. 1598.

193 Quoted by A. A. Sicroff, *Les controverses des statuts de pureté de sang en Espagne* (Paris 1960), 138n.

194 AGS *Secretarías provinciales libro* 1160/185v, king to the constable of Castile, 30 Oct. 1596, and 1161/223, king to the constable of Castile, 21 Jan. 1597.

194 AGPM 9/161, order of 28 Sep. 1596.

196 Escorial MS I.III.30, fols. 113–144, "Raggionamento" of Philip II.

PAGE
197 J. Lhermite, *Passetemps,* II (ed. C. Ruelens et al., Antwerp 1896),
     116–118.
198 F. González Olmedo, *Don Francisco Terrones* (Madrid 1946), xix.
198 J. de Sepúlveda, "Historia," *Documentos . . . Escorial,* IV, 203.
198 J. de Sigüenza, *Historia,* II, 517.
200 R. Watson, *The History of the Reign of Philip the Second, King
     of Spain* (2 vols., London 1777), II, 408.
203 Cambridge University Library, MS Gg.6.19: "Anatomía de España,"
     a manuscript tract of 149 folios.
203 AMAE *MDFD Espagne,* 239/417–67, "Pasquín" of Ibáñez and pa-
     pers on his trial.

INDEX

ᶘ

B
Philip II Parker, Noel
Geoffrey.

Philip II

DATE			

3/79

© THE BAKER & TAYLOR CO.

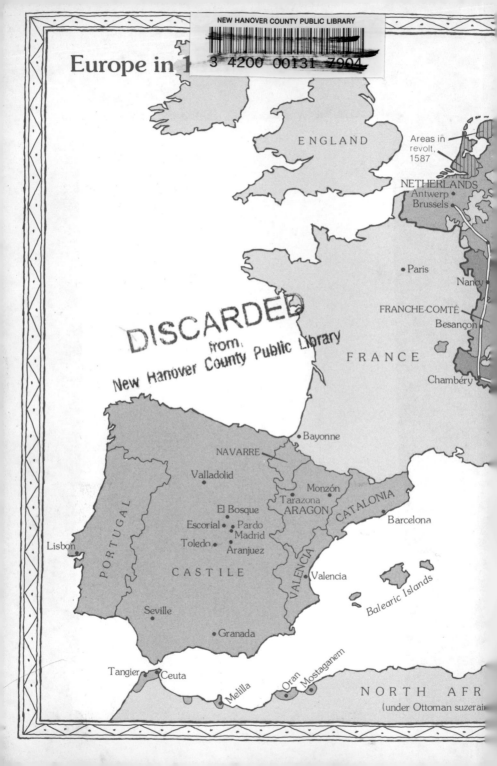

Europe in 1

ENGLAND

Areas in
revolt,
1587

NETHERLANDS
Antwerp
Brussels

Paris

Nancy

FRANCHE-COMTÉ
Besançon

FRANCE

Chambéry

Bayonne

NAVARRE

Valladolid

Monzón
Tarazona
ARAGON

CATALONIA

Barcelona

El Bosque
Escorial • Pardo
Toledo • Madrid
Aranjuez

PORTUGAL

VALENCIA

Valencia

CASTILE

Balearic Islands

Lisbon

Seville

Granada

Tangier • Ceuta

Melilla

Oran
Mostaganem

NORTH AFR

(under Ottoman suzerai